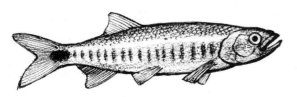

# THE FRESHWATER
# AQUARIUM

# THE FRESHWATER AQUARIUM

*A complete guide for the home aquarist*

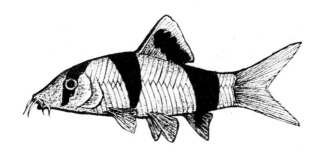

## R. F. O'CONNELL

GREAT OUTDOORS PUBLISHING CO.
4747 28TH STREET NORTH,
ST. PETERSBURG, FLORIDA 33714, USA.

This edition published 1971
by The Great Outdoors Publishing Co.
4747 28th Street North,
St. Petersburg, Florida 33714, USA.

SBN 8200-0113-9

Printed in Great Britain.

# CONTENTS

# Acknowledgements

The colour photographs in this book are by Bryon Harvey
and Alan Cupit

# LIST OF COLOUR PLATES

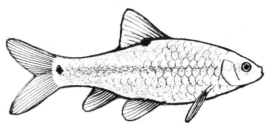

# AQUARIUMS AND EQUIPMENT

## Aquariums

An aquarium is more than a container for holding water, it represents the watery world in which the fish community are to live, therefore, when selecting an aquarium the needs of the fish should be the prime consideration. This does not mean that the end 'result' cannot be decorative, on the contrary, aquariums lend themselves admirably to attractive decorative treatment, but it is 'putting the cart before the horse' to design a beautiful aquarium, if it does not fulfil its basic function of housing the fish community in a state conducive to a healthy existence.

The shape of the aquarium is the first consideration. The oxygen content of the water is more dependent upon the surface area than on the actual volume of water (see oxygen), therefore, the aquarium should not be too tall or narrow. For example, a tank 12 in. × 12 in. × 12 in. will contain one cubic foot of water with a surface of one square foot, the same quantity of water will be contained in a tank 6 in. deep × 24 in. × 12 in. but the surface area will have increased to two square feet. This large tank will permit a greater number of fish to exist in comfort than the one foot square tank, although both contain the same volume of water. It is now obvious that the fancy shaped aquariums that many aquarists like to have for the odd corner or shelf, although they may be decorative because of their unusual shape or size, are often unsatisfactory because of their small surface area. In addition to the correct food and temperature, fish need plenty of space to develop. If the fish are restricted to an inadequate volume of water, or are limited by too small a surface area, the fish will be forced to adapt to the conditions and will remain small, stunted, or they will simply die. The most universal size tank in current fishkeeping is undoubtedly the standard 12 in. × 12 in. × 24 in., it is a size that is readily obtainable from any aquarist stores, and has the necessary proportions to suit most purposes.

There are of course, tanks of other sizes that are satisfactory that have become more or less standard, they are as follows:

18 in. × 12 in. × 12 in.
24 in. × 12 in. × 12 in.
24 in. × 12 in. × 15 in.
30 in. × 12 in. × 12 in.
30 in. × 12 in. × 15 in.
36 in. × 12 in. × 12 in.
24 in. × 15 in. × 15 in.
30 in. × 15 in. × 15 in.
36 in. × 12 in. ×'15 in.
36 in. × 15 in. × 15 in.
48 in. × 12 in. × 12 in.
48 in. × 12 in. × 15 in.

The next important consideration is the construction of the aquarium. Early aquariums were made with hardwood frames, and indeed a few are still being constructed today, but there have been many advances in both materials and techniques since those early days when only a relatively few aquarists were interested in keeping tropical fish.

Aquariums made in one-piece, moulded glass are quite useful as a spare container for occasional use, such as a hospital or quarantine tank, but they have two main drawbacks when used as a display tank. They are susceptible to damage, and also the flow marks introduced into the glass during the moulding process tends to distort the image within.

Tanks made from angle-iron with welded corners and glass panels cemented into the frame, have much to commend them. They are strong, the framework is unobtrusive giving maximum visibility to the interior, and if a pane of glass should get cracked, there is usually time to empty the tank and save the fish before all the water escapes, or better still, the crack can be temporarily patched until a permanent repair can be effected. Unfortunately they have one big disadvantage, in that unless the iron is well protected with a rust inhibiting paint, there is a tendency for the frame to rust under the lip of the top angles, and so cause water contamination.

Another method of construction used for the smaller sizes of tanks is similar, but the angle-iron is replaced with a plastic moulded section. These tanks are quite satisfactory if they are handled carefully.

The best all round construction uses a frame made from aluminium alloy angle, with glass set into the frame using a clear silicone rubber compound. The frame is usually anodised as an added protection against corrosion. There are other variations using stainless steel frames, iron frames coated with nylon or some other protective plastic, plexiglass and completely moulded tanks, but for durability, and general all round value for money, the iron or aluminium framed tanks are undoubtedly the best.

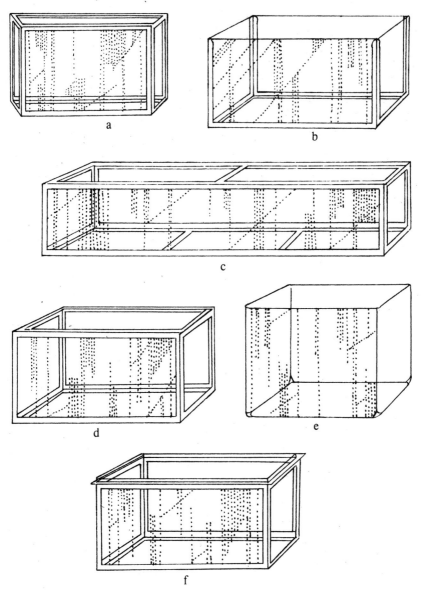

a. and b. tanks of different shapes c. long tank for breeding; d. ordinary angle-iron tank; e. all-glass aquarium; f. angle-iron tank with the upper rim turned out.

One final point worthy of noting in respect of construction is the cement. The glass panels are set into the metal frame with a putty or with a proprietary glazing compound. Badly cemented tanks are a continual source of trouble, water will seep through any small areas where the putty does not firmly and positively adhere to the glass or frame, therefore when buying a tank, inspect the interior for evidence of any points of poor adhesion which may be indicated by lighter patches where air has been trapped between the putty and the glass.

To calculate how much water an aquarium will hold use the following method of calculation:

$$\frac{\text{Length ins.} \times \text{Breadth ins.} \times \text{Width ins.}}{1728} = \text{Capacity in cubic feet}$$

The above formula gives the capacity in cubic feet, and as one cubic foot of water equals $6\frac{1}{4}$ Imperial gallons, you only have to multiply the product by $6\frac{1}{4}$ to find how many gallons of water the aquarium will hold. The U.S. gallon is slightly smaller than the Imperial gallon, therefore, to obtain a value in U.S. gallons, multiply the product by $7\frac{1}{2}$, this will give an almost exact equivalent.

One gallon of water weighs 10 lbs. (Imperial).

One gallon of water weighs $8\frac{3}{10}$ lbs. (U.S.).

One cubic foot of water weighs $62\frac{1}{2}$ lbs. (Imperial).

It will therefore be seen that an aquarium 24 in. × 12 in. × 12 in. will contain two cubic feet of water, weigh 125 lbs. and contain $12\frac{1}{2}$ Imperial gallons (15 U.S. gallons).

Having obtained a new aquarium do not press it into use immediately. Ensure that it stands on a strong base and that it does not rock, if it does, wedge pieces of thin hard-wood under the offending corner, then fill it with water and leave it for a few days to ensure that it does not leak. If all is well, disinfect as described and then it is ready for use.

## Disinfecting the Aquarium

First remove any odd pieces of cement or foreign matter that may have been left inside the aquarium.

In an old tank that has previously been used for fish, but has been stored dry for a considerable time, it is sufficient to wash the interior thoroughly with methylated spirits, but with a new tank in addition to the methylated spirit wash, a strong solution of potassium permanganate should be swabbed into the corners and left for a week.

The strength of the solution should be such that it is almost black in colour.

Finally, thoroughly wash the whole interior with clean water.

# Cements

If it becomes necessary to replace a glass side through breakage, or to completely glaze a tank, the glazing compound used should have four qualities—water resistance, adhesiveness, elasticity, and be non-toxic, the elasticity requirement is to allow for the slight movement of the glass due to water pressure and fluctuations due to temperature. Hard setting cements should never be used, because they do not take up these slight movements and they are difficult to remove if it is ever necessary to make a repair.

Good quality glazing compounds are available ready for use, supplied in tins or tubes, and the use of these saves the time and trouble of mixing your own, but if you prefer to mix your own, here are a few suggestions.

The best quality linseed putty is the easiest to use. Quantities should be well kneaded with the hands until quite soft, then pressed liberally into the frame with the fingers, ensuring that the corners are well filled.

Another cement that has been well and truly tried, is made by mixing two parts red lead, two parts white lead, and one part putty, using a minimum amount of Goldsize to unite the mass. The leads and putty can be mixed easily by laying them on a board, and working them together with a broad-bladed putty knife. A simple cement can be made from equal parts of white lead ground in oil and whiting. The lead and whiting are mixed together and small quantities of boiled linseed oil is added until the cement attains a dough-like consistency. The dough should then be hung in a muslin bag and left overnight to settle, and then given a final kneading before it is used. This particular formula has the advantage of remaining soft and in good condition for quite a long time if stored in an airtight tin, consequently it is a useful standby for the emergency repair.

Although it is not recommended for general use, a quick drying cement can be made from the following formula.

16 parts whiting.
4 parts litharge.
2 parts powdered resin.
2 parts powdered red lead.

The ingredients should first be mixed dry, and then a good quality varnish added until the mass attains the consistency of stiff dough. Because this cement hardens rather fast, it is advisable to make it only in small quantities and use as required.

Plaster of Paris should never be used as an ingredient in any cement, as it has a tendency to make such cement too dry and brittle.

## Leaks

To say the least, leaks are a nuisance, and generally they require the tank to be emptied before any repair work can be effected, however, if the leak is only slight, it should be given the opportunity to correct itself. This it may well do when the suspended matter in the water clogs the fault, or the water pressure on the glass closes the gap. As this process may take a few days, attach a sheet of newspaper to the frame of the aquarium just below the leak to absorb the water, if the seepage is not too fast the water will evaporate before it reaches the floor, and will prevent a pool of water forming. When the newspaper remains perfectly dry all over the leak can be considered cured.

If the leak does not cure itself, try scraping the cement away between the glass and frame to a depth of about $\frac{1}{4}$ inch and about $1\frac{1}{2}$ inches each side of the leak. An old hacksaw blade broken in half makes an ideal scraper. If the blade is bent back upon itself until it snaps, the broken edges will have a slight curve that acts as a scoop.

Then mix a small quantity of red lead with Goldsize until it forms a sticky paste, and gently force this paste into the crevice with a narrow-bladed putty knife.

Really bad leaks must be repaired from the inside. The tank should be emptied and thoroughly dried. It is advisable to leave the aquarium in a warm room for about a week to drive out any moisture trapped in the cracks, then prop the tank at an angle and run Goldsize down the inside corners. To apply the Goldsize a fountain pen filler can be used. The tank should be left for about a week before it is re-used.

An alternative sealer to Goldsize can now be obtained in tubes with narrow nozzles for easy application, in many respects these proprietary aqua-sealers are preferable as they usually contain a latex base which gives them an elastic property.

Cracked glass cannot be repaired successfully, the whole pane must be removed, old cement chipped out and a new piece of glass inserted.

All serious aquarists try to have a spare aquarium to cover emergencies, but eventually the temptation is too great to resist, and it is pressed into use for breeding, or some other purpose. Resist this temptation, and keep your spare aquarium *spare*, it is a good insurance against losing your fish in the event of an emergency.


## Heaters and Thermostats

Tropical and sub-tropical fish obviously must be given water temperatures near to that which they would experience in their natural

16

habitat, the general range, depending upon species, varies somewhere between 68°–87°F (20°–30°C). The relative temperature requirements of the fish will be discussed under 'Management,' here we are concerned with the means of providing water at a controlled temperature.

The easiest and most efficient way to heat a tank is undoubtedly with electrical heaters and thermostats. The heater is made with resistance wire, wound around a ceramic former, much in the same manner as the bar element of an electric fire. The former is housed in a heat resistant glass tube and sealed with a rubber bung through which the connecting wires are passed. This type of heater is designed to function under water, the heat being dissipated through the glass tube and into the surrounding water.

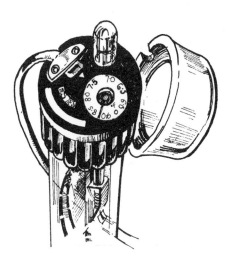

Heater with control dial & neon

Combined heater & thermostat

Never switch on the heater unless it is *totally* submerged because the heat generated cannot escape into the water, and the result is likely to be a cracked tube. This type of heater can be obtained in various sizes and wattages to suit tanks of various capacities. The thermostat is nothing more than a switch that is operated by varying temperatures. The main element consists of a bi-metal strip, which is two different metals of different coefficient of expansion, which causes the strip to bend as the temperature increases or decreases. This strip carries the contact point and is so arranged that it bends away from its opposed

17

contact with increasing temperature and towards it with a decreasing temperature. The actual temperature range is controlled by varying the mechanical pressure on the strip by means of a screw.

The desired temperature is set with the aid of a thermometer in an aquarium containing a heater and full volume of water. This trial and error method of setting is eliminated in the slightly more expensive models that have a calibrated control dial, together with a neon to indicate whether the heater is on or off, usually this type of thermostat gives very accurate control.

Another method of setting uses a special key which is ideal for stopping the younger members of the family fiddling with the knobs.

Another type of thermostat has the setting screw inside the tube, and a rubber bung similar to the heater, and is totally submerged in the tank. This particular type is useful when it is necessary to change the depth of the water for breeding purposes without any alterations to the tank. Its main disadvantages are that it has to be removed from the tank whenever it is necessary to make an adjustment.

All of the forementioned thermostats must be immersed in the aquarium in order to sense the temperature, but there is a compact type, that clips or is glued to the outside glass of the tank, this model is quite satisfactory, but the immersible thermostats are usually more reliable. A relatively new type of heater designed for use under the gravel consists of a loop of nickel chrome wire encased in a silicone elastomer tube, which is installed around the inside perimeter of the tank, and about one inch deep in the gravel. This warms the gravel and in consequence promotes vigorous root growth of the plants. This 'flexible heater is only obtainable in low wattages, and its use is therefore limited to small aquaria. Combined heater/Thermostats are units that incorporate a heater in the lower end of a glass tube and the thermostat in the upper part. To prevent the heater directly influencing the thermostat a baffle is incorporated. They are obtainable in several lengths and it is important to choose a length that ensures that the heater end is close to the aquarium floor whilst the top is above the water surface.

When setting up an aquarium with a new thermostat the temperature of the water should be controlled to about 2°F either side of its setting, normally the manufacturers will set the bi-metal strip to give these results, but occasionally a variation in excess of this tolerance will occur. If this should happen it usually means that the magnet which ensures a snap action and prevents arcing is too near the strip and has some difficulty in making its escape. A quarter turn on the contact screw is usually enough to decrease or increase the pull of the magnet sufficiently to bring it within the required range.

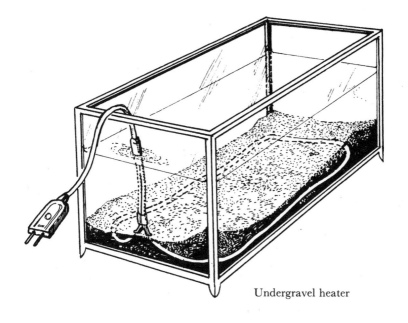

Undergravel heater

When the contacts of the thermostat make and break, they cause a tiny spark which can cause a disturbance to radio and television sets, some manufacturers fit a condenser to suppress this 'noise', if not, it is a simple matter to fit a 0·1 microfarad tubular condenser across the contacts. If there is space then it is obviously better to fit the condenser inside the glass envelope, if not, then bare the two wires leading from the thermostat as near to the top as possible, then wrap the condenser leads around the bared sections one from each end of the condenser to each wire, and solder. Then to avoid any accidents fully insulate the bare portions of the wire with insulation tape.

When buying the condensers, advise your radio dealer of the use to which it will be put, and the wattages of the heaters. He will then ensure that you get the correct type to withstand the mains current and load applied. When buying heaters a good 'rule of thumb' method of establishing the power requirements is to allow 10 watts per gallon of water. The following table shows how the wattage requirements vary under various room heating conditions and it is intended as a guide only.

| Aquarium Capacity | Heated Day and Night | Heated Daytime Only | Generally Unheated |
|---|---|---|---|
| 3 gallons | 25 W | 50 W | 75 W |
| 6 gallons | 50 W | 50 W | 100 W |
| 9 gallons | 50 W | 75 W | 125 W |
| 12 gallons | 75 W | 100 W | 150 W |
| 15 gallons | 75 W | 125 W | 175 W |
| 18 gallons | 100 W | 150 W | 200 W |

N.B.    The heat loss from a small aquarium is much more rapid than from a large one, and requires relatively more watts per gallon.

By insulating the sides, back and where possible the bottom of an aquarium, a considerable saving of heat and, consequently, electricity, will result. Expanded Polystyrene (Poron, Marleycell, etc.), $\frac{1}{2}$ inch thick, is ideal for this purpose.

## Thermometers

A good quality, accurate thermometer is an important piece of equipment to the tropical fish-keeper. The standard glass capillary, mercury filled, thermometer is the most reliable type. It is mounted usually by a rubber sucker to the front panel of the aquarium so that it can be read conveniently. A less common type can be stuck into the soil. Because heat rises, the top layer of the water will be warmer than the water just above the gravel, and, the thermometer bulb should therefore be positioned about mid depth, which will give an average reading.

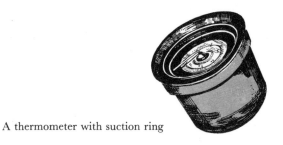

A thermometer with suction ring

Neat little circular thermometers are available with a suction ring around the outer case for mounting to the aquarium glass. They are unobtrusive, and can be positioned so that the desired temperature setting is on the top, i.e., 12 o'clock, it is then only necessary to observe that the indicating pointer is vertical to know that the required temperature is being maintained.

Both types of thermometers are available calibrated in °C or °F.

## Lighting

The most natural and effective light source is of course daylight. If it were possible to invent a lamp with all the characteristics of the sun, we would have the perfect lighting for aquaria. However, if we cannot have perfection we can still do a great deal with artificial lighting.

It must be remembered that whilst very decorative effects can result from placing the lamps in varying positions, the light source must be situated above the tank so that the light enters the water in a natural way.

Various tops and covers already carrying lamp fittings, are readily available, but if you wish to make your own cover to suit a particular decorative design do so by all means.

Aquariums should be covered with a sheet of glass to prevent water vapour condensing on the electrical fittings and falling back into the aquarium, to contaminate the water. It is also dangerous to permit water to enter any electrical fitting connected direct to a mains supply.

A simple light box can be made from wood, with one or two lamps mounted in sockets, and stood open side down on the glass. The box should be well ventilated and the inside top protected with asbestos sheet to dissipate the heat. Strip lights, mounted in their reflectors can be stood directly on the glass cover if small pieces of cork are fitted to each end of the reflector to permit a free passage of air around the lamp glass. A better method is to use a standard metal cover which contains the lighting and traps extraneous light rays. Fluorescent lighting is decorative and no doubt, it does help the plant growth, but as they are deficient in infra-red rays, I would not recommend them, however, there is one type of fluorescent tube that is gaining popularity among aquarists—the Grolux. This tube was developed for the indoor gardener, it produces mainly red and blue light which is particularly important to plant growth, by providing the energy for making carbohydrates by photosynthesis.

The makers recommend 2 watts of Grolux per gallon of water, and that the lights should be on for 10 to 12 hours per day. Personally, I do not like the visual effect of the red/blue light from these tubes, but this is a personal taste and many aquarists will not be so affected.

However, there is no reason why we cannot have the best of both types by fitting a normal and a Grolux tube in the same cover with independent switching. In this way the whiter light can be used for display, and the Grolux switched on during the day for the benefit of the plants.

Small aquariums used only occasionally for quarantine or some similar job, may be heated with an electric lamp only, with or without a thermostat but it is not advisable to use this method for tanks over one foot in length. The electric lamp is simply housed in a box and the aquarium stood on top. The box can be made from wood about 3 inches deep and corresponding in size to the aquarium base. Line the inside with thin asbestos sheet and bore a few holes for ventilation. Screw a base fixing lamp holder inside, and a strip of aluminium sheet in such a position that it prevents the direct heat from the lamp cracking the base of the aquarium. Under normal room heating conditions a 15 watt lamp is usually sufficient, but in extremely cold weather, it may be necessary to increase this to 40 watts.

When using this method of heating, always cover the floor of the aquarium with gravel, otherwise the unnatural position of the light will cause discomfort to the fish.

Wiring heaters and thermostats is simple, but remember that you are dealing with mains current and the normal precautions associated with any electrical appliances should be observed. Do not have any bare wires in the installation. Where it is necessary to join wires, use a safe connector block, and ensure that plugs are correctly fitted. If you are in any doubt consult your local electrician.

## Oil Heaters

Oil heaters have been used successfully for a number of years, but they are no longer made specifically for the aquarist. The main disadvantages of this type of heating, is the difficulty of controlling the heat output, and the need for daily attention to keep the wick trim and fume to a minimum.

These lamps were used underneath the aquarium, the heat from the flame warming the base and gravel, and subsequently the water. The flame obviously had to be a few inches from the bottom of the tank to avoid cracking the base, and protected from draughts for safety.

It was usual to make a fire-proof box the same dimensions as the base of the aquarium and sufficiently deep to house the lamp, due allowance being made to ensure that the flame was not too near the base. Ventilation holes were drilled around the sides of the box, and one end hinged for access to the lamp.

If oil heating is the only means available to the aquarist, there are still small ones on the market that can be adapted. The glass chimney is usually too tall, and can be replaced with a smaller one made from thin sheet metal.

When using oil lamps for 'under floor' heating, it is advisable to have an experimental run to get some indication of the flame height necessary to maintain the required temperature.

## Coal Gas

Gas can be used for heating aquaria, the techniques employs small gas burners situated under the aquaria in much the same set up as that used for oil.

This type of heating is hardly suitable for the home aquarist, but gas as a form of central heating is ideal for those who can afford the luxury of a fish house.

## Filters

Filters are used to remove unwanted matter from the aquarium and also as a means of introducing desirable substances into the water. There are now many types of filters available, from the simple bottom filter to the more expensive power filters.

The bottom filter is very efficient and inexpensive, like the majority of filters it requires an aeration pump to lift the water and induce a flow through the filter media. The filter box, usually made of plastic and, more or less cube shaped rests on the gravel in one corner of the aquarium where it can be camouflaged with rockwork or tall plants. Air is pumped into the centre section via a porous stone, the rising bubbles lifts the water from this centre section causing water to be drawn in through corners in the lid, or through vents around the base, the water then passes through the filter media and then to the centre section where it is returned to the aquarium proper.

A filter of this type will remove much of the mulm and larger particles suspended in the water, it will also remove slight cloudiness due to suspended organic matter. The filter should be cleaned once a week.

The only disadvantage of inside filters whether they are bottom filters or any type that is retained *inside the aquarium,* is the fact that the collected debris is still inside the aquarium until it is cleaned out. A neat little inside filter is now available with extensible elements, it is operated by the usual air lift principle, but additional cartridge elements can be added as required up to a total of four. The grooved elements can be used with or without the filter compartment that encloses the element.

External filters are clipped to the outside of the aquarium and in principle operate much the same as bottom filters, the water circulation through the filter media being generated by air-lifts. The external filter has advantages—the filter can be much larger, the choice of filter media much wider, and the collected debris is collected outside the environment of the fish.

An external filter is also useful for biological filtration.

Outside filters with their own built-in motors are more expensive, but they have the advantage of circulating a larger volume of water, and do not require an air pump.

The under-gravel or biological filter uses the gravel at the bottom of the tank as the filter media. In principle it consists of a number of plastic tubes with small holes along their length, the tubes are connected in a framework terminating in an air-lift tube, the framework is buried about $1\frac{1}{2}$ to 2 inches under the gravel and the action of the air lift draws the water through the gravel, depositing any organic matter between the grains. This type of filter is particularly beneficial to the plants and tends to keep the lower areas of the aquarium warmer by transferring the cooler water at the bottom to the top.

The biological filter functions by converting waste into minerals and plant nutrients, the main disadvantage of this type of filter is that detritus accumulates in the bottom resulting in a larger production of nitrate.

When buying an under gravel filter choose one that uses as much of the substrata as possible, the greater the area covered, the more efficient will be the filtration.

Power filters do not require to be coupled to an air pump, they have their own electric motors incorporated which drives a small centrifugal pump. One manufacturer is making conversion kits which will permit aquarists to convert their existing filters to power, at little extra cost. This is good news indeed, because the power filter is undoubtedly the most efficient system, but the relatively high cost has limited their more general use.

There are, of course, more expensive power filters incorporating high filtration rates, and facilities for changing the filter media easily. One type also provides a jet pipe for aeration.

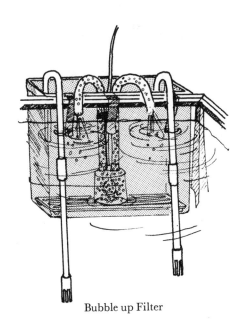

Bubble up Filter

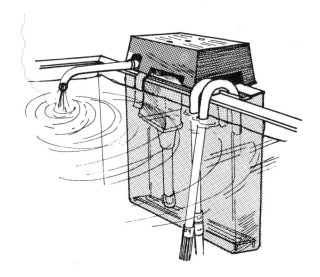

Filter with self-contained water pump

A small, versatile filter useful for small tanks, and for experimental work, employs the principle of filter pad, and/or a filter pack compartment, and sieves of various grades. It is possible to use several attachments if a variety of filtering materials are required.

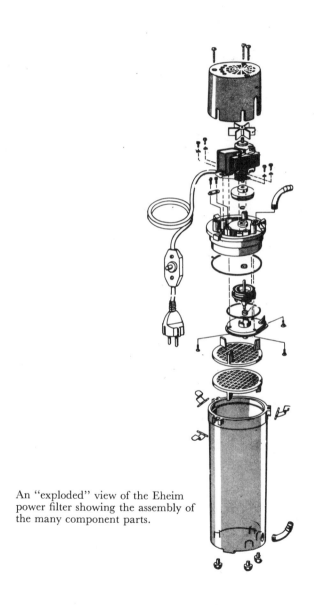

An "exploded" view of the Eheim power filter showing the assembly of the many component parts.

## Filter Media

*Fine gravel.* Usually used to pack the outer layer of a combination filter pack.

*Peat moss.* Peat moss is used in filter systems to condition the water, especially useful when breeding certain species of fish.

*Glass wool.* Used as a fine filter media, but it is not recommended because of the possibility of fine glass splinters entering the tank and lodging in the gills and on the skin of fish.

*Nylon wool.* Similar to glass wool, but much safer.

*Napped nylon.* A loosely woven material about the thickness of a good quality blanket. Obtainable by the yard and needs only to be cut to size. The same piece can be used over and over again.

*Exchange resins.* Used to soften and de-salt the water.

*Activated charcoal.* Used to purify the water of various organic matter including organic poisons and drugs. Does not remove mineral or inorganic substances.

## Air Pumps

Air pumps are necessary pieces of equipment for providing aeration and for providing the power to air-lift filters. The simplest type of electrically operated pump is the vibrator type, it consists of coils of wire wound around an iron core, and an iron strip which is connected to a membrane in a small circular container. When energised with electricity, the coil is alternately magnetised and demagnetised which causes the iron strip to be attracted and repelled rapidly like the hammer of an electric bell. One end of the strip is fixed and the other end is connected to the membrane which vibrates in its container producing continuous puffs of air. Vibrator type pumps are usually modest in price, and reasonably quiet running if they are not used to their full output. They are very economical to run, consuming only a few watts and depending upon size, are suitable for up to about 14 air-stones.

Piston type pumps, operated electrically, are very reliable and quiet, and usually have a higher output than vibrator pumps, they are particularly suitable for supplying air to a number of aquaria, but they are as may be expected, more expensive.

## Syphons

A 6 foot length of hose, filled with water and dangled over the side of the tank into a bucket will draw off water and if the end in the tank is held close to the bottom the flow of water will suck the mulm up into the pipe and into the bucket. This method is messy to perform if you have your aquarium in a carpeted room, and it is necessary to replace the water after filtering, or to make it up with new water at the correct temperature. The use of a syphon or dip tube simplifies this operation.

Syphons are a convenient means of removing the mulm from the floor of the aquarium without actually removing the water. They consist of an air lift tube powered by an air pump or by a rubber bulb (like a scent spray). The flow of water up the tube carries the mulm up with it, into a muslin bag which traps the mulm, but permits the water to pass through and return to the tank.

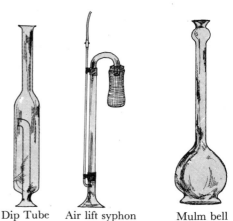

Dip Tube    Air lift syphon    Mulm bell

Other designs do not use the muslin bag, but trap the mulm in an enlarged section of the tube, but in principle, they perform the same function. Dip tubes and mulm bells are simply a length of tube, usually with a trap near the bottom which is inserted into the tank over the mulm, with the thumb over the other end. When the thumb is removed, water and mulm rush up the tube and into the trap.

## Clamps and Fittings

Neat installations of air tubing are made easier by using standard fittings, these fittings, 'T' pieces and 'Four Way' connectors are essential where more than one tank is supplied from a single pump.

Small clamps that fit over the tubing can be used to restrict the air flow. These clamps are adjustable with the aid of a knurled screw which compresses the tube and permits the supply to each tank to be individually adjusted, although the supply from the pump is constant.

## Nets

The best shape nets for aquarium use are undoubtedly rectangular. They are obtainable in various sizes, and it is useful to have a small, medium and large size always to hand, better still to have two of each size, as it is easier to net fish without too much chasing if one net is used to actually catch the fish and the other to guide it. Fish tend to thrash about when netted and it is while they are doing this that they are likely to injure themselves. They may even jump clean out of the net. The net therefore, should be deep enough to form a bag that can be closed with the free hand, or the top closed by holding the net handle in a vertical position.

Very small fish or fry should be brought to the surface with the net, but still actually in the water, and then removed in a large spoon together with water.

A net which will retain fry. Note the oiled silk lining

A small rectangular net can be adapted specially for handling fry. By lining the bottom to a depth of about $\frac{1}{2}$ inch with oiled silk, the fry are retained in a small amount of trapped water, without impairing the movement of the net through the water.

## pH Value Test Kits

The cheapest and simplest method of checking pH value is by using small books of indicator paper, prepared for the aquarist with a color grading chart on the inside cover. A strip of paper is dipped into the aquarium and resultant colour change compared with the chart.

A more accurate method of checking pH is by using a test kit, consisting of a small glass phial in which a measured amount of aquarium water is poured. A drop of indicator, for example bromthymol blue, is added to the phial and the resultant colour compared with a colour chart, or standard set of colour phials—green neutral, blue alkaline, and yellow acid. The depth of colour indicates the degree of concentration.

## Ozoniser

Ozonizers are small box-like units which when plugged into a source of electricity provide ozone. It is usual to connect the ozonizer in the air-line from the pump and distribute in the water via a diffuser stone.

Ozone $(O_3)$ is a pale blue gas with a particular pungent smell, formed by the action of an electrical discharge or by ultra violet light. It can be sensed in the fresh clean smell of the air after a thunderstorm and in the invigorating and bracing air found along the coast-line. The effect of ozone is to purify the air and sterilize the water, it is particularly useful for sterilizing live food, clarifying bacterially turbid water, and treating sick fish.

It has recently been discovered that Ozone is a carcinogenic substance and it can produce tumours in fishes if it is used constantly. Fortunately it is an unstable gas and high concentrations are unlikely to form. In the case of high concentrations it has been proved an irritant and becomes more injurious than beneficial. However, used with caution it is a most successful disinfectant and can also be used for destroying brown algae. Ozone treatment of water favours growth of Cryptocoryne, but not of Vallisneria.

## Feeding Accessories

Micro-worms and Grindle worms can be bred quite easily, but collecting them for feeding to the fish can be tedious. There are various makes of special containers for breeding these small worms that makes collecting them a simple matter. One such container is dish shaped with a raised centre section and fitted with a transparent cover. The culture medium is placed in the dish to an indicated level and the worms added. After a few days the worms multiply and will be found on the side of the container above the feed moat, from which they are removed with a camel hair brush.

## Ring Feeders

Personally I do not like this method of feeding, but there are a few advantages. Ring feeders are plastic, tubular section, rings that float on the surface of the water. Dry food is dropped into the centre of the ring which contains the food within its perimeter and so prevents the food spreading across the whole surface area of the aquarium.

The advantage gained by this method is that the drop-out falls towards the gravel in a reasonably restricted area, and the uneaten food falls in the same place every time. A flat rock placed in this spot makes it easy to remove uneaten food with a syphon. The disadvantages of these rings may be seen when a number of fish congregate under the ring, the furious dartings of the larger fish cause the food to spread and the main advantage is lost. If only a few fish are present, the feeding ring can serve a useful purpose.

## Worm Feeder

There are various designs, but in principle they are cup-shaped plastic containers, with a buoyance ring around the top. The bottom is perforated with fine holes to permit the slow escape of tubifex worms, which are usually sucked out by the fish as soon as part of the worm appears.

Feeder for worms

## Brine Shrimp Hatchery

Brine shrimps can be hatched quite simply in warm salt water, but the modern approach is to cultivate them in glass bottles well aerated for higher yields. Bent plastic tubes are specially marketed which provide for the entry of air right to the bottom of the bottle and also provides the means of collecting the tiny creatures without including the egg cases.

Brine shrimp collecting

In a short time after the larva have hatched, the egg cases will rise to the surface and the larva congregate near the base of the bottle. To extract the shrimps it is only necessary to remove the air tube connected to the pump and place it over a fine mesh sieve (suspended over a container to collect the water) and blow air down a second tube in the cork. This pressurises the bottle and forces the water and shrimps in the base of the bottle up the tube and into the sieve from which they can be easily collected. A detailed explanation of this process can be found under the Feeding Section.

## Sieves

In the past aquarists have used culinary strainers for grading live foods and for many other purposes, but it is now possible to obtain rectangular stacking strainers, or sieves, in plastic material with different grades of mesh. These sieves can be stacked to form a tower of strainers, providing four selections of size in one action.

## Breeding Traps

A breeding trap is a device for ensuring the safety of eggs and young fry.

Many aquarists devise their own traps by covering the floor of the aquarium with glass marbles, or by making plastic troughs or simply by introducing masses of fine leafed plants or artificial spawning media.

Plastic breeding traps specifically designed to prevent the adult parent fish from eating their offspring or eggs are useful. These traps are placed within a larger tank and provide a cage for containing the female, grills permit the eggs or fry to escape either into the main tank, or into a separate compartment below the female. These traps are not practical when spawning active and lively egg layers that need space for their courtship, but they are handy for the aquarist with only a few tanks who wishes to breed live-bearers, and for the less active egg layers.

## Water Hardness Testers

It is often necessary to know the hardness of the water in the aquarium and the general method of assessment is to use a standard soap solution. The water to be tested is placed in a calibrated bottle and drops of liquid soap added until by shaking the bottle, a permanent lather is obtained. The number of drops of soap required is used against a scale to provide the hardness figure. Kits comprising soap solution, burette tube for measuring the amount of soap used, and a calibrated bottle are all obtainable from most suppliers of chemical apparatus.

There is another method, more or less developed specially for aquarists and sold under the trade name of Durognost. This method uses an indicator which turns the sample water red. Tablets are then added to the water until it turns green. The number of tablets used indicates the total hardness of the water.

Water hardness is fully described under Aquarium Management.

# AQUARIUM PLANTS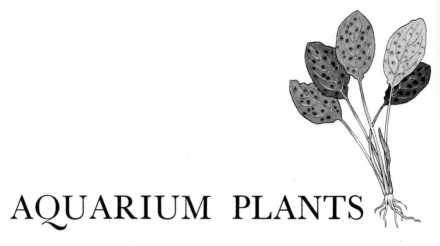

Much of the visual appeal of a well planned aquarium is provided by the plants and depends to a large extent on the manner in which they are arranged. Plants, together with natural pieces of rock, and other decorative devices will present a background to show off the fish to their best advantage. Plants also play an important part in the general function of the small, compact world contained within the glass walls of the aquarium.

The function of plants should not be given an exaggerated importance, biologically, fish will survive and remain healthy in aquariums which are entirely devoid of plantlife, providing alternative measures are taken to create aeration and to remove any waste products, but a tank devoid of vegetation is like a room without furniture—empty and uninviting. After all, the fact that underwater plants are growing successfully in your drawing-room makes them objects of interest in themselves, apart from their decorative and useful function.

The usual function provided by the plants is the assimilation of carbon dioxide given off by the fish, and the release of oxygen into the water. This process is known as photo-synthesis and only takes place under the stimulus of strong light, and requires water and the greenness (chlorophyll) incorporated in the plants. Naturally some types of plants are more efficient from the aquarist's viewpoint, than others, and many plants, e.g. *Vallisneria* produce oxygen so abundantly that it can be seen leaving the leaves as a slow thin, stream of tiny pearl-like bubbles.

Aquatic plants are nourished principally by various dissolved salts including nitrogen in the form of ammonia and nitrate; phosphate; potassium, and lesser quantities of calcium, magnesium, iron, sulphate,

34

copper, cobalt, manganese, boron, and molybdenum, they also require a few other trace elements and carbon dioxide. Some of the plant nutrients are found in natural waters, whilst others are provided by the gradual mineralization of organic matter. This organic matter is provided by the excreta from the fish initially and the subsequent action of micro-organisms. Therefore, it is obvious that the fish play their part in maintaining the plant life, whilst the plants offer a service in return.

Plants will thrive in an aquarium devoid of fish, but it will then become necessary to provide the necessary nutrient from some other source.

It is rarely, if ever, necessary to use anything other than aquarium sand or gravel as a planting medium, but if the aquarist has an inventive turn of mind, and feels he must experiment, then he should do so by all means. *Garden soil*, should never be used as it contains too many substances that are likely to give rise to trouble in time. It also takes a long time to settle and is easily disturbed.

The planting media, or bottom soil, has been a much discussed subject over the years, but no general agreement has been reached to indicate the best, all round, media. One suggestion is that the floor of the aquarium should be spread with an initial layer of clay bearing sand, and then covered by another layer of clean, washed gravel. Other suggestions include an under-layer of peat, or potting compost, and the local injection of fertilisers made from pulverised sheep manure, or even the pellet droppings of rabbits and guinea pigs, inserted into the sand, local to the plant roots. Frankly all these devices are best ignored. In a well set up aquarium the fish will supply the necessary plant nutrient in greater quantities than the plants require, and the risk of contaminating the water will not be increased by the addition of undesirable chemical and biological elements.

Never put newly acquired plants straight into an established aquarium. They should be examined first for any unwanted snails and the jelly-like adhesions of eggs, which should then be removed. Next remove any yellow or decaying leaves and rinse the plants under the tap. They should then be immersed in a solution of concentrated lime water diluted with fresh water to a proportion of six parts fresh water to one part lime water. The plants may be left in this solution for about 10 minutes, no more, and then placed in a solution of permanganate of potash for a similar period. The strength of the potash should be a quarter grain to a gallon of water. To make the lime water, mix liberally hydrated lime in water, and let the sediment settle, then syphon off the clear water and mix as previously described.

Plants should never be allowed to become dry during transit, or at any time for that matter. They should be wrapped in several layers of newspaper soaked in water with a final wrapping of greaseproof to prevent evaporation.

When adding plants to a filled tank, a pair of planting sticks may prove helpful. The plant can be pushed into the position with one stick whilst the other is used to heap the sand around the roots. The sticks can be made from any thin strips of wood sand-papered smooth, split bamboo is ideal. A 'V' notch in the end of one will allow stray root strands to be pushed under the sand.

If the plants are not firmly anchored into the sand their buoyancy will cause them to rise to the surface, but once they establish their root patterns this problem will not arise. Plants with small roots can be anchored temporarily with thin strips of lead wound around their base, but the lead should not be squeezed so hard that it bruises or injures the delicate structure of the plant. If the roots become black through contact with the lead, or for any other reason, you can restore them to their natural colour by floating them in water exposed to strong sunlight for 24 hours.

Plants should never be bunched too closely together. They should be planted so as to allow water and light to reach the stems. Another disadvantage of closely packed roots is that they form sediment traps, and may encourage the growth of unwanted bacteria.

Plants that form runners from the roots should not be planted too close to other plants as they will need space to spread their roots. *Vallisneria* and similar types should never have their crowns buried in the sand. The diagrams show the correct method of planting. Root filaments should always hang down and be planted vertically into the depression made for them in the sand, the tips should never be bent upwards. Finally, remember that *all* your plants will need to receive light so plan your layout so that the small plants are not overshadowed by the larger ones.

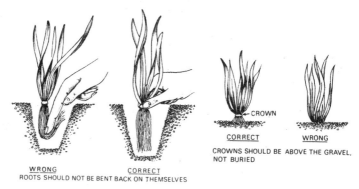

WRONG      CORRECT
ROOTS SHOULD NOT BE BENT BACK ON THEMSELVES

CROWN

CORRECT      WRONG

CROWNS SHOULD BE ABOVE THE GRAVEL, NOT BURIED

Diagrams showing method of planting roots

The layout, or the method of furnishing an aquarium will, of course be governed mostly by personal taste and artistic ability, but before the aquarium is planted, or even filled with water, consideration should be given to the site chosen for the tank. Only too often the aquarium is sited initially in a particular position for no other reason than there happens to be a convenient space in the room, subsequent considerations may well decide that a totally different position is more suitable to the room decor, and an aquarium full of water is not re-sited easily—it must be emptied before it can be moved. The inclusion of aquaria as a furnishing media, not only increases the pleasure of the hobbyist because he can observe the behaviour of his fish in the comfort of his home, but has the added advantage of enhancing the decor of a room or hallway and provides an animated scene that can be enjoyed by the whole family.

Firstly, always try to install one or two electrical plug points adjacent to the tank; this will enable the wires for heaters and any other electrical operated equipment to be either concealed entirely, or neatly run under a shelf or along a skirting board.

Air-lifts and outside filters can detract from the rectangular presentation of the tank if simply hung on the frame in a haphazard manner. Endeavour, therefore, to conceal such equipment with a frame or board incorporated in the furnishing, unsightly tubing and connectors can be concealed in the same manner.

Having decided upon the site for the aquarium and made certain that it is firm and does not rock on its support, we can turn our attention to the arrangement of the plants. How you approach this particular aspect of fishkeeping is, as previously stated, very much a matter of personal taste, but it is not unreasonable to assume that the majority of aquarists will want to combine an attractive appearance with a natural-looking underwater landscape.

First cover the floor of the aquarium with about a 2-inch layer of thoroughly washed aquarium gravel. This can be levelled or contoured. If using an under-gravel filter, it is an advantage to have the gravel more or less the same depth all over. Contours in the gravel will subside once the aquarium has been filled with water, unless some support is provided. One method is to use thoroughly cleaned stones of various sizes. The diagrams show how this can be achieved, as otherwise the water-saturated gravel will soon find its own level. As an example, assume it is required to make one corner of the floor of the aquarium higher than the general level, or to provide a gentle slope from the front to the back, then place large stones along the back, smaller ones in front of these and so on. Then fill in the spaces between the stones with gravel and finally cover the whole floor with a final layer of gravel.

37

It is important to ensure that the stones have been cleaned thoroughly in water, and any dirt removed with a stiff brush, finally they should be boiled in water for about 10 minutes to ensure that they are germ free.

Rocks used to support tiers of gravel

Remember to provide adequate pockets of gravel in which to set the plants, and do not use any more stones than is necessary to provide the desired effect. Another method commonly used to create slopes is to insert strips of clear plastic into the gravel to form barriers which hold the gravel in tiers.

The most effective and natural looking tank arrangement that can be used either with or without under-gravel filters, is to first provide a level gravel base about 2 inches deep and then lay thin pieces of flat Devon, or similar rock, diagonally across one rear corner to form a wall and then fill in behind the wall with gravel. Very natural layouts can be effected using this method and a little imagination and it has the additional advantage of leaving practically the whole of the gravel free to accept the plant roots.

Interesting slopes

When selecting rocks remember that your aquarium should represent, as near as possible, a natural cross-section of underwater terrain. Multi-shaped rocks and rocks varying considerably in colour should never be put in the same tank, they are unlikely to be found together naturally. Apart from providing banks of gravel at varying levels, rocks can be used to form terraces, and arches. It is not essential to install any rockwork, as plants alone could be used to provide very attractive arrangements.

Two favourite rocks used by aquarists are Cumberland stone and the green-brown flat, slaty rocks found in Devonshire streams. These flat natural pieces of rock can be pressed into the gravel to form pinnacles, or laid flat and built up, one upon the other, to form natural looking ledges.

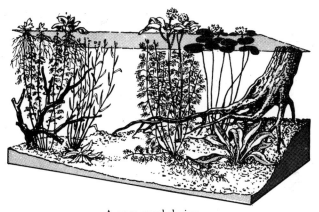

A very good design

Well weathered pieces are the best, but avoid pieces with jagged edges or protrusions which may injure your fish. The types of rocks suitable for aquarium decoration must be insoluble. Avoid using rocks of a soft or synthetic nature, as these tend to break up after prolonged immersion. If you have a doubtful piece of rock, put it in a bucket of clean water for a few days, if an oily ring appears on the surface, do not use it.

In the interest of hygiene it is advisable to avoid nooks and crannies in the rockwork that can harbour uneaten food, this will pollute the water and provide sediment traps. They could also hide a dead fish which could also cause water pollution. After the rocks have been sited to your liking, press them into the gravel, then if there are any pockets anywhere, fill them in with gravel.

It is possible to fashion your own rockwork, using sand and cement, but it is not an advisable practice. However, it can be done. After the rocks have been moulded into the desired shapes and due care taken to ensure that no sharp projections have been left, leave for about a week for the cement to harden, then boil for at least an hour in clean water to remove most of the free lime. Next soak the 'rock' in a strong solution of permanganate of potash for about 6 hours. In addition to disinfecting the rock this also adds to its attractiveness by giving it a natural weathered appearance. After a final soak under a running tap for about an hour the rock is ready for use.

The next stage is to add the plants. Avoid moulding the overall design of the interior so that the result is completely symmetrical, a plant or rock placed in the centre of the tank with equal numbers of identical plant on each side is a sorry sight and will certainly not look very natural, neither will an aquarium with all the 'weight' tucked into one corner without any balancing piece. The aim should be to provide a well balanced scheme with tall plants at the back and the smaller and daintier specimens to the fore, keep an eye on proportion. The aquarium should look well balanced. Remember that the use of excessively large rocks will have the effect of reducing the impression of depth, and do not scatter the plants around in a haphazard manner, as this will result in an untidy and unnatural design, it is much better to group the various species.

Tank layout

Many aquarist supply stores carry a wide range of plastic plants, some of which are quite excellent artifices. Personally, I see no virtue in using these plants in a fresh water tank when one can see the real thing, however, tastes differ, and the odd sprig may well be used to advantage if used with discretion. Plastic tree trunks can be used to hide filters and other apparatus and are effective when reproducing the terrain of tropical rain forest rivers.

The number of plants one should use is somewhat arbitrary, in one sense the more the merrier, but if the aquarium is too crowded with plants, the fish cannot be seen, therefore, the following suggestions are average requirements for a tank measuring 24 in. × 12 in. × 12 in.

  18 Sagittaria     about 12 inches long.
   2 Cabomba      about 12 inches long.
   8 Myriophyllum about 12 inches long.

or

  18 Vallisneria    about 12 inches long.
   2 Indian Fern   Large
   1 Amazon Sword Medium
   6 Ambulia      Medium.

Hair grass and other small decorative plants can be added for effect.

The inclusion of gnarled branches and twisted roots is most effective, but they can have some effect on the condition of the water by releasing organic acids from the wood. The only really safe woods to use are those that have lain in water for a number of years and have a petrified appearance, it is advisable to further cleanse these branches by washing for an extended period in a clean stream or lake, followed by boiling in salt water, and further washing in clean water for about a two week period. Finally boil in clean water before actually putting them into the aquarium.

An effective use of twigs etc.

Even after taking all these precautions, there is no guarantee that their inclusion will not turn the water cloudy by releasing certain mineral compounds.

Under no circumstances use fresh branches or roots. These release decomposable substances into the water which can cause pollution, which is harmful to the fish.

One final word on layout—whatever objects you put into your aquarium always ensure they are clean, free from dirt, have no hidden crevices to hold substances which could cause pollution and that they have been thoroughly disinfected as previously described.

# PLANTS

*Acorus gramineus* (**Japanese Rush**)

This pretty little plant is found naturally in the calm waters of East Asia, where it grows in swampy terrain, sometimes partly submerged, sometimes completely on dry land, but in the aquarium it grows totally submerged.

*A. gramineus* is a small, very attractive little plant, rarely exceeding a few inches in height, therefore, it is an ideal decorative piece to use near the front of the tank. It is decidedly rush-like with narrow, grass-like, pointed leaves, that sprout direct from the rootstock, their colour is bright to dark green.

This particular plant may well be described as *A. pusillis*, *A. japonicus*, or *A. intermedius*, they are not however, different species, but simply varieties of *A. gramineus*.

This is not a difficult plant to grow providing it is maintained in a moderate temperature, it does not like very warm water.

Propagates by splitting the rootstock, but because this species does not root very fast it is necessary to anchor with strips of lead, or with glass rods.

*A. calamus* is a similar species growing somewhat taller, but it is not suitable for tropical aquariums.


*Aponogeton fenestralis* (**Madagascar Lace Plant**)

This plant comes from the Island of Madagascar and has been a firm favourite among aquarists for a number of years, but it is not a very easy plant to grow.

It is the leaf structure that makes this plant so unusual, the tissue between the nervures and veins is always absent giving the leaves the

43

appearance of fine lace, hence its popular name. The leaves are oval, and slightly pointed at the base and the tip, they can grow to 12 inches long and 3 inches wide. The rootstock is cylindrical.

*A. fenestralis* is not an easy plant to cultivate in the aquarium, it requires soft slightly acid water, and a weak or diffused light. The open lattice structure of the leaves collect algae very readily and this chokes the plant and stunts its growth.

Propagates by runners which can be divided from the rootstock as soon as they reach 1 inch in length.

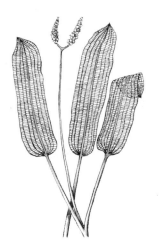

Aponogeton fenestralis

## Aponogeton ulvaceus

Found naturally in Madagascar, this plant is one of the larger plants available to aquarists. The leaves are a very delicate light green in colour and may well reach a length of 12 inches and a width up to 3 inches. The attractiveness of the plant is enhanced by the wavy edges to the leaves.

Because of their large size these plants require a spacious aquarium, they also thrive best in a water temperature around 75°F (24°C) in summer, and a little less in winter.

*A. ulvaceus* is not a particularly difficult species to cultivate but they can prove frustrating to aquarists not particularly skilled in plant culture. Like *A. fenestralis* it prefers soft slightly acid water and the leaf surfaces kept free of algae and settled mulm.

Propagates by seeds and runners.

44

## Aponogeton undulatus

This species is an ideal plant for the smaller aquaria, the plant only growing to about 9 inches tall. The leaves are a beautiful brilliant green, tapering to a point at the tips, and more rounded at the base. The leaf edges are slightly crinkled like the edges of torn paper. The actual leaf rarely exceeds 12 inches in length or 2 inches wide.

This is not a fast growing plant and rarely flowers in the aquarium.

*A. undulatus* offered by most stockists is generally a species cross-bred with *A. crispus*.It is an attractive little species nevertheless.

## Azolla caroliana (Fairy Moss)

Normally found in the tropical and sub-tropical zones of America, and Southern Europe where it was subsequently introduced. This rather unusual floating plant is composed of very small sage green leaves over-lapping one another like the scales on a fish, or tiles on a roof. On the underside of the leaves many long thread-like root strands hang down in the water. When used in an indoor aquarium, they should be spread thinly otherwise they will shadow the other plants below. Under natural conditions Azolla thrives well in moist, warm air, under the open sky with plenty of bright light, unfortunately it does not do so well in the aquarium, it tends to wither very easily and rarely survives the winter.

## Bacopa amplexicaulis

*B. amplexicaulis* is a species of swamp plant found naturally in Southern and Central U.S.A. It is a hardy plant with stiff stems which are somewhat brittle, consequently they are easily broken. The leaves are attached to the stem in pairs, one leaf opposite the other, and they are a beautiful shiny green, and rounded in shape. The stem is finely fluted and covered with fine hairs.

When in bloom the pretty blue to violet flowers appear in the angles of the leaves, but this plant will not bloom in the aquarium where it is totally submerged. The flowers only appear on emerged plants.

*B. amplexicaulis* does not like very high temperature, ideally, the temperature should be maintained at about 64°–68°F (18°–20°C). Temperatures above this level cause the plant to degenerate.

Because the plant refuses to bloom in the aquarium, and so provide seeds, propagation is effected by cuttings.

### *Bacopa monnieria*

This species is found naturally in America, Australia, Asia, Africa and possibly in Southern Europe. It is very similar to *B. amplexicaulis* with the exception of the stems and leaves which are devoid of hairs, also the leaves are slightly smaller. It is just as hardy, and has the advantage of tolerating slightly warmer water, consequently it is the better of the two mentioned species for inclusion in a tropical aquarium. Because the plant only blooms when emerged, seeds are unlikely to develop in aquarium specimen, but they can be propagated by carefully selected cuttings.

### *Cabomba caroliniana* (Fan-Wort)

This is a very attractive plant with its leaves of delicate light green which fan out from the main stem. The fan-like leaves form an excellent retreat for young fish, but it is not considered a good spawning plant because the leaves are not sufficiently dense.

*Cabomba* is one of the few plants that can be bunched, but not too tightly. When purchased these plants are often tied in small bundles with a thin strip of lead, if this is so, the ends should be broken off before planting into the gravel, this will give the stems a better chance to take root. It is also advisable to strip back the leaves for about 2 inches from the bottom of the stem to ensure that no leaves are buried in the gravel to become a potential source of decay.

This is not a particularly hardy plant neither is it a very good oxygenator, therefore, it is best to consider it as a decorative plant only.

Propagates by cutting.

Cabomba caroliniana

### *Ceratophyllum demersum* (**Coarse Horn Wort**)

*C. demersum* is a species that is found over the major parts of the world, and could become an exhibit in almost every aquarium, unfortunately it has two main drawbacks. The leaves are so brittle that they snap off at the slightest touch, and it has no real roots.

The leaves resemble *Myriophyllum* in structure except that they are coarser and are equipped with tiny thorns. It is not one of the best plants for exhibition purposes, but it is useful for breeding if it is weighted down with small pieces of lead.

If left floating in an aquarium, thin tendril like shoots grow from the stem towards the gravel in an attempt to root.

Propagates by cuttings.

*C. submersum* is a less common species very similar to *C. demersum* except that the leaves are thinner and more delicate.

Ceratophyllum submersum

### *Ceratopteris thalictroides* (**Indian Fern**)

Found practically all over the tropic regions of the world, *C. thalictroides* was first introduced as an aquarium plant in the 1930's and since then has become an established favourite. The leaf formation is not unlike those of the chrysanthemum, with deeply indented edges; they are soft and a delicate light green in colour. The stems are rather brittle and rise from a compact root stock.

If planted in deep water, the stems may well reach a height of a few feet, in shallow water the leaves will either float just below the surface, or extend themselves above the surface and bear a fine cluster of rather coarse foliage.

47

This plant will grow readily under the stimulus of artificial light, and generally it is the best way to grow it.

It is advisable to replace old plants occasionally with younger ones as the old plants will turn brown and decay. Snails find them an appetising meal so if snails are present, it will become necessary to replace the plant at fairly frequent intervals.

For propagation *C. thalictroides* develop a perfect miniature of itself among the foliage. These miniatures then detach themselves and float to the surface. This, however, does not generally occur until part of the leaf or frond has turned brown and withered away.

Ceratoptris thalictroides

### *Cryptocoryne* (Water Trumpet)

The *Cryptocorynes* are individualist in aquatic plants. The beautiful shaped leaves have a particular character that is all their own. They are found widely distributed over South East Asia and some 46 species are known, but these are not all suitable or obtainable for aquatic use.

The *Cryptocorynes* are not lovers of strong light, so if the aquarium is positioned in the shade, these are the plants to use, but it is as well to remember that they do require some light stimulus so do not overdo the shade. Because the quantity of light required by *Cryptocorynes* is less than that required by most aquatic plants, it is obviously better to group plants of this nature in a single tank otherwise a compromise must be made between the supply of strong light for some plants and a weaker light for others, with the result that neither are satisfied.

These plants have a strong rootstock that grows within the gravel and throws off many runners. To propagate, the rootstock of large plants can be split up, or the new plants provided by the runners, can be replanted.

## Cryptocoryne beckettii

Found naturally in Ceylon, *C. beckettii* is one of the smallest of the family, its leaves, a delicate green, are elongated and pointed, and tend to grow in a horizontal position giving the plant a somewhat untidy appearance.

It prefers soft water, but will thrive in moderately hard water. Grow to about 6 inches.

## Cryptocoryne cordata

The leaf form of this species is similar in shape to *C. griffithii*. The large, broad leaves are somewhat heart-shaped near the base and slightly pointed at the tip, they are a rich dark green in colour, and sometimes the underside of the leaves are reddish brown. The veining is well marked.

It grows to an average height of 10 inches. Remember that these plants are naturally tropical and should be maintained at a temperature ranging between 70°–80°F (21°–26°C.). Reproduces by runners.

## Cryptocoryne nevillii

This is another very small species, the leaves are slightly arched and lanceolate in shape, their colour ranges from light to dark green. This species should not be shaded too much by other plants. Propagation as the other *cryptocorynes*.

## Cryptocoryne griffithii

*C. griffithii* is a native of Indonesia and Malaya. The leaves are dark green in colour with a reddish underside and they have somewhat crinkly appearance. This species is very similar to *C. cordata* and can easily be mistaken for it, identification can be established by the more rounded leaf tip and tougher leaves.

49

It is a robust species, that will stand considerable rough handling and knocking by the net.

Reproduction by runners.

### *Cryptocoryne willisii*

This is probably the most popular of the *Cryptocorynes*. The leaves are a bright medium green and have a wavy edge. Propagation is by means of a short runner, or by splitting off a part of the parent plant. Once this species has become established in an aquarium, they should not be removed unnecessarily as they have an objection to new locations.

They grow to about 6 inches in length.

The young plants can then be collected and planted where required. If the plants are allowed to remain on the surface they will surely die, but take a comparatively long time to do so.

Cryptocoryne willisii

### *Echinodorus brevipedicellatus* (**Narrow Leaf Amazon Sword Plant**)

This beautiful plant from Brazil is shown to its best advantage in large aquaria. The shortish stems are between 2 and 6 inches long topped by long, narrow, lance-like leaves. In natural waters the plant will grow well above the surface, but in the aquarium they tend to lay flat along the surface.

Propagates by runners and is best maintained at a temperature around 70°F (21°C). Cooler water tends to keep the plants small, and less robust.

## *Echinodorus longistylus* (Long-Shafted Sword)

*E. longistylus* is a swamp plant found naturally in Brazil. It is ideally suited to large aquaria, but the plant has a tendency to grow above the surface of the water. Its shape is typical of the genus with long elliptical leaves about 7 to 9 inches in length on stalks that can reach up to 20 inches high.

It likes a water temperature of about 75°F (24°C) during the summer, and a few degrees less during the winter, and water a little soft. Natural sunlight will help to provide robust specimen.

Propagation in an aquarium is not easily achieved, but occasionally really heathy plants will grow new plants which can be separated, and planted out.

Echinodorus longistylus

## *Echinodorus martii*

Found naturally in Brazil, this species is a relative newcomer to the aquarium. It has lanceolate leaves, varying in length between 12 and 20 inches, with slightly wavy edges and rounded tips. The stalks are extremely short—only about 3 inches long. It is a plant that enjoys the higher temperature range of 75°–85°F (24°–29°C) and soft water, and should only be considered for very large aquaria.

Reproduction by runners, which should be pressed down into the sand where the new plants begin to develop.

### *Echinodorus paniculatus* (**Giant Amazon Sword**)

This plant has a wide range over South America. It is the largest of the Sword plants with leaves attaining a length of 20 inches, the shape of the leaves is typically lance-like, tapering both ends to a point, and running down the stalk towards the root.

Because of its large size, *E. paniculatus* needs a large aquarium, it also requires reasonably soft water, and a regular daily supply of either sunlight or artificial light. Temperature around 75°F (24°C) is ideal, lower temperatures tend to restrict the growth of the plant.

Reproduces by runners which should be pressed down into the sand where the new plants begin to develop.

### *Egeria densa* (**Argentina Anacaris**)

Previously known as *Elodea densa*, this plant is found naturally in subtropical South America. It is a beautiful plant with densely clustered leaves set closely to a central stem. The roots are sparse and consequently do not anchor very well into the gravel, a little lead may be necessary when first planted, they have the advantage however, of drawing their nourishment from the water, so they can be cultivated free-floating. The colour of *E. densa* is a fresh green, and one of its main attractions is that it is a quick growing plant—a growth of one inch a day not being unusual, the closely packed leaves offer a hideout to young fish, but they are too coarse for spawning tropical fish.

Early aquarists considered this plant to be one of the best oxygenators, undoubtedly it is a good oxygenator, but by present day

Egeria densa

standards, it is not considered so highly, however, do not exclude it from your selection on that account, as it makes an interesting specimen, if only for its speed of growth.

E. *callitrichoides* and E. *canadensis* are two species that are restricted to the outdoors pool or cold water aquarium, and normally E. *densa* is only suitable for cold water, but it has been used quite successfully in tropical tanks. E. *densa var crispa* however is suitable for either, the leaves and stem are shaped the same as E. *densa*, except that they bend back upon themselves and form a curly pattern.

## *Eichhornia crassipes* (Water Hyacinth)

This water Hyacinth is a beautiful and interesting plant, but it is not considered so in its natural habitat. It is found in most tropical regions of the world where it grows along the banks of rivers and other waters, and floating in dense matts, it grows so rapidly and densely that navigational problems are caused to boats.

The leaves are a shiny light green and spray outward on a short stem to form a rosette. The base of the stems are somewhat swollen and contain a sponge-like substance which gives the plant buoyancy and keeps it afloat.

The roots, blackish-blue in colour are long, dense and bushy, and make an ideal spawning refuge for fish that spawn adhesive eggs near the water surface.

The flower, which grows on a stalk from the centre of the rosette, is a delicate blue or violet.

Although this plant has been used in the aquarium for many years, it is not an easy plant to grow, because of its height above the water surface it is necessary to reduce the water level. The Water Hyacinth needs plenty of light, and moist warm air which makes it more suitable for the swamp aquaria or aquaria that have an extensioned glass top to contain the warm moist air. It usually dies in winter unless kept in a tropical greenhouse.

## *Elatine macropoda* (Big Footed Elatine)

Found naturally in Southern Europe and North Africa, this plant does not seem to be very readily obtainable in the United Kingdom or the U.S.A. and this may well be because the plant prefers temperatures just below 70°F (21°C) which is a little cool for the average tropical aquarium.

The small leaves, about $\frac{1}{2}$ inch long and $\frac{1}{8}$ inch wide have rounded tips and are attached in little bunches to a horizontal stem from which the root filament grows down into the gravel.

When first planted they should be left undisturbed for a period until they become firmly established and specially guarded from the attention of inquisitive fish who will disturb the water surrounding them.

Propagates by division of the stem and roots.

### *Eleocharis acicularis* (Needle Grass)

*E. acicularis* is widely distributed all over Europe. North and South America, Asia and Australia, where it grows along the edges of stagnant waters.

The leaves are thin, similar to the stiff blades of some grasses, and like grass the leaves sprout directly from the rootstock stemless. The roots spread out from plant to plant similar to the runners of *Valisneria*, the filaments burrowing down below each plant. In ideal conditions the plant will spread to form a matt which covers the whole floor of the aquarium. Dense patches make ideal spawning plants, the fine needle like blades give excellent protection to eggs scattered by egg laying fish. Temperature requirement for tropical aquaria should not be lower than 75°F (24°C). Propagates by division of the rootstock.

Eleocharis acicularis

### *Heteranthera zosteraefolia*

This plant is found naturally in Brazil and Bolivia. In some respects it resembles *Anacharis*. The pale opaque green leaves are attached in alternative positions on a somewhat brittle stem. It prospers best in a well-lit aquarium, with the water at a temperature of about 70°F (21°C). It is a hardy plant, with the additional advantage of growing quickly.

### *Hydrocleis nymphoides* (Water Poppy)

Found naturally in the tropical regions of South America the Water Poppy is a pretty addition to the aquarium with its shiny green heart shaped leaves floating on the surface of the water.

It is not a particularly difficult plant to grow in the aquarium providing the conditions are favourable. It requires plenty of sunlight, or a source of strong artificial light. The plant also seems to prefer soft water. Propagation is by shoots which sprout from the nodes of the stem.

### *Hygrophila polysperm* (Water Star)

This species is found naturally in the shallow waters of S.E. Asia, and it is one of the easiest of plants to grow. It has all the appearance of a terrestrial plant and it is interesting, because it is the only aquatic in the genus. The leaves sprout from a central stem in opposed pairs, their shape being not unlike those of the antirrhinum, they are a pretty light green in colour.

Reproduction is achieved by cuttings snipped off just below a node with outgrowing root tendrils on the stem. It does require plenty of light and will thrive abundantly in temperatures between 70°–80°F (21°–26°C).

### *Isoetes setacea* (Quiltwort)

Found naturally in Southern Europe, *I. setacea* is a suitable plant for mid positions in the aquarium. The pale green, slim, rush-like leaves generate direct from the compact rootstock and may reach a length of 12 inches. Their tendency to flow upwards in slightly wavy vertical lines makes the plant ideal for forming curtains of green tracery.

It is a hardy species suitable for relatively high temperatures, but it does grow rather slowly.

Propagates from spores encased in capsules situated at the base of the leaves. Young plants will often shoot up from around the base of the older, established plants.

There are other species of *Isoetes*, but these are not suitable for the general requirements of the tropical aquarium.

### Lemna gibba (Duckweed)

This species is found naturally in Europe, Asia and Africa, and is a common sight around the edges of our ponds and lakes, forming a green mantle which from a distance is easily mistaken for scum.

The dainty little leaves only about ⅛ inch long, are dark green and shiny, and a quantity of these makes a rather pretty roof to an aquarium in which it is being used to cut down light. Surprisingly the addition of this plant to an aquarium does not seem to impair the surface of the water from absorbing oxygen from the atmosphere. Reproduces by budding, resulting in chains of little plants.

### Lemna minor (Small Duckweed)

A slightly smaller species than *L. gibba*.

### Lemna trisulca

The pale green leaves of this species are quite different in shape from the usual Duckweeds, they are connected in little triangular columns.

### Limnobium stoloniferum (South American Frogbit)

Found naturally in the tropical regions of South America, *L. stoloniferum* is a beautiful floating plant with attractive heart shaped leaves attached to a central root by short stems, forming a rosette pattern. The leaves are sponge-like which gives the plant buoyancy. Long, thread-like roots hang down into the water.

This plant likes plenty of light, but if this is too intense, the leaves are likely to turn brown. Like most tropical swamp plants they require a moist warm atmosphere, consequently, the aquarium should be covered, but it will be necessary to lower the water to provide adequate space for the plant above the water level, alternatively, a special glass cover can be added to the top of the aquarium to increase the air space.

*L. stoloniferum* prefers soft water and a temperature around 75°F (24°C) or slightly higher.

Propagates by shoots from the parent plant.


## Limnophila sessiliflora

*L. sessiliflora* is found naturally in S.E. Asia and parts of tropical Africa and Australia. It is a similar plant to Cabomba consequently the two are sometimes confused. The main difference is in the shape of the leaf. When viewing *Cabomba* from above the fan-like leaves form a semi-circle, but the leaves of *L. sessiliflora* viewed from the same position, form a complete circle. The arrangement of the leaves are bunched rather close together making it an ideal spawning plant.

This species will not thrive unless it is supplied with plenty of light, natural or artificial, and a water temperature no lower than 68°F (20°C).

The fine feathered leaves are particularly susceptible to the settling of mulm stirred up by fish and air-lifts, it clogs the fine interstices and caused the plants to die.

There are about thirty known species of *Limnophilia*, but only two are currently being used by aquarists in addition to the above, they are *L. gratioloides* and *L. heterophylla*.

Propagates by cuttings. Smallish shoots snipped off from where they join the main stem make the best plants.


## Ludwigia natans (Floating Lugwigia)

This plant is found in the Southern regions of the U.S.A. The leaves are lance-shape and pointed at both ends. They are joined to the main stem in pairs opposite each other. Their colour is a brownish green, sometimes brilliant red on the underside. *L. natans* requires plenty of light, if you plant them in a shady part of the aquarium the leaves are likely to droop.

It is not a very difficult plant to propagate which is accomplished by snicking off a piece of plant just where the leaves join the stem, where you can see the young trendrils shooting, the cuttings can then be planted in the usual way.

*L. alternifolia* is a species not really suitable for tropical aquaria, the leaves are attached to the main stem alternatively instead of directly opposed as in *L. natans*.

*L. palustris* is the only European species.

Ludwigia natans

### *Lysimachia nummularia* (**Moneywort**)

'This pretty little plant is found naturally in Europe, E. Asia and North America. The light green rounded leaves are attached to a central stem in opposed pairs. It is a hardy plant with strong decorative appeal.

*L. nummularia* is not difficult to grow providing adequate lighting is supplied and it will certainly benefit from occasional exposure to sunlight.

### *Myriophyllum brasiliense*

Is found in South and Southern America, it is a deep green colour with distinctly separated feathery leaves forming a shape like a snow crystal star when viewed from above. Suitable for tropical freshwater aquariums.

Myriophyllum brasiliense

### *Myriophyllum* (**Water Milfoil**)

This genus of plants have a delicate fern-like beauty with fine abundant leaves attached to a central stem that make them ideal spawning plants. The plants will float naturally just below the surface and in aquariums where the water depth has been reduced, give excellent protection to livebearer fry. If the plant is to be used to catch the eggs of spawning fish, they should be planted in thick clusters.

When planting, the stems should be stripped clean of leaves for about 2 inches from the bottom, and pressed into sand.

*Myriophyllum* does not like very warm water, most species should be maintained in aquaria with a water temperature no higher than 75°F (24°C). Although a hardy plant, it requires constant attention. If it

59

is to prosper, mulm deposited on the leaves by water disturbances should be removed, similarly mulm collected around the roots should be syphoned off.

Propagates by cuttings.

## *Najas microdon* (Nymph Worts)

Found naturally in America, this plant is a vivid green in colour, with narrow generally opposed leaves which sit on the stems in much the same manner as the leaves of carnations. Occasionally fine indentations will be found on the edges of the leaves.

*N. microdon* is a fast growing species, providing they are given plenty of light and warmth, the temperature of the water should never be allowed to drop below 70°F (21°C). Given these conditions, they will grow into dense clumps useful for spawning fish that lay their eggs in thickets.

Propagation is by cuttings. The cuttings should be planted so that the gravel just covers the first two leaf position, they will then root quickly.

This plant is very similar in appearance to *Elodea callitrichoides*, but as this is a cold water species, the warmth of a tropical tank would soon kill it.

*N. minor* is a smaller species, but it is unsuitable for the aquarium.

## *Nitella flexis*

This species is found all over Europe, North America and Asia. It is a particularly dainty plant. The leaves, more like small stems from which flowers have been removed, are divided into two or three extensions at the tips positioned radially around the main stems. Leaves and stems are dark green.

These plants have thread-like roots which are insufficient to anchor the plant when first planted therefore, a temporary method of anchoring is necessary.

*N. flexis* requires plenty of light, but if this is excessive they tend to become inundated with algae. Apart from its decorative appeal, it is a useful plant for the breeding tank. The long tendril-like stems can be anchored along the floor of the aquarium to form a dense matt for protecting the eggs of spawning fish and young fry.

*N. gracilus* is another similar species.

Nitella flexis

### *Nomaphila stricta* (**Giant Indian Water Star**)

This is a swamp plant from S.E. Asia where it is found naturally in very shallow water and along the shore. The top of the plant protrudes well above the water surface. In many respects it is similar to *Hygrophilia polysperma*, the stems are strong and the leaves a beautiful vivid green, a little paler in shade on the underside, and somewhat varied in both shape and size, they are pointed at the base and the tip, and grow up to 5 inches in length. It is not unusual for fine hairs to grow on the stems and leaves.

*N. stricta* prefers a temperature around 75°F (24°C) and softish water.

Propagates by cuttings from the stems of strong plants, or even leaves. It is a plant that thrives best under the influence of strong light.

### *Pistia stratiotes* (**Water Lettuce**)

This interesting species of floating plant range over most of the tropical and sub-tropical regions of the world.

The leaves cascade from a central base like the petals of a flower and are light green in colour, fluted and velvety. Under suitable conditions, the plant will reach a diameter of 4 inches.

The roots hang down below the plant and are white to blue in colour, and although they are fine and bushy, they are not really dense enough to provide a spawning ground for surface egg layers.

This species does not prosper well in the aquarium, the raised top covers with built in lights are not ideal because they tend to dry the leaves which then go white.

Propagation by surface runners, preferably in shallow water.

Pistia stratiotes

### *Riccia fluitans* (Crystalwort)

This pretty floating plant is found naturally all over Europe, America and Asia. In the aquarium it forms a tangled matt of interlocking fibrous-looking greenery, sometimes to a thickness of ¾ inch. The small leaves are pronged and shaped like the minute antlers of a deer.

*Riccia* should not be allowed to grow too thickly, otherwise light and free passage of water will become restricted and decay will set in. Due also to the close packed formation of the leaves, it is difficult to keep it clean of algae, but an abundance of snails will help to keep it clean. However, care should be taken to exclude any Ramshorn snails. They will simply make a meal of it.

It is a really good oxygenator that multiplies by separation, one part separates from the parent and becomes a parent itself and so on.

It requires plenty of light, but not so near that the leaves become burnt.

### *Sagittaria* (Arrowhead)

*Sagittaria* is a genus of plants that closely resembles *Vallisneria*. The plant leaves irrespective of the species, are shaped more or less in the form of an arrowhead, hence its name *Sagittaria* after the mythical heavenly archer.

### *Sagittaria subulata*

Found naturally in the eastern regions of the U.S.A. this species could easily be confused with *Vallisneria spirallis*, the differences being mainly in the leaf structure, the leaves are narrow and ribbon-like, terminating in a tapering point, their colour being somewhat darker than *S. natans* which is vivid green.

### *Sagittaria lorata*

Found naturally in the N.E. regions of U.S.A. this species may well be known by other specific names of *S. eatonii, pusilla,* or *gracilis*. It is a hardy plant, with vividly green leaves, ribbon-shaped, sometimes broadening at the tips.

### Sagittaria gigantea

This species as its name suggests is a large species averaging a length of 15 inches, with leaves ½ inch or more in width. When well rooted, they are sturdy and will stand quite a lot of knocking from the net.

There are other species of *Sagittaria* that are more fitting for the cold water and aquaria, consequently they have been omitted.

All the above species reproduce by runners, but it has been observed that *Vallisneria* and *Sagittaria* rarely do well if planted in the same tank.

### Salvinia auriculata (Small Eared Salvina)

Found naturally in stagnant waters of Tropical South America, *S. auriculata* is one of the most interesting and prettiest of the floating plants available for tropical aquaria. The small hairy oval leaves are attached in opposed pairs to a common stem, and where they join the stem, root-like appendages hang down into the water. These brown, feathery threads are not true roots, but leaves that have become modified and adapted to absorbing the necessary nutrients from the water. Spore capsules sometimes develop at the base of the submerged leaves, but little is known about their development at the present time.

Because *salvinias* natural habitat is still water, it thrives very well in the aquarium, but it does require plenty of strong light and a temperature range between 64°–77°F (18°–25°C). It does not take kindly to drips of water from the cover glass, therefore, the cover of aquaria containing *Salvinia* should be tilted.

Multiplication is effected by sprouting, and under favourable conditions it will grow profusely. Aquaria sited in a greenhouse, and subjected to a reasonable amount of sunlight, are particularly suited to rapid growth. In natural conditions, the plant prefers shallow water containing decaying plant matter and infusoria, the clear water of the aquarium does not compare with these conditions, but it will still prosper although the leaves are likely to be smaller.

*Salvinia* is a plant that must be used with a little discretion, as a thick layer on the water surface shades the plants below from the available light source. On the other hand, it is an ideal plant for providing a refuge for small fry, and other tiny water creatures. It is also an ideal plant for the breeding tank for fish that spawn near the surface. Bubble nesters frequently make use of this plant to reinforce their nest of bubbles.

*Salvinia* is described under many different names, but these are often no more than colour varieties.

*S. natans* is a species found in Europe, North Africa and Asia Minor, but it is not recommended for use in the aquaria.

## *Sertularia cupressina* (Sea Cypress)

Sea Cypress is not a plant, but its usefulness in the aquarium justifies its inclusion. Sea cypress is in fact, the external skeleton of a hydroid polyp. It is found naturally in the tidal waters of Holland, Germany, Iceland and Great Britain and along the coasts of the North Sea. It grows on the sea bed, sometimes in bunches or beds up to 10 inches in depth, and in its natural state it has a delicate mossy appearance. The 'plant' consists of a skeleton made of chitin—the same substance that forms the outer case of insects. The tiny inhabitants of this skeleton are removed by a process of washing and drying, which leaves it clean and more or less dehydrated. It is in this form that it is available to aquarist. When dropped into water the fronds spread out to make a real life-like leathery plant.

If a single feather is viewed under a low powered microscope, the little pockets that once housed the tiny polyp can be seen quite clearly.

Although basically used as a decorative piece, its real value lies in its use as a breeding refuge.

When used in the breeding tank it is unnecessary to cover the floor of the aquarium with sand. The Cypress can be weighted with small pieces of lead attached to the base, the buoyant stems will then float vertically, making an ideal egg trap, or refuge for young livebearers.

Another advantage of Sea Cypress is the fact that it can be stored dry, preferably in a plastic bag for safety, and will last indefinitely if carefully handled.

After being used in the breeding tank, it can either be washed gently under a running tap and returned to the aquarium or thoroughly dried and stored.

## *Synnema triflorum*

This attractive plant, sometimes described as Wisteria, normally ranges through S.E. Asia, where it is found in tropical swamps, paddy fields and along the banks of rivers and lakes.

It is closely related to *Hygrophila*, with a strong vertical stem which can reach about 14 inches in height, the short leaves are light green on the upper surfaces and a whitish green on the underside. The irregularly shaped, lightly indented, leaves grow from the stem in such a way that when viewed from above they form beautiful rosettes.

Stems and leaves are covered with short hairs.

Propagates by cuttings which grow roots quickly. It does not like very hard water, and need plenty of light and a temperature around 75°F (24°C).

## *Utricularia exoleta* (Bladderwort)

This species is found naturally in S.E. Europe, Africa and Australia. It looks like a tangled mass of light green cotton with little knots attached to the strands, as if someone had tried to untangle it and lost patience. The little knot-like appendages are little bladders through which the plant feeds in an unusual way.

The bladder, called utricles, are in fact traps for catching the prey on which the plant draws its nutrient. The bladders are equipped with a tiny trap door that is normally closed, and when the prey—small micro animals, infusoria etc.—comes in contact the door flies open and the inrush of water carries the prey inside to be digested. This plant is ideal for spawning surface egg layers and as a protective maze for very young livebearers, being of a closer formation than Riccia.

When using Bladderwort it is advisable not to have other floating plants in the same tank, as they become hopelessly entangled with each other.

*U. exoleta* grows best in softish water and in a temperature no lower than about 70°F (21°C). Propagation takes place by fragmentation of the plant which only requires to be put in water to grow new shoots.

*U. vulgaris* is another species but it is not suited to the warm temperatures of the tropical aquarium.

## *Vallisneria* (Eel Grass)

*Vallisneria* is a genus of perennial water plants belonging to the family of the Frog Bits. It is distributed naturally over wide areas of the tropics, sub-tropics and the warmer parts of the world.

They are ideal furnishing plants for the aquarium with their light-green leaves and tall grass like blades. They are hardy plants useful for forming backgrounds, and need no special attention except a reasonable amount of light.

They propagate by shooting out runners, the baby plants setting themselves. Female flowers grow on thin, spiral stems which reach up to the surface. Male flowers form at the base of the leaves, detach themselves and float on the surface to join the females.

66

### *Vallisneria spiralis* (**Common Eel Grass**)

The shape of *V. spiralis* is typically grass-like and has the advantage of being an excellent oxygenator. It is a tall plant with leaves that rise vertically from the crown to the top of the water, where they float along the surface.

### *Vallisneria gigantea* (**Giant Eel Grass**)

As its name suggests, this is a somewhat larger species, the leaves may well reach 5ft in length, and widths in excess of 1 inch. They are found naturally in New Guinea and the Philippines.

### *Vallisneria spiralis-forma tortifolia*

This is a corkscrew variety of *V. spiralis* with spirally wound leaves and it does not grow quite so large. They are hardy but tend to remain small with less pronounced corkscrewing if maintained in water too cool.

Vallisneria spiralis forma tortifolia

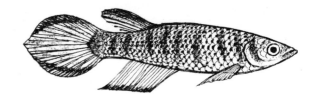

# AQUARIUM
# MANAGEMENT

## Water

Water, the most important element of all life, is also the most important aspect that we have to consider in fishkeeping.

Water or $H_2O$ as every schoolboy knows is an oxide of hydrogen and it is rarely if ever found in nature in its pure state. The nearest to pure water is rain water, but even water precipitating as rain collects dissolved atmospheric air and small particles of impurities on its way down to earth, and in heavily industrialized areas where large volumes of smoke pollute the atmosphere the impurities can reach a very high level.

Once the rain has reached the earth it either soaks into the terrain or forms rushing torrents over rocky surfaces. The water in springs and wells, and indeed the water of rivers, have traces of various substances dependent upon the composition of the layers over which the water has passed. Mineral salts of calcium and magnesium increases the hardness of the water, decomposed vegetable and animal matter provide humic and tannic acids, peat, fallen trees, etc., will tend to make the water acid, whilst chalks tend to have the opposite effect by neutralising the acid and making the water alkaline.

Whilst distilled water, $H_2O$, is a simple compound, the composition of the waters of the worlds rivers is by no means simple. Depending upon their location, they contain many chemical substances, and many organic compounds, bacteria, suspended algae, protozoans and so on. Fish living naturally in rivers are obviously acclimatized to the particular quality of their water, and drastic changes can prove disastrous as we know by some of our own polluted rivers. For example, fish living in deep lakes and mountain streams are acclimatized to clean, fresh, highly oxygenated water, whilst estuary fish, bottom-living fish and species with auxiliary respiratory organs can withstand a much lower quality of water. The fish from mountain streams could hardly be expected to survive in the same conditions as lung fish, or Paradise fish.

The first requirement of aquarium water is that it should be clear and clean, and in general terms it is true that both fish and fishkeeper require these conditions. Sparkling, clean aquariums are a beautiful sight indeed. Any attempt to simulate water from a particular area is bound to be only partly successful due to the constant changes in natural waters, and the difficulty of providing the microscopic life. Some species of fish must have reasonably controlled water, but this particular aspect will be discussed under species of fish, we are mainly interested now in providing a water generally suitable for the majority of our fish and plants.

Distilled, or pure water is useless, as minerals are necessary for both fish and plants. Micro-organisms are needed also as they help to quickly decompose waste products. Once set up, the aquarium water should remain clean and hygienic without the use of chemicals, controlled only by a 'biological balance' of fish, plants, water, minerals, micro-organisms, and a little assistance from the aquarist.

## Tap Water

The most readily available water is, of course, from the household tap. It is clean, filtered, but also chlorinated by various amounts dependent upon the needs of the district. The hardness of the water will also vary. Hard water can be improved by boiling which will remove calcium and magnesium bicarbonates, after boiling allow the water to cool then draw off from the top by siphoning with a length of plastic tube. The lower portion of the water should be discarded. Tap water should be allowed to stand for a few days to allow chlorine and any excess gases to disperse.

## Water, Other Sources

Clean rain water from a water butt has much to commend it, but always filter through fine muslin first, and preferably follow with a further filtration through fine nylon floss. It is advisable to add a little sea salt to make up for any mineral deficiency. About 2 level teaspoonsful to 12 gallons of water is about right. Should the water become cloudy when the salt is added, do not let this worry you, it will soon clear. Pond water, and waters from rivers, lakes and brooks are suitable providing they are well filtered, and look clean, but keep a wary eye for possible pollution. Frankly it is safer to use either tap or rain water.

### Matured Water

Aged water is simply water that has stood for sometime. If the container was sealed for example in a stoppered bottle, the water is unlikely to have changed in composition in any way. It is often useful to have a quantity of such water available, especially when breeding as the parents can often be stimulated to spawn by a partial change of water.

Mature water is water that has undergone a change, both chemically and biologically in the aquarium in association with the fish, plants and micro-organisms. The composition of aquarium water is not static, it is continually being changed by the activity of bacterial action on waste, and chemical production and assimulation by plants and micro-organisms. The aquarists task is to maintain the 'biological balance' by removing excess waste products and to ensure that each aquarium is balanced with fish and plants to obtain optimum conditions so that the aquarium will look after itself within the limits of its confinement.

### Green Water

Green water in itself is not necessarily undesirable, its main drawback is that it clouds the view and prevents you from seeing the beauty of the fish. The green colouring matter is a form of plant life oxygenating the water and behaving much in the same way as other leafed plants.

These microscopic vegetable cells need light and food to develop as with all life. If you eliminate all light, you eliminate green water, but it is not as simple as that, fish and plants still require light so we have to compromise by reducing the amount of light falling onto the tank.

Another method of clearing green water is to tip a large quantity of daphnia into the tank, but as these creatures are oxygen consumers it does mean removal of the fish for a while. Slightly acid water tends to keep the water clear, but has a tendency to discourage plant growth.

An effective way to reduce light is to cover the water surface with a mantle of duckweed, riccia, or salvinia.

70

Whilst I am basically against the use of chemicals or drugs unless there is no other course of action I have found the proprietary solution Acurel F very effective in controlling suspended organic debris and clearing up the green water condition by removing the green suspension of algae.

It is a wise precaution to keep feeding down to a minimum whenever the water becomes discoloured, until the condition has cleared.

## Cloudy Water

Water that has turned brownish or muddy in colour indicates that there is trouble brewing. Whilst green water can be considered healthy, this opaque mistiness is decidedly the opposite. It is caused by an excess of organic matter in the water probably due to overcrowding the fish and a resultant excess of waste products.

Excessive bacteria can result from feeding a dry food containing some ingredient that the fish refuse to eat, or simply by feeding too much food. Another possible cause is too few plants to absorb the level of waste present, or an insufficient light source to stimulate the plants into the necessary action. All kinds of organic matter including plant remnants, dead leaves, excreta and general debris, form a nutrient body for bacteria which will multiply rapidly with the aid of oxygen and break it down into mineral salts. If the waste is plentiful, then the oxygen supply will be inadequate and anerobic fouling will follow. The bacteria will then produce large quantities of toxic substances which are detrimental, if not lethal to the fish.

A possible remedy is to dissolve one-fifth grain by weight of pot: permanganate into each gallon of water. Fish and plants will be unharmed by this concentration. Whilst this may clear the problem, remember it will re-occur unless the underlying cause is removed. Should the water take on a yellowish tinge, there is nothing for it but to completely change the water without delay.

When setting up an aquarium for the first time, cloudiness in the water may result because the gravel has not been cleaned properly. Newly set-up aquariums may well exhibit a little mistiness, but they usually clear themselves within a few days when the plants settle down.

## pH Value

The determination of pH value is a valuable guide to aquarists when breeding certain types of fish or growing plants requiring particular conditions. It enables the condition of the water with respect to its alkalinity and acidity to be ascertained and corrected if necessary.

Technically pH is the logarithm of the reciprocal of the hydrogen ion concentration. Some knowledge of chemistry is necessary to understand fully the meaning of the formula, but it is sufficient to know that it is a measurement of acidity/alkalinity represented by a scale 0–14 where 0 represents maximum acidity, 14 represents maximum alkalinity, and mid position 7, equals a point of neutrality, neither one or the other.

Aquarists will only be concerned with readings around the neutral position, say pH5 to pH8, conditions outside this range will not concern us here as fish could not possibly tolerate the extremes.

The pH value of water is not a constant factor, it is influenced by adding new water, by deposits of various substances, rotting vegetation, the amount of dissolved calcium and magnesium in the water and so on.

The methods of obtaining pH value has been described under 'Equipment'. To make adjustments the following suggestions may be used without risk.

*To correct an over-acid condition.* Add salt, or sodium bicarbonate ($NaHCO_3$), Sea salt is probably better because it contains minor elements of beneficial minerals, mix first with water before adding to the aquarium.

*To correct an over-alkaline condition.* Add acid sodium phosphate ($NaH_2PO_4$) again mix first with water before adding to the aquarium.

The addition of acid sodium phosphate usually causes a thin film of precipitate to form on the surface of the water, this can be avoided if it is possible to boil the water first and then add potassium hydrogen tartrate ($KHC_4H_4O_6$), instead of acid sodium phosphate.

Natural conditions are well imitated by filtering the aquarium water through peat moss which will give a weak acidification and result in a soft acidic water.

A final word of importance—do not make any drastic changes to the pH values of water containing fish. A quarter degree of the scale every twelve hours should be considered a maximum, and it is preferable to make an even slower change if possible. Do not forget to check the aquarium after treatment to ensure that the desired results have been achieved.

## Filtration

Filters are used basically to remove suspended matter from the water and secondly to provide a varying amount of water turbulence.

Naturally if the water is to be filtered it must be circulated through a filter medium and returned to the tank. This water movement which can be gentle or fierce depending upon the type of filter selected, provides currents that are beneficial to the fish and to some extent simulates their natural environment where the water is rarely static. Some fish that are found naturally in fast running streams enjoy swimming against the current, whereas fish from swampy areas are conditioned to more gentle water movements.

In community tanks a good rule of thumb method is to filter the total volume of water about four times an hour.

Now to the main purpose of the filter which is to remove waste materials from the water. Individual requirements and availability of the necessary spare cash will largely dictate the approach to filtration. If the aquarist has only one large decorative furnishing aquarium and he requires a fairly high water circulation, then the obvious choice is a power filter.

On the other extreme he may have a room full of tanks then it is obviously better to install a good air pump and air-operated filters.

Internal box type filters operated by an air lift are quite efficient for the removal of mulm, but many experienced aquarists object to them because they do not remove the waste from the aquarium water, but rather contain it in a confined volume. Another disadvantage is the fact that they are rather unsightly and need to be hidden behind plants or rockwork for better visual presentation.

Outside box filters, whether operated by air lift or integral motor driven pump, are easier to clean without disturbing plants or layout and can be much larger. In my opinion, this latter feature has considerable advantages over the internal bottom filter.

A further application for filters is to use them for conditioning the water by including a layer of ion exchange resins in the filter pack for removing salts. Once installed the filter should be left on permanently as the continual water movement will keep the surface mobile and encourage oxygen absorption, and the bubbles from air lift tubes will certainly provide oxygenation.

All box type filters need to have their filter media changed periodically. The media must have the property of removing suspended matter from the water without restricting the water flow unnecessarily. An ideal medium, currently obtainable in America is napped nylon. It is a loosely woven fabric about the same thickness as a good quality blanket. It is inexpensive and obtainable by the yard and needs only to be cut into convenient sizes to fit the filter. It can be washed and used over and over again.

Polymer Dacron wool is another useful filtration material that can

73

be used several times if washed. The fibres of the material are excellent for trapping dirt. Ordinary gravel is commonly used as a base, with filter wool on top. Glass wool should be considered suspect and never used, it has the tendency to break into fine slithers which can find their way into the tank and lodge in the gills of the fish or even be eaten by them.

Carbon and activated carbon is used to remove toxic material from the water, there are many proprietary brands available. The efficiency of the various carbons can be judged by taking a sample quantity and putting it into a container with water, then add a dilute solution of Methylene Blue and shake. The more active the carbon, the more dye it will absorb.

Undergravel or biological filters are filters that process the waste material within the aquarium. They consist of a perforated frame under the gravel which sucks the water and waste down into the gravel. These filters should be used in well planted aquaria to obtain the best results.

In operation the waste organic matter is carried down between the grains of gravel where bacteria converts it into plant nutrients. The ideal grain size for the gravel is 6–20, or 8–20 if using quartz gravel. If the gravel is too fine the waste cannot permeate it and if it is too coarse the waste penetrates too well and causes a high concentration of bacteria with a resulting change in pH of the water towards the acid which can be highly toxic to some plants and fish. It is important that the depth of gravel should not be less than 2 inches otherwise the bacteria will not have enough room to multiply in sufficient numbers to perform efficiently.

It is always better to feed the fish with high protein foods as they will require less and consequently the waste products are less, and the acids formed are kept down to a minimum. It is advisable to check occasionally to see if too much food is penetrating the gravel. This you can do by stirring the gravel, if the top $\frac{1}{2}$ inch layer is caked, too much uneaten food is penetrating—reduce the quantity and improve the quality. The caking is caused by the bacterial colonies in the surface of the gravel.

## Metals

Very few metals can be used unreservedly in the aquarium. Avoid brass, galvanized iron and zinc as they corrode and will contaminate the water. Lead is usually safe, but unfortunately, it lacks rigidity and therefore, is unsuitable for some of the uses to which we would like to put it.

Iron will rust and although the iron oxide is not poisonous, it is not desirable to have drops of water and rust falling into the aquarium, therefore, treat the underside of the top lip of iron framed tanks with a good coat of paint or aquarium sealer.

If the aquarium frame is made of brass all but the top underside lip will be protected by glass and cement, make sure the lip is insulated from water vapours by several coats of paint, or a good sealer.

Nickel plating corrodes after a time in water, so it should not be relied upon for permanent protection against corrosion.

## Cleaning

Aquariums do require a little attention periodically. Regular maintenance does not take much time, but it does ensure the well-being of the fish, and repays the aquarist with clean and trouble-free tanks.

Once a week any mulm that has collected in hollows and around the roots of plants should be removed by an air rejector tube or syphon.

Green algae on the glass should be removed with a razor blade or scraper. Special scrapers with extended handles make the job simple and quick. Thread algae, which if left unhampered will soon choke plants, can be removed with a rough piece of twig. Poke the twig into the algae treads and twirl it, the threads will adhere to the twig and can be removed.

Scum on the surface hampers oxygenation, it is caused by excessive lime in the water or by overfeeding dry food. You can remove the scum by dragging a piece of blotting paper across the surface from one end of the tank to the other, and lifting it out carefully. Alternatively, a sheet of newspaper can be laid on the water surface, left for a few moments and then carefully peeled away.

Dead and decaying plant leaves should be snipped off, not pulled, otherwise the plant roots may be disturbed and even pulled right out of the gravel. Check filters are clean, if not, clean them out and recharge.

A word of warning—do not put hands into the water unless it is absolutely necessary, if you must, thoroughly wash the hands and rinse in clear water to remove all traces of soap. Nicotine stains on the fingers are particularly harmful to fish.

## New Arrivals

It is always advisable to quarantine newly acquired fish for a short period to ensure that they are free from any diseases. The majority of importers and breeders are usually very careful and do not intentionally supply retail sources with diseased fish, but the occasional outbreak is inevitable, so it is better to safeguard your stock by taking the few days necessary for quarantine.

If you suspect all is not well, then subject the new arrivals to a prolonged bath in a solution of potassium permanganate, $\frac{1}{8}$ grain to a gallon of water.

When transferring fish from container to aquarium, never tip them straight in, but float the container in the aquarium until the temperatures are more or less the same, then release them. Although many tropical fish can adapt to a reasonably wide temperature range, sudden changes are likely to cause chills and other problems.

## Petty Cruelties

Many little cruelties are perpetrated by thoughtless actions such as suddenly switching on a bright light over the aquarium, the fish are startled, if not frightened, and show this by darting about in an agitated state. Tapping on the side of the aquarium glass has a similar effect, and carelessly dropping the cover back on top of the aquarium, will send a shock wave through the tank. These are just a few examples of thoughtless actions that should be avoided in the interest of the fish.

## Overcrowding

Overcrowding is a common beginners fault. Once the aquarium is set up, every week-end sees a few more fish added, without making certain the aquarium has sufficient capacity to accommodate such an influx. Experienced aquarists know better. Tropical fish can stand a higher density than cold water varieties. The latter require about 24 sq. ins. of surface area per inch of fish, but tropicals need only about 8 sq. ins. of surface area per fish. This is of course, a rule of thumb method of calculation as number of plants, method of aeration, and size of fish are all factors that must be considered.

Some fish are notorious bullies and like to chase and nip their smaller community dwellers, and what is more, they seem to enjoy it. If the aquarium is roomy the smaller fish have the chance to escape, but it is better to keep only fish of a similar size in any one tank.

Persistent bullies should be removed and placed in another tank with larger fish.

# Netting

Always use rectangular nets to catch fish in an aquarium. The best way to net your fish is to use two nets, one net to gently guide the fish into the other.

Very small fry should never be handled, bring them to the surface in a net and then remove them, still in water, with a large spoon such as a soup ladle.

When netted, fish tend to jump about in an effort to escape, they may even jump right out of the net, and it is while they are doing this that injury is likely to occur. To avoid any problems always ensure the net is deep enough in the bag to be closed at the top with the free hand.

A useful net for handling very small fish can be made by lining the bottom of a small rectangular net with oiled silk for about $\frac{1}{2}$ inch at the bottom. The oiled silk retains both water and fish.

# Snails

Snails are a somewhat mixed blessing, they will not keep the aquarium clean by themselves, but they will help to consume some of the uneaten dry foods. Snails also help to keep down the algae in the inside of the glass and on plants, but they do not do the job well enough to save the aquarist from the task of scraping the glass with a scraper.

**Red Ramshorns** (*Planorbis corneus. var ruber*) are European snails that can be included in the tropical aquarium. They are quite exotic creatures, the best of them being bright red. Red Ramshorns produce from 60 to 120 eggs during a season in jelly masses containing 20 to 40 eggs, and these hatch in 10 to 40 days depending upon the aquarium temperature, unfortunately, tropical fish will destroy the newly hatched snails, therefore, if you wish to rear them, transfer the plant and eggs to an aquarium devoid of fish.

The **Malayan Burrowing Snail** (*Thiara tuberculata*) is quite distinctive and easily identified by the shape of its shell which is a long, tapering cone, having eight whorls. The shell is basically a light brown to grey-green overmarked with brown spots running more or less symmetrically along the length of the shell.

As its name suggests, it is a burrowing snail, and will bury itself in the sand leaving only the tip showing. Fully grown specimens rarely

77

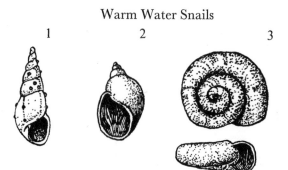

1. A burrowing snail from Africa and Thailand
2. A small Australian snail
3. Small Brazilian snail, approx. ¾″

exceed 1½ inches in length. An interesting feature of the snail is the fact that they are viviparous, the tiny babies are replicas of the parents, almost transparent at birth, but gaining some colour when about ⅛ inch in length.

They apparently feed in decaying animal and vegetable matter, or mulm.

Generally, snails will eat plants, this is an annoying habit especially when they attack a particularly favoured show piece, but the Malayan snail can be trusted to restrict his activities to the gravel. Pond snails can be used if desired, they perform quite well, but are not particularly spectacular.

The decision to include snails in an aquarium is a personal one, they are not essential with modern techniques of filtration, but they do in some way belong to the underwater scene.

## Water Hardness

Water is said to be soft when soap readily lathers in it, and hard when it does not. Rain water is soft and in many respects resembles distilled water, which has a silky quality that makes washing in it a pure joy. On the other hand, hard water gives a meagre lather and the water feels 'coarse'.

The actual cause of water hardness is the impurities it contains, these can be divided into three main groups—dissolved, suspended and colloidal. Colloidal suspension is a state between true suspension and solution. Both suspended matter and matter in colloidal suspension can usually be removed by filtration.

The major cause of hardness is dissolved compounds of calcium and magnesium. Total hardness of a water includes both the permanent and the temporary hardness. The temporary hardness is due to the presence of bicarbonate of calcium and magnesium and can be removed by boiling the water. A similar process takes place naturally in the aquarium when plants under the influences of light absorb carbon dioxide.

The permanent hardness of water cannot be removed so easily, boiling has no effect, neither can it be removed biologically. The cause is the presence of dissolved sulphates and chlorides of calcium and magnesium, as these are in solution, they cannot be removed by filtration or by boiling.

The Permutit process softens water by treatment with zeolite in which ion exchange takes place; calcium and magnesium ions are removed and replaced by sodium from the zeolite, which can be recharged by treatment with brine.

However, it is possible to reduce the permanent hardness by the addition of sodium carbonate $(Na_2CO_3)$ which is ordinary washing soda. This reacts with the calcium sulphate and forms a deposit of insoluble calcium carbonate leaving sodium sulphate dissolved in the water.

The equipment for assessing the hardness of water has been described in the Equipment section. There are more accurate methods such as completely evaporating a given volume of water and accurately weighing the residue, but this is beyond most aquarists, and is probably more accurate than is necessary for successful fishkeeping anyway.

Water hardness can be expressed in various ways, the most common is to use parts per million of calcium carbonate in Britain, and German degrees on the continent.

## German Degrees

| | | |
|---|---|---|
| 0°–4° | DH | Very soft |
| 4°–8° | DH | Soft |
| 8°–12° | DH | Medium-hard |
| 12°–18° | DH | Hard |
| 18°–30° | DH | Very hard |
| 30°–DH and above | | Extraordinarily hard. |

## Parts per Million

| | |
|---|---|
| Under 50 | Soft |
| 50 to 100 | Moderately soft |
| 100 to 150 | Slightly hard |
| 150 to 250 | Moderately hard |
| 250 to 350 | Hard |
| 350 upwards | Very hard |

The simplest way to obtain a definite hardness below that which is readily available is to start with distilled or rain water and add tap water or sea salt until the desired hardness is obtained.

Water hardness is only one aspect of water, there is an inter-relation with pH values due to the buffering effect of certain alkaloids; and the trace elements, and micro-organisms present can make different waters of the same hardness quite unlike in many other respects.

Generally, softish water is better for fish and plants newly imported from the tropic zones, but as a vast majority of available fish are bred quite successfully in our somewhat harder water, we should continue to use it and only experiment when there is a specific need.

For the convenience of the experimental aquarist, a water hardness conversion table is given below.

| | | *Parts/ million* | *Grains/ Gal Deg Clark* | *Parts/ 100,000* | *Parts/ 100,000 German Deg.* |
|---|---|---|---|---|---|
| Parts/million as $CaCO_3$ | | 1·00 | 0·07 | 0·10 | 0·056 |
| Grains/gal as $CaCO_3$ Deg Clark | } | 14·3 | 1·00 | 1·43 | 0·80 |
| Parts/100,000 as $CaCo_3$ | | 10·0 | 0·70 | 1·00 | 0·56 |
| Parts/100,000 as CaO German Deg | } | 17·8 | 1·24 | 1·78 | 1·00 |

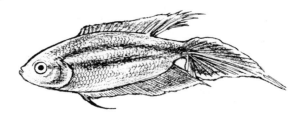

# DISEASES

'Prevention is better than cure'—this old saying was never more true than when related to fishkeeping. A watchful eye on aquarium hygiene and care when buying and introducing new fish to an established aquarium will do much to reduce the need to resort to doctoring. Nevertheless, even when great care is lavished on a most prized collection, the unexpected outbreak of white spot or some other malady, may unfortunately occur.

Considerable knowledge, experience and equipment is needed to diagnose some fish diseases and only specialists in this field are qualified to do such work, but many of the more common maladies are relatively easy to recognise and lend themselves to treatment by the aquarist.

Many of the chemicals required are easy to obtain, but treatments requiring the use of drugs will prove difficult in the U.K. due to the difficulty in obtaining the drugs without a medical prescription signed by a doctor and such a prescription would be illegal if it was intended for fish.

However, other countries have different regulations and if drugs are the only known cure for a particular disease, then there is no alternative but to recommend it.

Antibiotics are special types of chemical substances produced by one type of organism that is detrimental or lethal to another. The most common of these is penicillin, discovered in the U.K. by Sir Alexander Fleming. Scientists have known of the existence of antibiotics for the past 60 years, during which time they have been used spasmodically for the treatment of animal infections. The most notable of these early antibiotics was known as pyocyanase, an anti-biological blue pus.

Antibiotics are produced primarily in large quantities by fungi and bacteria. The causes of the diseases to which fish are prone are many, but in general they are caused by viruses, parasites, and fungi, and whilst it is practically impossible for the aquarist to give an absolutely accurate diagnosis, it is reasonable to assume that most of them are the result of disease-producing bacteria or nuero-organisms invading the system and therefore, can be treated in an experimental manner with antibiotics.

Remember that fish treated with these chemicals should not be left in contact with them any longer than is necessary.

Fish can be treated by adding the chemical to their water, or by direct application to the affected part. Where possible, use the treatments recommended later in this chapter, but if they do not apply and you wish to experiment, then restrict the use of antibiotics to those diseases which are not easily recognised, or incurable by any other known method. Use only the concentration recommended for stated treatments of known diseases. All chemicals and drugs should be dissolved completely before beginning any treatment, minute particles of undissolved chemicals can cause disastrous results if eaten. If necessary, filter the solutions before using them.

Proprietary cures are available from aquarists supply stores, most of these are excellent, but this is not true of all. Remember there is no panacea for curing all ills, one must treat any such claims with more than a degree of reserve.

The recent use of ozone as a curative agent is very promising indeed. Ozone $(O_3)$ is oxygen with an extra atom, and is produced for the aquarist by static electrical discharge and supplied to the tank via the filter or diffuser.

Its main purpose is the destruction of bacteria, and it does this without harming the fish if it is used at the correct concentration.

The importance of a spare tank for treating ailing fish cannot be over emphasized. Adding chemicals to a well established tank containing numerous healthy fish just because one or two exhibit signs of disease is foolhardy. The addition of some chemicals require the total volume of water to be changed subsequently, which is inconvenient to say the least. Conversely it is just as foolhardy to permit one or two fish to spread a disease among the whole community.

### *Argulus* (Fish Louse)

The cause of this disease is a free swimming crustacean that attaches itself to the fish. There are several species, they also possess a spine between the eyes for injecting poison.

DIAGNOSIS. The disease is recognized by reddish inflammation marks around the site of the sting, which develops into greyish patches, usually round. Favourite areas for attack are around the belly, gills and throat. Infected fish are restless, and flick themselves against the gravel or rocks. Fins usually flattened.

TREATMENT. Prepare a bath with potassium permanganate, 1 gram to 100 litres of water, and immerse fish for 10 to 30 minutes. Repeat as necessary every 8 to 10 days. No harm will come to fish or plants.

Alternatively, remove the fish from the aquaria and paint the affected areas with a camel hair brush dipped in paraffin oil, or turpentine, and then remove the offenders with a pair of tweezers.

## *Branchiitis* (Inflammation of the Gills)

This is not strictly a disease but rather a malady caused by an insufficient supply of oxygen.

DIAGNOSIS. The gills become inflamed and swollen, sometimes accompanied by white patches on the body and a general listlessness. The cause is a lack of oxygen in the water which asphyxiates the fish and causes the overworked gills to redden and become inflamed.

TREATMENT. The fish should be transferred to a hospital tank in which the water level has been reduced to 6 inches. Well aerate the water and feed the fish with small quantities of live food. It should only be necessary to continue the treatment for a few days.

## Constipation

Constipation in fish is not a disease but rather the result of being out of condition perhaps due to wrong feeding, but it can also be the herald of a more serious condition.

DIAGNOSIS. The fish becomes thin, sometimes refuses to eat, and swims with fins almost closed.

TREATMENT. Transfer the fish to a small aquarium and add Epsom Salts to the water—half a teaspoon to each gallon. The effectiveness of this treatment can be judged by the fish passing heavy excreta. Before returning the fish to the community tank, change the water and feed live foods for a few days.

Another method of giving a laxative is to soak a small bread pill in halibut oil.

If the above treatment fails it indicates that the fish may be suffering from an internal stoppage, which may not lend itself to treatment.

## Costiasis

Costiasis is caused by a small parasitic flagellate that attacks the skin and gills of fish.

DIAGNOSIS. It is recognized in the later stages by a reddish streak something like a burn, which spreads along the side of the fish from the tail towards the head.

In the early stages the fish behave more or less as if they have white spot by rubbing themselves against the gravel and plants. It is practically impossible for the amateur to reach an accurate diagnosis in the early stages, and when it does become apparent it is usually too late to treat effectively.

TREATMENT. Try immersing the fish for 20 minutes in a bath made with cooking salt, 10 to 15 grams to a litre of water. Alternatively, try a formalin bath for about 45 minutes—2 ml. of a 40% solution to 10 litres of water. Do not be disappointed if these baths fail to cure.

## Dropsy

Infectious dropsy is caused by bacteria that is found in most waters. It is a disease that takes many forms, and it is almost incurable. Normally really healthy fish are immune from the disease, but they can contract the disease if a tank becomes infected.

DIAGNOSIS. The fish become bloated with distended belly so much so, that the fish looks as if it will burst. The scales stand proud from the body, and skin lesions may appear, surrounded by a white ring, with a black outer ring.

TREATMENT. There is no real cure for this disease, it usually proves fatal within three weeks, it is therefore, advisable to destroy any infected fish immediately it becomes evident that it is suffering from dropsy. If you wish to experiment, try injections with streptomycin, 1 mg. per 50 grams body weight, and chloromycetin, 0·1 gram per 10 grams body weight.

## *Exophthalmia* (Pop Eye)

Pop-eye is caused by a haemorrhage in the capillaries of the eye socket. The capillaries are ruptured by an internal gas, and can affect either one or both eyes.

DIAGNOSIS. This is a really easy disorder to identify, the eye becomes enlarged and stands out in the socket like the half spheres of a rabbit's eye.

TREATMENT. The simplest treatment is to give the fish a salt bath as prescribed for Saprolegnia, for a period of 36 hours followed by bathing the eyes carefully with a 5% solution of Argyrol, which is a mild silver proteinate.

An alternative treatment consists of immersing the fish in a bath made up with one drop of ammonia to each gallon of water. The temperature of the bath should be set at 80°F (26°C) and the fish left in for 3 hours. After this period, gradually reduce the ammonia concentration by adding fresh water until it reaches normal. The fish can then be returned to the community tank.

## Fin Rot

Fin Rot can be caused by bacteria which attacks the fins and any injured areas of the skin. Bacterial fin rot is very difficult to cure but you can try a prolonged bath lasting a few days in Trypaflavin. To prepare the bath, dissolve 1 gram of Trypaflavin in a litre of water, then use 10 ml. of this stock solution per litre of water.

Phenoxephol has also been used and found to be an effective cure for Fin rot.

## Flukes (Trematodes)

The cause of this disease is infestation by the parasitic flat worms *Gyrodactylus* and *Dactylogyrus*. These lodge in the gills and under the skin of the fish. *Dactylogyrus* mostly infest the gills and if not checked, they can completely destroy the gills. *Gyrodactylus* mostly infest the skin, but can also affect the gills.

DIAGNOSIS. The parasites cause the fish to swim in a wild and jerky manner, suddenly stopping with every appearance of exhaustion. Growth is retarded, and in serious cases the worms can be seen beneath the raised gill cover of the live fish.

TREATMENT. There are various treatments for this illness. Make a bath of clear water and add 2 ml. of a 40% solution of formaline to every 10 litres and immerse the fish for 30 to 45 minutes, or until the fish shows distress. Alternatively, try a bath made up of 10 to 15 grms of cooking salt to every litre of water and immerse the fish for about 20 minutes.

## Frayed Fins

Occasionally it will be noticed that a few fish have been nibbling the fins of other members of the community. At odd times many species develop this annoying habit. The fins of the victims become frayed and untidy, but if they are removed to a tank free of the 'fin nibblers' the condition will soon correct itself. This condition should not be confused with fin rot which is difficult to treat.

TREATMENT. Separation from the bullies is usually sufficient, but if the condition is very bad, a salt bath will do no harm (ordinary cooking salt 10 to 15 grams per litre of water).

## Gas Bubble Disease

The cause of this problem (it cannot really be considered a disease) is fine gas bubbles trapped within the fishes body. Under high pressure a liquid will absorb more gas than it can when the pressure is low. Liquids will also absorb more gas when the temperature is low than it can do when the temperature is high. Providing conditions are stable, i.e., constant temperature and pressure, then it follows that a constant amount of gas will go into solution in a liquid. Under normal conditions the atmosphere pressure is about 14 lbs./sq. in. (this, of course varies with altitude, the higher the altitude the lower the pressure) and assuming a constant temperature in the aquarium, the amount of gas dissolved in the water will be normal for these conditions. If, however, the gas content is in excess of the normal, it is known as supersaturated, and the excess gas will be given off until a state of normality is attained.

The aquarium water can become supersaturated with oxygen with strong plant growth and fairly intense insolation. The liquid in the body of the fish then also becomes supersaturated. When the water is stirred, or moved by air pumps, the excess oxygen given off is accelerated, leaving fine gas bubbles within the body of the fish.

A condition similar to that experienced by deep sea divers and known as the 'bends' then occurs.

DIAGNOSIS. Bubbles under the skin, and a tendency for large fish to make tiny creaking noises when netted.

TREATMENT. Simply transfer the fish to normal water, or rapidly reduce the super saturation by disturbing the water with a power filter.

### *Ichthyophthirius* (White Spot)

*Ichthyophthirius multifiliis* is the name of the parasitical organism responsible for the common disease known among aquarists as White Spot.

The parasites are one-celled animals, spherical in form, with cilia

86

covering the surface. They burrow under the skin of the fish where they set up an irritation and spread, if unchecked, all over the body and fins. They live off their host until they become fully developed. When mature the parasites fall away from the host and individually form a cyst which adheres to plants and rocks. The cyst capsule eventually bursts releasing up to a 1000 tiny spores to re-infest the fish.

DIAGNOSIS. The first indication you may get of white spot is the fish darting about among the plants or flicking themselves against rocks obviously trying to ease the irritation, and a tendency to hold the fins and tail flat.

If white spot is not checked at this stage, the spots will become visible and multiply rapidly until the whole body and fins are covered.

The main casue of this disease is a chill caused by sudden temperature changes. Such changes need not be excessively low, a drop from 82°F (28°C) to 74°F (23°C) may well trigger an outbreak. Another source of infection is of course, the introduction of newly acquired fish which already has the disease.

TREATMENT. There are various effective treatments but the simplest requires no chemicals or drugs.

(1) Raise the temperature of the affected aquarium to 85°F (29°C) and maintain it for several days. (This should always be done irrespective of the method employed) Then transfer the fish to a tank free of parasites every twelve hours (also at the same temperature). The objective of this method is to increase the growth rate of the parasites by increasing the temperature, then when they fall off the fish into the tank, remove the fish to another tank to prevent re-infection.

It takes 72 hours for parasites in a tank devoid of fish to hatch and die, therefore any tank that has stood for over three days can be used again.

(2) Add mercurochrome to the infected tank, three drops of a 2% solution to every gallon. After a week draw off approx. half of the water and replace with clean water. Do not exceed the recommended concentration otherwise it may cause loss of fish due to mercury poisoning.

(3) Add 2 to 3 grains of quinine sulphate or quinine hydrochloride per gallon of aquarium water. Mix first with water and slowly add to the infected tank. Keep tank dark during this treatment.

(4) Add 2 drops of 5% aqueous solution of Methylene blue per gallon of water. Increase temperature to 85°F (29°C). This treatment

(5) Make a stock solution by dissolving 1 gram of Rivanol in 1 litre of water, then add 2 ml. of this solution to every litre of water. It is better to use the hospital tank for this treatment, and leave the fish in it for at least 3 days.

There are proprietary brands of white spot cures available, and generally they are effective, but most of these cures are affected by light, and should be supplied in dark bottles.

## *Ichthyosporidium*

This disease is caused by a fungus which infects marine cold and tropical fish. It forms roughly spherical cysts, microscopically small, which attack the liver, kidneys, spleen, heart and other organs, and even the muscles and skin. The daughter cysts develop inside the mother cyst which when they mature, bursts to release the parasites.

DIAGNOSIS. Internal symptoms are difficult for the average aquarist to assess, and it is possible for a fish suffering from this disease to die without exhibiting any external changes of appearance.

Generally, fish become very emaciated, swellings may occur which burst and form ulcers, pop eye may develop and if the brain or swim bladder is affected, the fish may have difficulty in swimming.

Angel fish are most likely to contract this disease, but no fish are immune.

TREATMENT. There is no effective treatment for this disease, therefore, it is best to remove the sick fish and destroy it to prevent other fish becoming infected.

The effect of ozone introduced into the tank via the air stone, or into the filter has not been fully explored but it is possible that the sterilizing property of ozone could prove beneficial in preventing the spread of the disease, if not actually curing it.

## Indigestion

This is not really a disease, simply a disorder usually caused by wrongful feeding, i.e., too much dried foods. It can also be caused by constipation.

DIAGNOSIS. Indigestion can be recognized by a swollen belly, air bubbles in the faces, and general sluggishness. It is not serious in itself, but must cause the fish some discomfort, so it should be speedily treated for that reason alone, but if left untreated, it could lead to a more serious condition.

TREATMENT. Salt bath, or halibut oil as prescribed for constipation.

# Itch

Itch is a malady caused by unhygienic conditions in the aquarium. It is a problem that should not present itself in well maintained aquaria.

DIAGNOSIS. The fish dart about the tank obviously suffering from some irritation, they flick themselves against the gravel and plants in much the same manner as if they were suffering from *Ichthyophtirius* or flukes, but the actual cause in this instance is a microscopic organism in the water set up by excessive uneaten food and excreta allowed to remain too long in the tank.

TREATMENT. Add ⅛ grain potassium permanganate per gallon of water to the tank, leave for a few hours, and then syphon off any mulm in the bottom of the tank, and the same time, remove about half of the water and replace with clean seasoned water. This will leave the water slightly pink, but this condition will clear itself eventually.

The plants and fish can remain in the aquarium during this treatment, but remember it should not have been necessary to carry out this treatment if the aquarium has been clean and healthy.

# *Lernaea* (Anchor Worm)

Anchor worms are parasitic, free swimming crustaceans. Generally they do not attack tropical aquarium fishes except perhaps large cichlids.

DIAGNOSIS. Anchor worms attach themselves to fish and burrow into the skin, leaving only the egg sacs protruding. Look for these sacs, and obvious signs of discomfort in the fish.

TREATMENT. Remove the fish, and carefully paint the anchor worms with either paraffin or turpentine. A small camel hair pencil brush is ideal for this operation. After painting remove the offending crustaceans with a small pair of tweezers. 0·1% solution of potassium permanganate can be used instead of paraffin.

Painting the worms in this way kills them and softens them so that their removal causes the least damage to the fish's muscle fibres. After removal the lesions should be disinfected to prevent bacterial attack.

Alternatively, the fish can be placed in a bath made with (D.F.D.) Difluordiphenyl trichlor methylmethane, 1 ml. to 10 litres of water, for between 2 and 3 minutes.

## Mouth Fungus (Cotton Wool Disease)

This is a most unpleasant disease, luckily it is rather rare in well maintained aquaria, but once it develops it is highly contagious and if not checked, will soon reach epidemic proportions.

DIAGNOSIS. First a white cotton-like fluff appears on the lips, which progresses into the mouth, eventually it starts to erode the jaws away. A major cause of this disease is damage or bruising to the lips of the fish, either during transportation or by clumsy handling.

TREATMENT. This is a difficult disease to cure by mass treatment, it is much safer to treat fish individually by carefully netting and swabbing the mouth with hydrogen peroxide straight from the bottle.

Alternatively, try Argyrol, a mild silver protienate, reduced to 10% strength dabbed on to the lips.

Phenoxephol has been used with some success and is recommended for advanced cases of the disease. Mr. Ian Rankin first introduced this oily liquid for the treatment of fish diseases and recommends a stock solution of 1 cm³ Phenoxephol to 99 cm³ of water a concentration of 45–90 cm³ should be used in the tank water for each gallon (imperial).


## *Oodinium* (Velvet)

There are various species of *Oodinium* but in effect the result of infection by these parasites is much the same, irrespective of the species causing the problem. The parasites attack the gills and skin, but will also penetrate deeper into the body if the disease is not checked early.

DIAGNOSIS. The disease can be recognized by a yellow brown film which usually starts near the dorsal fin and then spreads all over the body in a velvet like film. It may have the appearance of talcum powder. This dust is of a pale yellowish colour.

TREATMENT. Dissolve one tablet of Acriflavine (0·46 grain) obtainable from most chemists, in 80 drops of hot water, then add five drops of this solution to every gallon of water in which the fish is to be treated.

During the treatment, the aquarium should be kept dark and aerated artificially. Repeat treatment after 5 days.

Alternatively, try bathing the fish in a bath made up of Formalin, 2 ml. of a 40% solution to 10 litres of water, for a period of 30 minutes.

A 1% solution of methylene blue has been found to be effective against velvet disease. It can be used in tanks containing plants and is completely harmless even to the smallest fish. Power filters containing charcoal should be switched off while treatment is proceeding. Six to 10 days is usually sufficient to remove the disease completely. Activated charcoal filters absorb methylene blue dye and can be switched on after treatment has been completed.

## *Saprolegnia* (Fungus)

The cause of this disease is a fungus that settles on dead organic matter such as uneaten food, forming fine white filaments. It usually only attacks fish that are already in a weakened condition. Bruises, chills, wrongful feeding, attacks from other fish, weakness from another malady and dirty aquariums are all possible causes of fungus. The fungus can develop independently in fish, but it is somewhat rare in tropical species.

DIAGNOSIS. The fungus becomes evident as a white shiny, cotton-wool-like film covering the infected area. When the fish is removed from water, the film collapses.

TREATMENT. The fish should be placed in the hospital tank without any plants, and salt added in the proportion of two level teaspoons to every gallon of water. Sea salt is preferable to common salt . If after 24 hours there is no evidence of improvement, add two more teaspoonfuls of salt.

If by the third day no change is noticed, add another teaspoon. When the fish is cured, it should be re-acclimatized to fresh water before being returned to the community tank. This is accomplished by adding fresh water, over a period of a few days to lower the salt content. Alternatively, make a bath with potassium permanganate, 1 gram per 100 litres of water and immerse the fish for between 10 to 20 minutes.

Colloidal silver, 0·1 mg. per litre, made up into a bath is another accepted treatment. The fish should be immersed for 15 to 20 minutes only.

If the affected part is small, take the fish from the water and dab the affected part with a solution of mercurochrome (one part of 2% solution with nine parts water) or use an iodine solution. The solutions are best applied using a soft camel hair brush. After practice it is possible to keep the head and gills under water while medicating the fungus affected parts. Dichromate of potash can be used in weak concentrations of 1 gram to 5 gallons of water as a follow-up to this treatment.

## Shimmies (Swinging Sickness)

Shimmies is not a disease, but rather an indication that all is not well.

DIAGNOSIS. The fish usually stay in a static position waving their body from side to side in a slow constant motion. Fish suffering from Ichthyophtirius also perform this peculiar movement, indigestion, chills, etc., are also possible causes.

TREATMENT. Sometimes it is only necessary to change the water completely. If this fails raise the temperature to 80°F (26°C) and feed sparingly. It is possible that micro-organisms in the tank can bring on an attack of shimmies, therefore, ensure that you pay due attention to the hygiene of the aquarium. If it is inconvenient to change the aquarium water completely the pH should be checked and the value adjusted as necessary. This may help cure the trouble.

## Swim Bladder

The swim bladder is the organ by which the fish control their depth. It is situated approximately in the centre of the body and it is used by the fish to vary its buoyancy, which it does by inflating the bladder with gas.

When watching lively fish diving and darting about the plants, it will be appreciated that the swim bladder is a very delicately balanced organ, if too much gas inflates the bladder the fish will be unable to leave the surface, and if too little, it will sink and remain on the bottom. The formation of internal gases caused by indigestion, or some other cause, will often affect the swim bladder temporarily, but a prolonged upset will be the result of a defective swim bladder. Unfortunately, a defective swim bladder is untreatable in most instances, therefore, it is a kindness to destroy the fish, unless the cause of the trouble can be observed. Malfunctioning of the swim bladder may be caused by the cysts of Ichthyophonus preventing the full inflation of the bladder and this may be cured by treating the source of the trouble (see Ichthyophonus).

## Threadworms (Nematodes)

Threadworms are usually found in the body tissues in the larval form, or in the gut as an adult worm.

DIAGNOSIS. The thin, thread-like worms, can be seen trailing from the anus of the fish (Not to be confused with excreta from constipated fish). Fish may also feed badly and become thin and hollow bellied.

TREATMENT. Practically incurable, it is wise to destroy infected fish. Valuable fish can be isolated and given a bath in parachlorometaxylenol, 10 ml. per litre, for a few days, but it is unlikely that a cure will be effected if the disease has reached a stage where the larval has become encysted.

### *Tuberculosis* (**Wasting**)

Tuberculosis is caused by the tubercle bacilli, and manifests itself externally by the fish becoming hollow bellied, listless and generally emaciated. They will rest on the rocks or on the bottom in a most dejected manner with fins frayed and laid flat, sometimes the eyes protrude and skin will show open lesions.

Contributing factors to this disease are excessive temperatures, over-crowding, under feeding, or an unsatisfactory diet. There is virtually no cure for this disease, and fish seldom survive, it is therefore better to destroy it to save unnecessary suffering and to prevent other fish becoming infected.

If you have a particularly valued fish you can try hospitalizing it in a separate tank and feeding live food and the scrapings of raw lean beef, you may be fortunate and save it, but it is unlikely you will do so.

Pencillin ointment can be used where tuberculous wounds of the skin are present. It has been found to be very effective for healing these. The ointment should be applied directly to the fish. Penicillin does not last long in the warmth of tropical aquaria and its use in the water is therefore not very effective. Other tried and tested remedies include terramycin and streptomycin but these are outside the sphere of the average aquarist.

### Tumours

Fish also are subjected to both benign and malignant tumours Internal tumours cause the body to swell, whilst external tumours are visible as swellings protruding from the body. Melanosarcomas are tumours affecting the black pigment cells in the skin causing the fish to become excessively black in colour.

There is no cure for tumours and fish thus affected should be destroyed to save them unnecessary suffering.

As mentioned elsewhere it has been proved that the constant use of ozone in high concentrations can cause tumours and this is worth bearing in mind if you favour the use of an ozonizer for disinfecting your tank.

### Wounds

Wounds can be caused by fish dashing around the tank in an effort to escape the net, and by knocking themselves against the rock. Wounds can also be the result of nips from larger fish.

Sores and wounds should be treated as soon as they are discovered to prevent them developing into a fungus.

TREATMENT. The easiest and most effective method is to dab the wounds with a small piece of cotton wool soaked in a 2% solution of Mercurochrome, or by pouring a strong solution of permanganate of potash directly onto the wounds, and then washing off with clean water. The fish have to be netted before treatment, so remember to handle them carefully and protect the gills with a swab of muslin soaked in water.

## UNDESIRABLES

Occasionally undesirable creatures are introduced into the aquarium with live foods, or on plants. The majority of these are relatively harmless, but they are unsightly and they can be detrimental to eggs in the breeding tank, and to very young fry.

### Great Pond Snails *(Limnaea)*

*Limnaeidae* are a family of mud snails, and *Limnaea stagnalis* is probably the one most likely to be found accidentally in an aquarium. Unfortunately, they have a healthy appetite for plants and will attack anything green.

Another disadvantage associated with the *Limnaeidae* is their tendency to harbour parasitic worms. They have the reputation of exterminating hydra, but even if this is so, this advantage is outweighed by the damage they will do to the plant life.

### Leeches *(Hirudinea)*

**Leeches** are a pest but usually nothing more, however, on rare occasions several may attach themselves to smallish fish to suck their blood which has an obvious weakening effect on the fish and can make them prone to serious infections and skin wounds. Also leeches can be carriers of blood parasites.

There are many species of leeches, all flattish, with a sucking disc at one end and a suction cup at the other which enables the creatures to crawl over solid objects like a caterpillar with looping 'strides'. They do not like strong light consequently they hide under stones and rocks and appear mainly when the tank is in darkness. Like snails, leeches are hermaphroditic.

94

Leeches attached to fish can be removed physically with a pair of blunt tweezers, if they adhere strongly their adhesion can be weakened by bathing the fish in a weak solution of cooking salt, 10 to 15 grains per litre for about 15 minutes. Cleaning a tank of these pests is easily accomplished by trapping them on raw meat. Suspend a piece of raw meat on a piece of cotton in the aquarium before going to bed. The next morning leeches will be found crawling or hanging on to the meat. It is then a simple matter to remove the meat *and* leeches together. Repeat each night until the tank is clean.

## Flat Worms

**Flat Worms,** or **Planarians** as they are known to aquarists are small, usually no more than $\frac{3}{16}$ inch in length, and coloured pale grey, like that of the body of the garden snail. They are a nuisance in the aquarium and in the breeding tank a definite hazard as they prey on the eggs and fry. They are nocturnal, and usually remain hidden during the day. The simplest method of trapping them is to suspend a piece of raw meat in the aquarium, so that it just touches the gravel, before going to bed. In the morning the meat will be crawling with them, simply remove the meat and worms. Repeat every night until the worms are eradicated.

For those interested in their systematic position. Flat worms belong to the class *Turbellaria, Phylum Plathelminthes.*

## Beetles

Most beetles are carnivorous, and in consequence, should not be allowed to remain in a tropical aquarium. It is most unlikely that any of the creatures will find their way into any aquarium if reasonable care is taken to keep them out. Any that slip through should be netted and removed.

## Water Tiger *(Dytiscus marginalis)*

The **Water Tiger** is well named, it is far more dangerous than the larva of the dragon-fly. Both the adult beetle and the larva are ravenous eaters, but it is the larval form that is likely to cause the aquarist prob-

95

lems. The larva is not content to wait for a victim to come within reach like the dragon fly larva, it will chase and attack by sinking its two hollow mandibles into the flesh of a fish. Once the mandibles are firmly fixed, the larva injects a digestive fluid which breaks down the flesh to a fluid that can be sucked in by the larva. Larval *Dytiscus* grow to a maximum length of about 2 inches and at this size they are easy to see and remove, but they should never be allowed to reach such maturity in the aquarium. The real danger is when they are smaller, say $\frac{1}{4}$ inch long, they can mingle with fry and very small fish almost undetected, and will eventually kill them all. There is only one precaution—vigilance.

The *Dytiscidae* is a family of water beetles of the sub-order *Adephaga*.

### Dragonfly Larvae

**Dragonflies** are beautiful creatures, but their larvae are not welcome guests in aquaria. The larvae are predatory insects that attack and feed on fish. They lie in wait until a fish comes within striking distance, they then strike by extending the lower lip which grips the fish tightly. The lower lip forms a mask, which carries the mouth and pincers, and can be thrust forward at will. The pincers grip the victim whilst the flesh is eaten.

Most larvae propel themselves by ejecting a stream of water from the body, but some species transport themselves by wriggling their tails like an oar. The life cycle of the larval stage is about a year, after which time the beetle-like creature is ready to leave the water to become a beautiful dragon-fly.

The larvae are particularly dangerous to young fish and fry.

Under normal conditions it is unlikely that the larvae will be introduced into the aquarium, but it is possible to do so if you collect your own daphnia. Any strainer that passes daphnia, is also likely to pass small larvae. Dragonflies belong to the *phylum Hexapoda*, order *Odonata*.

### Hydra

**Hydra** are polyps. They are a low form of life that will devour tiny fish and daphnia only, so they do not represent much of a hazard in a community tank.

There are many species of fresh water hydra, but from the aquarists view-point they are all much the same. The body is thin and elongated with thin tentacles spreading from the mouth in a star-like formation. The number of tentacles varies with species. Hydra can anchor themselves to solid objects in the aquaria by means of the foot plate situated on the opposite end of the body, but they are also capable of progression by floating along the surface of the water. Hydra vary considerably in size, colour, and actual shape, but they rarely exceed a body length of about 1¼ inches.

Hydra attack by waiting for a victim to pass near enough to be caught by the tentacles, it is then passed into the mouth to be digested, indigestible portions being ejected.

Hydra are greedy creatures, and it is not uncommon for a single specimen to have captured daphnia and held by each tentacle awaiting to be consumed. Hydra propagate by budding and division, and under favourable conditions multiply rapidly.

Not many fish like hydra, the known exceptions are the **Blue Gourami** (*Trichogaster trichopterus*) and its sub-species *T.t. sumatranus*.

The pest can be exterminated by removing the fish and increasing the water temperature to 105° (40°C), but this is usually inconvenient. If so, you may prefer to add one teaspoonful of household ammonia to every five gallons of water in the tank. Leave for two hours and then completely change the water. This concentration of ammonia will harm the fish so they must be removed before the ammonia is added. Plants, however, will not be harmed. The **Great Pond Snail** (*Limnaea*) whilst being a general feeder, has a strong leaning towards animal matter, and is reputed to eat hydra.

# Glossary of Chemicals Useful in the Treatment of Diseases of Aquarium Fishes

This is not an exhaustive list, but covers the more important chemicals which are of use to the aquarist in the cure and prevention of disease. Some are only available on prescription.

## Acriflavine

There are two types of acriflavine, one acidic and the other neutral, in all cases the neutral types should be used to avoid creating an excess of acid in your aquarium water. The neutral acriflavine compound is deep orange while the acidic compound is a more reddish brown. For a stock solution 3 mg. are added to 330 cubic centimetres of water. This stock solution may be used for disinfecting aquaria at the rate of 10 cubic centimetres to one gallon of water. While this is an effective disinfectant prolonged use is not recommended as it causes sterility which can last for several months. Can be used for treating sliminess of the skin.

## Ammonia

The main drawback to the use of ammonia apart from its offensive pungent smell is the fact that it cannot be used in planted aquaria as it affects plant growth. Ammonia treatment can be used for the treatment of flukes by preparing a bath of 10 parts commercial ammonia to 90 parts of water (by volume).

## Aureomycin

Aureomycin is an antibiotic usually supplied in deep yellow crystalline form. It can be used as an effective treatment against oodinium and Ichthyophthirius It is best used in a 5% treatment bath solution.

## Brilliant Green

Can be used for the treatment of Mouth Fungus. A remedial bath solution is made with 2 grains dissolved in a small quantity of alcohol which is then added to one gallon of water. The treatment should last for about a minute in this solution.

## Chloromycetin

A colourless crystalline antibiotic substance which has proved effective against Velvet disease, Ichthyophthirius and other bacterial infections. 40 mg. to an imperial gallon is an average dosage.

## Hydrogen Peroxide

The commercial 3% solution may be used direct from the bottle for swabbing infected parts of fish affected by skin flukes or Cotton Wool disease.

## Iodine

The commercial strength is 10% of Iodine dissolved in alcohol and is dark brown in colour. It is used as a direct disinfectant diluted with 9 parts of water. Applications are made using a camel hair brush.

## Malachite Green

This green crystalline dye has proved successful in the treatment of fungus diseases. Used in the home aquaria as a disinfectant in the treatment of fungus diseases. The author recommends methylene blue rather than malachite green.

## Mercurochrome

This is another dye containing mercury. It is red in colour and has strong disinfectant properties.

Applied by camel hair brush. The commercial solution strength is 2% mercurochrome and should be diluted with 5 parts of water to form a solution for direct application.

## Methylene Blue

Used in the treatment of white spot, and flukes, and velvet disease. Power filters containing activated charcoal should be switched off while treatment is taking place. 1 gram to 100 cubic cm. of water makes an ideal stock solution which can be added to the aquarium water at the rate of 2 cubic cm. to 1 gallon of water.

## Ozone

Ozone is a pale blue gas with good sterilizing properties. It is produced by the action of ultra violet light and has been successfully used in the treatment of bacterial diseases, fin rot and mouth fungus. It is now known to produce tumours in fishes after prolonged use and is therefore best used periodically for aquarium hygiene.

## Potassium Dichromate

Used for the treatment of wounds, fungus disease or sores. A 1% solution can be applied by camel hair brush or a bath made by adding 1 part of 1% solution to ten parts of water.

## Potassium permanganate

Used as a disinfectant in tanks. The crystals should be dissolved in water before adding to the aquarium.

A useful general purpose disinfectant with no side effects.

## Sodium Chloride (Salt)

Common salt is useful as a treatment against a number of fish ailments, it has been used as a remedy for skin flukes, and sliminess of the skin. Salt solutions may gradually be increased in strength to allow the fish to become acclimatized to it, prolonged treatment can be given with no apparent ill effects.

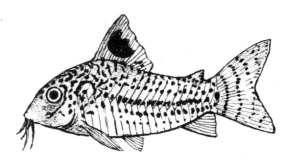

# FEEDING

## Feeding

The first rule, to remember about feeding is that overfeeding is one of the most common causes of pollution in aquaria. Foods with a high protein content are the most satisfactory as they are more fully used up by the fish. Dry foods with a large volume of cereal fillers are cheaper to produce, but a larger amount has to be fed to the fish to keep them healthy. The appetite of fish and their metabolistic rate is linked with their environment, the warmer the water, the faster they grow, and the more they eat.

Cold water fish do not normally eat as much as tropical varieties under conditions that are normal to both, tropicals will lose their appetite with reduced temperatures, and regain it when the temperature is raised.

Where possible, it is advisable to feed a little and often, always keeping the fish just that little bit hungry, so that they forage for the odd tit-bit tucked between the gravel or resting on rockwork.

During the inevitable absence occasioned by holidays and the week-end in the country, the fish can be fed rather more often for a week before departure, the fish will then be able to survive a week without food and little harm will come to them.

For absences of a larger period, it will be necessary to enlist the aid of a friend, but do take the time to instruct your friend on *how much* food to give per day. If you are not confident of your friends assessment, make up little packets in screws of paper with instructions to feed one or two a day.

Personally, I do not recommend feeding rings for dry foods. They serve little or no purpose when the aquarist provides the correct amount of food, the natural dispersion over the water surface gives all the fish the same opportunity to feed, if the quantity has been judged acurately, it will all be eaten within 5 minutes.

Live foods are invaluable for keeping fish in the pink of condition, they contain protein, and the kind of animal food that the fish would find in their natural habitat, indeed, some species of fish are exclusively carnivorous but the vast majority of fish available to aquarists take quite readily to the very excellent dry foods available commercially today. Even fish like a little variety in their diet, so a well balanced menu including dry and live foods, fed alternatively or simultaneous will provide the ideal combination feeding programme.

## Dry Food

There is a wide variety of prepared dry foods available the ingredients of which vary considerably. Naturally each manufacturer considers his own product to be the best, and without doubt considerable research has been devoted to providing suitable high quality feeding stuffs.

Flake foods can be fed as a staple diet to a large variety of tropical fish without any additional foods.

The fish should be fed 2 to 4 times a day with as much as will be consumed in a few minutes. Many fish like to take the flakes as they float on the surface, others prefer to catch the flakes as they sink. When keeping bottom feeders such as catfish, a proportion of the flakes should be made to sink quickly by soaking them in water.

Reputable dry fish food manufacturers have devoted much time and effort in scientific research to find the ideal food. Their laboratory technicians have approached the subject with the same dedication that would be given to research given to foods for human consumption, with the result that flake food is now used by 80 per cent of the world's aquarists. Flake foods should be the first choice, because they disperse well in water and in general contain highly nutritive ingredients.

Naturally, each manufacturer has his own formula and flake ingredients will vary in content between each manufacturer, therefore, obtain a supply of a range of well known flakes and feed from a different pack each day.

This will provide the fish with a varied diet and also indicate to the aquarist the most acceptable brand names. Flakes are made from either animal or vegetable substances, or a combination of both. The manufacturer usually indicates the basis on the pack.

Apart from the obvious necessity of providing food, flake foods have the added advantages of being dust free, and unless grossly overfed, of not clouding the water.

Tetratips offer a new approach to feeding dry foods. It consists of small tablets that are fixed to the interior glass wall of the aquarium by simply pressing them on. The tablets are prepared from freeze dried foodstuffs, a process which preserves the natural goodness of the live food. They contain brine shrimp, fish, roe meal, dried beef, liver, crustacean meal, aquatic plants, selected dried seaweeds, crab and fish liver meal, milk, fish glue, wheat germ oil, cod liver oil and vitamins.

If it is necessary to leave your aquarium for a few days without attention, Tetratips will provide a constant reserve food supply without causing the problem of water pollution, the tablets only disintegrate as they are nibbled by the fish.

## Blood Worms

Blood worms are the larvae of a midge species of Chironomus, and can be fed to the larger fish without chopping or shredding. They are found in ponds containing daphnia, and other watery places.

## Freshwater Shrimps *(Gammarus pulex)*

Freshwater shrimps are ideal for the larger fish. They grow to about ¾ inch and as they feed on decaying animal and vegetable matter, help to clean the tank by scavenging.

## Brine Shrimps *(Artemia salina)*

Brine shrimps are one of the most useful and amazing additions to the aquarist pantry. The eggs, which in themselves are not a food, are obtained in a phial and under reasonable storage conditions, can remain dormant for many months. When newly hatched they provide an excellent early live food diet, and can be fattened up for feeding to larger fish.

There are various ways of hatching the eggs (see Equipment) but they can be hatched in ordinary two pound jam jars, containing a saline solution. The solution is made by adding a tablespoon of salt to a pint of water preferably in a bottle so that it can be well mixed by shaking the bottle, then strained through fine muslin to remove any sediment.

Pour the saline solution into a jar and sprinkle some eggs on the surface then place the jar in a spot where the temperature is maintained at 75°–80°F (24°–27°C). The eggs will hatch in 48 hours.

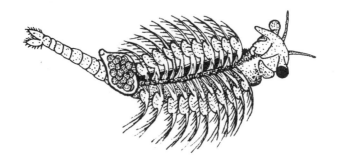

To feed, the shrimps can be syphoned off, or by straining through several thicknesses of muslin which is then rinsed in the aquarium. The former is the better method because only shrimps are collected, old egg cases and eggs that have failed to hatch can be left in the jar.

Never pour the salt solution into the aquarium it will only upset the pH and water hardness.

If you wish to obtain adult brine shrimps the youngsters can be fed with dust-sized food, but they also require algae. Some liquid proprietory foods contain particles of food that is particularly beneficial to rearing brine shrimps.

Remember brine shrimps will only survive for a few hours in fresh water, so be careful not to feed more than is consumed within say five minutes.

## Cyclops

Cyclops are very small crustaceans. They have the appearance of possessing only one central eye and it is for this reason that they are named Cyclops after the one-eyed giant of mythology. They are usually found in ponds containing daphnia and can be collected in much the same way. They can be cultivated in a shallow container of infusoria water where they will breed rapidly. An old porcelain sink will do, with the drain hole plugged.

These tiny crustaceans can be fed to all fish and they are particularly useful for small fry just out of the infusoria stage, providing they are graded to a suitable size by sieving. At some stage of their life cycle female cyclops develop a double sac containing eggs. These are situated at the rear part of the body and no doubt add to their desirability as a fish food.

# Daphnia

Daphnia is the most universally accepted and best known of all the live foods. They are found in almost every country in not too clean ponds, particularly in farm ponds where a certain amount of manure finds its way. They appear as a cloud of bugs, all moving, but getting nowhere. The colour of these crustaceans varies from grey, green, to red, the latter are more sought after as they are thought to be more nutritious.

Daphnia are more abundant between April and October, but isolated batches may well be found well into the winter. As they require oxygen in much the same way as fish, it is advisable to only feed small quantities at any one time, so that they are quickly consumed, any dead ones remaining should be syphoned off as they are likely to spoil the water.

Daphnia can be stored for a few days if they are kept cool and in reasonably large containers, some aquarist use old porcelain sinks, and even enamel baths. Never use metallic containers: it is always preferable to use ceramic, porcelain, plastic or glass, and if you intend to use tap water, let it stand for a day to let any chlorine evaporate.

Because daphnia en mass require a large amount of oxygen, it is foolhardy to catch too many at any one time and crowd them into a container only to find that half have died by the time they reach their destination. The best way to transport daphnia is on frames made of wood with an absorbent material stretched across. The material is soaked in water and the daphnia spread thinly over the material. A number of frames can be mounted one above the other in a box with a lid to reduce loss of moisture by evaporation.

Daphnia purchased from any aquarists supply stores is usually clean and can be fed direct to your fish, but if you have collected your own, never feed direct from the container, but let them stand for a day so that any undesirable creatures collected with the daphnia or dead specimens, can be removed. Draw off the healthy daphnia with a syphon tube and strain through a net or sieve. At the same time, you can grade the daphnia for any small fish you may be rearing.

It is possible to cultivate daphnia if the supply required is worth the time and trouble. It is necessary to have a few containers of a minimum capacity of about 14 gallons with a water depth of about 6 inches. Prepare each container with a handful of old sheeps or cows droppings, or chicken manure. Leave for two weeks, then add a little baking yeast, and a little animal blood. After a few days add the daphnia. When the water becomes denuded of nutrients, feeding should be renewed.

## Earth Worms

The lowly earthworm, the favourite bait for schoolboy fishermen, is generally acceptable to most fish, but they have to be chopped up or shredded before they can be fed. An old pair of scissors can be used to cut them up into sizes small enough for average size fish, or they can be shredded with worm shredders (two steel plates with circular grooves like a file).

Whichever method is used it is a messy business and overfeeding will soon lead to pollution. The worms should be cleaned well before shredding. Do not use worms that exude a yellowish secretion, the fish will not eat them anyway. Nottingham red worms and red worms found in compost heaps are the best.

Feed earthworms only if cleaner foods are not available.

## Gentles

Gentles are an excellent food for the larger species of fish and especially favoured by cold water varieties.

Gentles are the larvae of the blue-bottle or blow fly, they are pale whitish grubs about $\frac{1}{2}$ inch long when fully grown, because of their large size it is advisable to feed only a few at a time as they will quickly satisfy the appetite of most aquarium fish.

Gentles are popular among coarse fishermen as a bait and they can usually be purchased from suppliers of fishing tackle, but a word of warning—it is a practice of fishermen to use artificially coloured gentles to attract their quarry, these coloured varieties should not be used for feeding aquarium specimens, use only those that are a natural pale colour.

## Glass Worms *(Chaoborus or Corethra larvae)*

These worms, also known as ghost worms, are not really worms at all, but the larval form of the plumed gnats. They are transparent creatures, about $\frac{1}{2}$ to $\frac{3}{4}$ inches in length, not unlike bloodworms, but without the blood of course.

They are found in ponds well shaded by overhanging foliage. They can be seen lying in a parallel position only a few inches below the surface. Suddenly they disappear but a close examination will show that they have moved about a foot and now face the opposite direction. Over short distances their speed is so fast that they create an illusion of the classic disappearing act—here one moment—gone the next. These ghost like creatures are so transparent that when viewed in strong light they become almost invisible.

When netting glass worms the net must be swept through the water swiftly and steadily, if any have been captured they will appear in the bottom of the net as a mass of jelly.

Not all ponds yield glass worms, but those that do so usually have an abundant supply. Unlike daphnia they do not appear to mind being a little crowded, therefore, they lend themselves quite well to storage in a small aquarium. One advantage of glass worms as a live food is the fact that they are obtainable during the winter months.

## Infusoria

Infusoria is a rather loose term used to describe organisms in the water small enough to be fed to the very tiniest of fish. It is kind of 'primaeval soup' containing the necessary ingredients for the first link in the chain of life.

Infusoria can be prepared from squashed lettuce leaves placed in a quart of water which is then left out in the sun and air. The minute infusoria spores will settle on the water from the atmosphere and multiply on the products of the decaying lettuce. Chopped hay can also be used, first boil it in water and then leave in a dark spot. The water from a vase in which chrysanthemums have been stood usually is an excellent source. Potatoes, banana skins and crushed chrysanthemum leaves left in water for a few days will all produce infusoria.

A few tropical infusoria snails (*Ampullaria paludosa*) put into a tank will promote infusoria, their partly digested droppings providing the necessary food. These snails feed on lettuce, so ensure some is available. Excellent cultures can be made from dried duckweed and lettuce leaves. Dry the leaves thoroughly in an oven and store in clean jars until required.

This method has the advantages of providing infusoria the whole year round.

To check the richness of a culture, place a spot of water taken from the top surface of the culture onto the slide of a low power microscope. It should be teeming with minute life about the size of a fine dust.

## Micro-Worms *(Anguillula silusiae)*

These tiny, almost invisible worms, are an ideal baby food, and can be fed to fry just out of the infusoria stage.

They are grown from a culture obtainable from your local dealer. The food in which the culture is to grow and multiply can be made from soya flour, semolena, or oatmeal. Oatmeal should be mixed with water, $1\frac{1}{2}$ ozs. to a half pint, and then cooked and left to cool. It is only necessary to mix soya flour or semolena with water to the consistency of a floppy paste, no cooking is required.

The culture is placed in the food mass to multiply.

Because of the nature of the food stock it will naturally deteriorate, when this happens simply make up a fresh supply and transfer a spoonful of the old worm-bearing stock. It is obviously an advantage to have a few cultures progressing in stages so that a guaranteed supply is available for when it is most needed.

There are proprietary accessories that make the collection of the worms easier (See Equipment) but an old trick is to use damp matchsticks.

Any small pot with a plastic lid will do. Simply drill about 12 holes in the lid of a size that will hold a matchstick firmly, put a small quantity of a culture in the pot, a $\frac{1}{8}$ inch layer will do, and fix the matchsticks so that they just touch the culture. Leave the pot in a warm room for a few hours; after this time enough worms will have migrated onto the sticks to provide a meal. Simply rinse the sticks in the aquarium to release the worms for feeding.

Better collections of worms will be made if the match-sticks are thoroughly soaked in water before use.


## Mosquito Larvae

Mosquito larvae can be collected from ponds, puddles, water butts, and almost any container near dwelling houses. Once the female has deposited her eggs it is only a few days before the larvae hatch. These wriggly creatures average about $\frac{1}{4}$ inch in length and have a knob-like head and 'Y' shaped tail. They either remain near the surface of the water or make constant trips to obtain air. They cannot utilize the dissolved gases in the water like fish, so they are compelled to utilize atmospheric air. This they do by means of a tube situated on the last abdominal segment, the tip of which they thrust just above the water surface. If there is any risk of pollution in the water from which they have been collected, rinse them well in clean water before putting them into the aquarium. It is advisable to only feed fish over $1\frac{1}{2}$ inch in length with mosquito larvae, smaller fish are liable to choke on them.

## Rotifers

Rotifers are minute aquatic animals feeding and swimming by means of bands of beating cilia, giving the impression of revolving wheels, hence their old name of 'wheel animalcules'.

Rotifers are an ideal early food for some of the larger species of fish and will thrive in an infusoria culture as their main nutrient is algae and unicellulars.

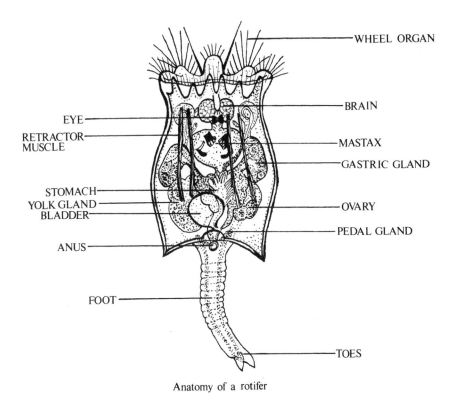

EYE

RETRACTOR MUSCLE

STOMACH
YOLK GLAND
BLADDER

ANUS

FOOT

WHEEL ORGAN

BRAIN

MASTAX

GASTRIC GLAND

OVARY

PEDAL GLAND

TOES

Anatomy of a rotifer

Rotifers are found in ponds, usually among the weeds, and it is essential to use an extremely fine net to collect them. Very fine muslin will do.

One species *Brachionus rubens*, is often found adhering to the body of daphnia. These can be removed by washing the daphnia in a fine sieve with a strong jet of water. The rotifers are knocked off and pass through the sieve leaving the daphnia behind for feeding to the larger fish.

## Tubifex Worms

Tubifex worms are another live food source that can be obtained the year round. They vary in length from ⅜ inch to about 2 inches long, they are extremely thin, and rusty-red in colour.

Tubifex worms are found where there is plenty of mud, such as small estuaries and the flats of streams and ponds. They are collected by lifting the mud with a spade, and putting it into a muslin bag; then swilling the bag in the stream to remove all but the worms. If the Tubifex are left in a shallow container in about one inch of water, they will congregate into a ball-like mass, it is then simple to transfer them to their transport container.

Do not put too many worms in a jar as the weight of those on the top will kill those below. They should be stored in a bucket or large bowl into which a slow steady stream of water is allowed to enter. The bunched worms can be separated occasionally with a jet of water, which will also wash out any dead ones.

If a bunch is dropped into the aquarium, they will eventually scatter and bury part of themselves in the gravel, the protruding ends waving around as if in a strong breeze. Fish eating these individual worms usually only manage to bite a section off leaving a part of the worm in the gravel to decay and cause problems later. Therefore, it is preferable to us a floating worm feeder (see Equipment) and place a large flat piece of rock under it so that any worms that fall through cannot burrow.

It is not necessary to dig your own worms, most aquarists supply stores stock tubifex worms.


## White Worms (Enchytraeids)

White worms are soil dwelling creatures belonging to the family *Enchytraeidae*, and they are related to the earth worm. All species are hermaphroditic. 'Mating' takes place between two specimen lying side by side whilst they exude a secretion. The eggs are spawned in cocoons.

White worms cultures are valuable as a winter and supplementary food they are easy to breed and provide food that is highly nourishing.

The cultures are cultivated in large tins or wood boxes. Fill the boxes to about ¾ of their depth with a mixture of garden loam, bulb fibre, or peat, in an approximate proportion of one to one. The nature of the mix should be such that it does not pack too tightly.

Make a small depression in the centre of the soil in which to place the food for the culture, this can be a stiff mash of oat flakes to which is added a little sugar, or mashed potatoes, bread wetted with milk or Bemax.

The worms, obtainable from most aquarist supply stores, are placed in the depression and the mash spread over them. Now cover with a small sheet of glass and place the box in a cool place for about three weeks, the best temperature is around 60°F (15°C). The worms will multiply without any further attention except for keeping the soil moist. Do not overfeed, it will turn the soil sour. If this should happen, however, start a new culture with some of the worms from the original one. It is advisable to set up a few boxes and rotate them for feeding the fish, this will give the cultures time to reproduce and ensures an adequate supply.

To collect the worms for feeding, simply remove the glass cover and remove them with a pair of tweezers from the underside of the glass where they will have assembled in large numbers. Before feeding the worms, make sure they are free of any soil, a quick rinse in water will remove any adhering particles or take a few and place them in a shallow container, such as a food container lid, and place it where it will receive a gentle heat, this will cause the worms to amalgamate into a ball for easy collection.

## Conditioning

Healthy fish in the pink of condition are more likely to spawn and give a higher percentage of fertilized eggs than fish in indifferent conditions. Ideally all fish should be in such a condition, but it is worthwhile treating fish intended for breeding to a period of condition feeding for about a week or longer before any spawning is attempted.

Frequent meals of live foods, raw finely lacerated beef, fish, shrimp, crab and lobster can be hung in the tank on a piece of cotton and removed after about an hour, or whenever eaten, whatever is soonest.

The diet should be as varied as possible not forgetting meat scrapings from lean meat, liver, dried egg yoke, white of egg, and shredded baked fish, all obtainable from the household pantry.

## Feeding Young Fish

Most of the foods required to rear fry have been mentioned previously in this section, but for the general guidance of the aquarist the following table may prove helpful.

When feeding flour-size dry food to fry never sprinkle it on the surface of the water, it is most difficult to assess how *much* to feed, with the result that an excess is usually given some of which will remain uneaten and cause pollution.

The best method is to make a stiff paste by adding a little water to the flour food, then put the paste in a piece of muslin or muslin bag. To feed, screw the muslin so that the paste forms a ball and put an elastic band on the ends of the muslin so that the paste ball is trapped. To feed, drip the bag into the aquarium and the food will disperse into the water in a fine cloud, in easily controlled quantities.

There are many excellent commercially produced fry foods available and the aquarist should not be backward in using these to give variety to the diet.

Information in respect of fry feeding habits in the wild is very limited, but it can be assumed that the available supply covers a wide range giving the fry the opportunity of choosing, to some extent, their own menu.

## Small Sized Fry (Anabantids)

| Stage 1 | Stage 2 | Stage 3 | Stage 4 | Stage 5 |
| --- | --- | --- | --- | --- |
| Green Water | Infusoria | Infusoria | Brine- | Larger |
| Flour size | | Micro-worms | Shrimp | Daphnia |
| dry feed | | Rotifers | Sieved | Small |
| | | | daphnia | Flake |
| | | | Chopped | Food |
| | | | white worm | |

## Medium Sized Fry (Barbs, Characins)

| Stage 1 | Stage 2 | Stage 3 | Stage 4 | Stage 5 |
| --- | --- | --- | --- | --- |
| Flour size | Fine dry | Brine- | Larger dry | Adult |
| dry food | food and | Shrimp. | food (Flake) | Daphnia. |
| Infusoria. | tiny flakes. | Sieved | Chopped | Med. Dry foods |
| Egg Yoke. | Fine grated | daphnia. | White worm. | and flakes. |
| (hard boiled | Shrimp. | Micro- | Medium | |
| and mixed | Rotifers. | worms. | Daphnia. | |
| with water) | | | | |

# Large Sized Fry (Cichlids, Live-Bearers)

*Stage 1*
Brine-
Shrimp.
Sieved
Daphnia
Flour-size
dry food and
flakes.
Micro-worms.
Rotifers.

*Stage 2*
Med daphnia.
Chopped
white worms.

*Stage 3*
Chopped
white worms.
Fine flakes
and dry foods.

*Stage 4*
Adult
Daphnia.

*Stage 5*
Larger dry
foods and
flakes.
Chopped
Tubifex.

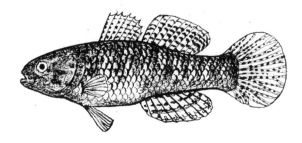

# CLASSIFICATION

## Classification

Systematics is the branch of biological knowledge concerned with the recognition, description, nomenclature, and classification of the different kinds of all life, both animal and vegetable.

Something like one million different animal species have been classified, out of which approximately 30,000 are fish. It will be obvious, from the vast numbers involved that to attempt a detailed account of each species is well beyond the scope of this book, and many would be quite unsuitable for the home aquarist to keep in his tank. It is, however, possible to introduce the reader to the subject, and if he so desires, he can pursue it in greater depth on his own initiative.

Although there are tremendous differences in the size, shape and behaviour of the various species of the animal kingdom, study has shown that a complex relationship exists between them and that these differences are the result of an evolutionary process. Systematic classification is important to zoology, for not only does it provide an exact identification of the species, but by determining the relationship of systematics to ecology, it helps to position them in a natural classification, and in so doing often indicates the life-history of a species of which nothing is previously known, and when we consider that over one million species have already been catalogued, it will be obvious that some filing system is necessary to provide science with an international working basis.

Broadly speaking, classification involves the grouping together of the similar and the separation of the dissimilar. To illustrate this point, let us take a simple example, using something familiar to most of us—a box of nuts and bolts.

First we would separate the nuts from the bolts, we could then separate the nuts into piles depending upon the material from which they are made, brass; steel; or aluminium. Each pile could then be sorted into thread size and finally subdivided into 'plated' or 'unplated'. A similar exercise would follow with the bolts. This example, is of course, a tremendous over-simplification, living animals are more complex in structure and shape, their behaviour, histories and habitats so varied that the number of possible classifications are much greater than our simple example.

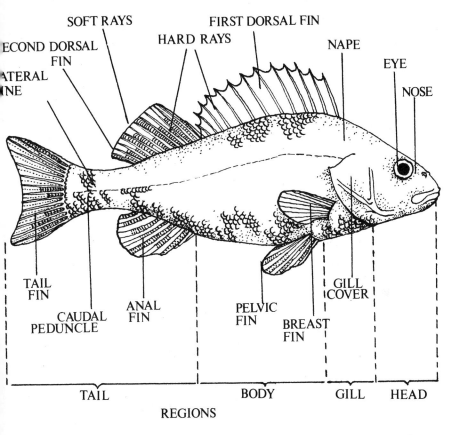

The name of Linnaeus, the Swedish naturalist, is world famous for his early work on classification. He had a natural ability for indexing and his Systema Naturae, published in 1758, provided a basis for the indexing of zoological and herbarium museums that is still used to this day. Although scientific circles agree that his system is not ideal for modern needs, so far, no one has found a better method.

Although Linnaeus made a not inconsiderable contribution to the organization of knowledge, the seventeenth century English naturalist

John Ray, was responsible for laying down the foundations on which Linnaeus built. It was Ray who defined the 'species' as the unit for biological classification. As our interest is with fish classification, first we must know a little about the names to describe the external features of our fishes for this is the only way amateur ichthyologists have of recognizing the group to which they belong.

Most fishes have seven pairs of fins, four of which are paired, that is lying directly beside each other.

The first pair, those nearest the gill cover, are the pectoral or breast fins, and correspond to hands. The second pair are the ventral or pelvic fins, situated on the underside, just below or behind the pectoral fins, these correspond to the legs. Between the tail and the ventral fin is the anal fin and this is situated behind the ventral. Next comes the tail or caudal fin, which is used by most fish to propel themselves through the water. The fin on the back or top part of the body is the dorsal, and this may be either short and upright or broad and extending the length of the back, or even separated into two separate halves.

Some species have an extra fin—the adipose, which is situated on the back between the dorsal and the caudal. Fins are composed of a fin membrane, stiffened and supported by fin rays which are jointed and spread out as they approach the margins of the fin. Some fishes have the dorsal and anal fins modified by having the foremost rays sharp and unjointed.

These bony rays are known as spiny and the remaining part as soft. The gill cover is called the operculum, and one of the sensory organs that is generally visible is the lateral line which runs down the side of the fish from just behind the gill cover to the tail root.

It is the formation and position of the fins, plus other differences, mostly of an internal nature, that control the whole system of classification.

The main group of fish that interest us will be the Teleostei, or bony fishes; most of our aquarium species are of this class.

The class of Teleostean fishes are grouped under three main divisions, these are further divided into Superorders, Superorders into Orders, Orders into Suborders, Suborders into Families, Families into Genera and Genera into Species.

Very old fish of a bygone age, of which only fossils remain, are placed first and the other follow on in order, according to their evolutionary development.

At first reading, this may seem a little complicated, but for a clearer explanation, imagine an army division as the class, which is broken down into Regiments and Companies, until finally we have the soldier, who represents the species.

For example *Scatophagus argus* would be described as follows:—

| | |
|---|---|
| Class ... | Teleostei |
| Division | Three |
| Order ... | Perciformes |
| Suborder | Percoidei |
| Family | Scatophagidae |
| Genus ... | Scatophagus |
| Species | argus |

To use the full information contained in the above every time one wanted to make reference to a particular species would prove cumbersome, so for all general purposes the last two are considered to be enough. Genus always being placed before species.

Sometimes it is necessary to sub-divide the species into what is called 'a variety', this is abbreviated '*var*'. For instance, if we added this to our example '*Scatophagus argus var. ruber*', it would denote that it was a colour variety only of the species, not a different species. Variety is only used in this sense. When the word 'species' is used after the genus instead of the name, it means the genus is known but the species has not been determined.

To save needless repetition, the ichthyologist uses the abbreviation of the first letter of the genus, instead of the complete word, providing it has been been quoted in full previously. For example, *S. argus*.

The plural of genus is genera and of species is species.

The names of families are formed by adding the termination *-idae* to the stem of the name of the 'type' genus, and sub-family names by adding *-inae*.

The name of an author of a specific name would follow the latter without a comma, and be printed in Roman type. The classification used in the Fish Gallery of the British Museum (Natural History) is that proposed by Dr. C. Tate Regan, F.R.S., and is explained in articles by him on 'Fishes Selachians', etc., in the fourteenth edition of the *Encyclopaedia Britannica* (1929). As more knowledge is gained, it is natural that revisions and modifications to the existing placings must be continually under review. Aquarists wishing to obtain the most recent thoughts on their hobby in respect of classification should obtain a copy of the Provisional Outline Classification of the Teleostean Fishes by Greenwood, Rosen, Weitzman and Myers, published in 1966 in the *Bulletin of the American Museum of Natural History*.

| | |
|---|---|
| FAMILY | *Anabantidae* |
| SUBORDER | *Anabantoidei* |
| ORDER | *Perciformes* |
| SUPERORDER | *Acanthopterygii* |

The Anabantids are all relatively small fish, characterized by possessing ancillary organs for breathing atmospheric oxygen. Oxygen, is taken in by gulping air at the surface of the water.

Various species can live out of water by varying periods of time, but only the **Climbing Perch** can leave it entirely and travel overland in search of better water.

| | |
|---|---|
| FAMILY | *Atherinidae* |
| SUBORDER | *Atherinoidei* |
| ORDER | *Atheriniformes* |
| SUPERORDER | *Atherinomorpha* |

This family represents the Silversides, the majority of which are found in coastal waters, but a few have taken to fresh water. The dorsal fins which is a major characteristic of the family, is separated into two distinct fins, the first spiny, the second soft.

| | |
|---|---|
| FAMILY | *Characidae* |
| SUBORDER | *Characoidei* |
| ORDER | *Cypriniformes* |
| SUPERORDER | *Ostariophysi* |

**Characins** belong to the large group of Carp-like fish. They vary considerably in shape, and generally are recognised by the presence of the adipose fin, but this characteristic is not always present. They do not ever possess barbels, and have well developed teeth, sometimes only in the upper jaw.

| | |
|---|---|
| FAMILY | *Cichlidae* |
| SUBORDER | *Percoidei* |
| ORDER | *Perciformes* |
| SUPERORDER | *Acanthopterygii* |

These are perch-like fish, but differing by the structure of the throat bones and the presence of only one olfactory pit on each side of the head. The dorsal fin is spiny on the fore, softer on the rear part. The anal fin generally has three hard spines and large soft rayed part. Most species of **Cichlids** are predatory, but some species will eat vegetable foods in addition.

| | |
|---|---|
| FAMILY | *Cobitidae* |
| SUBORDER | *Cyprinoidei* |
| ORDER | *Cypriniformes* |
| SUPERORDER | *Ostariophysi* |

This family contains the **loaches**, they are worm or snake-like fish that have much in common with the carps, but differ in having three or more pairs of barbels.

They do not have any teeth in their mouth, and many species survive periods in damp mud and oxygen-poor water, by swallowing a bubble of air which passes into the intestines where fine blood vessels absorb the oxygen.

| | |
|---|---|
| FAMILY | *Cyprinidae* |
| SUBORDER | *Cyprinoidei* |
| ORDER | *Cypriniformes* |
| SUPERORDER | *Ostariophysi* |

This family, the *Cyprinidae* represents the **Barbs** and **Minnows**. They are toothless and possess protractile mouths. A great number of carps have barbels, generally a maximum of two pairs but there are a few species that possess more.

Although these fish are toothless in the general sense, they do have curved pharyngeal bones in the throat which carry grinding teeth, that chew against a palate plate.

| | |
|---|---|
| FAMILY | *Cyprinodontidae* |
| SUBORDER | *Cyprinodontoidei* |
| ORDER | *Atheriniformes* |
| SUPERORDER | *Atherinomorpha* |

This family represents the **Tooth Carps, Top Minnows**, or **Killifish**. The majority of the species found in aquarium belong to the old sub family *Fundulinae*, which have single pointed teeth. These are a few exceptions **Jordanella** and **Aphanius**, which are grouped under the sub family *Cyprinodontinae*, which have three pointed teeth.

All species in this family are small, and never possess barbels. The jaws are toothed and lateral lines are not present.

Some 400 different species have been named.

| | |
|---|---|
| FAMILY | *Gasteropelecidae* |
| SUBORDER | *Characidae* |
| ORDER | *Cypriniformes* |
| SUPERORDER | *Ostariophysi* |

This family is closely related to the *Characidae*, and represents the **Hatchet Fish** or **Flying Characins**. The Hatchet Fish are so named because of their body shape which resembles the blade of an axe or hatchet. When viewed from the front they are thin and blade-like, but very deep in the belly when viewed from the side.

They possess powerful and elongated pectoral fins, not unlike the wings of a large insect which are used by the fish to skim along the water surface or to even become airborne.

| FAMILY | *Nandidae* |
|---|---|
| SUBORDER | *Percoidei* |
| ORDER | *Perciformes* |
| SUPERORDER | *Acanthopterygii* |

The **Nandids** are small fish, perch-like and predatory. They are more or less nocturnal. They differ from their related species mainly in skeleton structure, generally they have large mouths capable of opening widely, they have almost transparent caudal fins and clear parts in the rear of their anal and dorsal fins.

| FAMILY | *Poeciliidae* |
|---|---|
| SUBORDER | *Cyprinodontoidei* |
| ORDER | *Atheriniformes* |
| SUPERORDER | *Atherinomorpha* |

This family represents the live-bearing tooth carps. They are found only in the New World.

They are easily recognized by the sex organ of the male, this is in fact a modification of the anal fin into a moveable tube-like appendage named the gonopodium. It is mainly the differences in this organ that decides the various generic classifications.

| FAMILY | *Scatophagidae* |
|---|---|
| SUBORDER | *Percoidei* |
| ORDER | *Perciformes* |
| SUPERORDER | *Acanthopterygii* |

The 'Scats' have laterally compressed bodies. The dorsal fin has spines on the forepart and soft rays on the rear part. Both parts of the dorsal are joined at the base. The anal fin is similar.

They are found naturally in brackish and salt water.

| FAMILY | See below (Catfish) |
|---|---|
| ORDER | *Siluriformes* |
| SUPERORDER | *Ostariophysi* |

There are 31 families of catfish, the principal ones concerning the aquarist are as follows:

| | |
|---|---|
| *Bagridae* | Unarmoured catfish with long barbels. Old World. |
| *Bunocephalidae* | Unarmoured catfish with flat heads. |
| *Callichthyidae* | Small armoured catfish. |
| *Clariidae* | **Gill Sac Catfish** possessing an ancillary breathing organ permitting the fish to leave the water for long periods. |

| | |
|---|---|
| *Doradidae* | Heavy bodied catfish with a single row of bony plates, each of which carry a spine, running along the centre of each side of the fish. |
| *Loricariidae* | Spiny armoured catfish with sucking disc mouths. |
| *Mochokidae* | Family noted for its feathered barbels. |
| *Pimelodidae* | Unarmoured catfish with long barbels. New World. |
| *Schilbeidae* | Family containing the **Glass Catfish**. |
| *Siluridae* | Catfish with very long anal fins and small, or absent dorsal fins. |

FAMILY       *Tetraodontidae*
SUBORDER    *Tetraodontoidei*
ORDER        *Tetraodontiformes*
SUPERORDER   *Acanthopterygii*

This family contains the 'four toothed' **Puffers**. Instead of the usual teeth, they have two broad tooth plates on each jaw which forms a kind of beak.

Most of the species are of a large size and inhabit salt water, but a few are small and inhabit fresh water.

FAMILY       *Hemiodontidae*
SUBORDER    *Characoidei*
ORDER        *Cypriniformes*
SUPERORDER   *Ostariophysi*

Family of Characin like fish, with or without an adipose fin. They swim generally by continuous vibrations of the vertical fins. Some species possess the ability to change colour at night, the horizontal stripe markings being replaced by darker vertical stripes.

FAMILY       *Centropomidae*
SUBORDER    *Percoidei*
ORDER        *Perciformes*
SUPERORDER   *Acanthopterygii*

Fish of this family inhabit the coastal regions around the Indian and Pacific Oceans, however, many species have adapted completely to life in fresh water and some to both.

They are similar to the **Cardinal Fish,** but differ in having both the spiny and soft dorsal connected at the base. Most species are translucent.

| FAMILY | *Monodactylidae* |
|--------|------------------|
| SUBORDER | *Percoidei* |
| ORDER | *Perciformes* |
| SUPERORDER | *Acanthopterygii* |

This family comprises only one genus—*Monodactylus*. The genus is characterized by a high, almost round, body which is strongly compressed laterally. The scales extend well over into the fins.

| FAMILY | *Centrarchidae* |
|--------|------------------|
| SUBORDER | *Percoidei* |
| ORDER | *Perciformes* |
| SUPERORDER | *Acanthopterygii* |

A family of small to medium fish known as **Sunfishes**. Their bodies are more or less compressed laterally, and the cheeks, gill covers and body are covered with scales. They possess small teeth arranged in ribbons.

All species of Sunfishes are strikingly beautiful and they are exclusive meat eaters.

| FAMILY | *Gobiidae* |
|--------|------------|
| SUBORDER | *Gobioidei* |
| ORDER | *Perciformes* |
| SUPERORDER | *Acanthopterygii* |

Family of mostly small fish in which the ventral fins have grown together to form a sucking disc.

# BREEDING

Some aquarists will regard a single decorative aquarium as the ultimate end to their hobby, but the great majority of serious aquarists will not be content to sit back and just look at their fish swimming among the rocks and plants, beautiful though it may be, they will want to extract the added pleasure and achievement derived from breeding successfully both the easy and more difficult species of fish. Even in the present day world where technical achievements, often of a startling and dramatic nature, are regarded as commonplace, the miracle of new life is still a subject for wonder, and where better to witness this miracle, than in the relatively tiny world of the aquarium.

Breeding tropical fish is not necessarily expensive, the equipment is usually very simple, and the space requirements can be adjusted to suit the needs of the aquarist—limited breeding can be achieved with only one spare tank.

Breeding more difficult species does not require any special equipment, but in many instances it does require patience and dedication that can only come from an absorbing love of the subject.

Freshwater tropical fish can be bred true to type, which is the normal way nature propagates the species, ignoring the evolutionary process, they can be hybridized, that is the breeding of near species, strains, or subspecies or they can be artificially bred by selective breeding with the object of developing a particular colour or shape from mutants, in fact, many of our aquarium species are the result of this latter method.

The needs of the fish must be given careful consideration if successful breeding is to be achieved. The provision of suitable and as near natural conditions as possible; the condition of the water, temperature, plants and lighting are all important factors which control the desire to spawn and the successful rearing of the resultant fry.

Determination of the sexes is another important factor which can be easy, for example the livebearers, or virtually impossible. The average aquarist is limited to external appearances and as a very general, but by no means infallible rule, the males are more colourful. Quite often the males can be identified by body shape, usually slimmer than the female and fin differences.

Many aquarists breed the same species, successfully using quite different approaches, but this usually applies only to fish that spawn readily and are reared easily. On the other hand many of the 'difficult' species require very precise, controlled conditions.

The approach to breeding the majority of available aquarium fishes has been described under family heading in the following pages, and where a particular species does not conform to the general description for the family, the departure from the normal has been covered under additional paragraphs. It must be appreciated that the breeding habits of many fish have yet to be discovered, and whilst the breeding habits of other species may well be known in the wild, they have as yet defied breeding attempts in the confines of the aquarium.

It is possible that the more adventurous aquarist may wish to breed, or attempt to breed some of the species of which little is known, or so far have not been bred in captivity. In this instance, the aquarist is advised to start his experimental breeding by using the same techniques employed for closely related species, and if this is unsuccessful, modify his attempts within the scope of his knowledge.

**Breeding the Anabantidae**

(A) The majority of **Anabantids** are bubble nesters. At breeding time the male becomes quite violent and it is likely that during the courtship one of the pair will be killed, usually the female; therefore the breeding aquarium should be large, say 12 in. × 12 in. × 24 in. (30 cm. × 30 cm. × 60 cm.) and well planted to provide a refuge. The water well matured, should be maintained at a level approximately 2 inches (5 cm.) below the aquarium top and raised to a temperature between 78°F (26°C) and 82°F (28°C).

Once the temperature has been set it should be maintained consistently, with the minimum of fluctuation, finally, the aquarium must be covered with a sheet of glass to prevent draughts destroying the nests and to maintain the humidity and temperature.

The bubble nest is built by the male, usually under or adjacent to a floating leaf. The male rising to the surface takes in a gulp of air, and envelopes it in mucuous formed in the mouth during spawning time, with the result that the bubble floats. Continual bubble blowing in this way produces a floating raft of bubbles resembling a little heap of soap bubbles.

When a male starts building a nest, or even a few bubbles it indicates he is ready to breed.

Having prepared the aquaria, it is advisable to introduce the female a few days previous to the male. If they are ready, the male will build a nest and proceed to court the female with heightened colour and spread fins. The female is driven towards the nest and if all goes well, the male will wrap himself around her and fertilize the eggs as they are released. The eggs of some species are oily and will rise to the surface, whilst others will sink to the bottom. The male will collect the eggs and plant them in the nest, sometimes assisted by the female.

Once the spawning is over, the female should be removed.

The male will guard the nest, and return any eggs or fry which fall out. Fry hatch in 2 to 3 days. Once they become free swimming the male must be removed otherwise he will forget all the care and attention he has lavished on them and eat the lot!

The fry require infusoria in large quantities as an initial food, and this is best provided by having a plentiful supply of algae in the breeding tank. The production of infusoria can be encouraged by sprinkling a little dried lettuce leaves and dust size dried food onto the surface when the eggs are laid.

After about 6 days the fry should be fed dust size dried food, mashed daphnia, egg yoke, and mashed enchrytae.

Once the fry have hatched a very gentle aeration is beneficial to the rearing of large broods, the ancilliary breathing labyrinth does not develop until 3 to 4 weeks after birth.

(B) The **Giant Gourami**, among a few other species, builds a rather untidy and indefinitely formed nest. The eggs are lighter than water and float upwards into the nest.

The female should be removed immediately the spawnings are completed, and the male a few days after the eggs hatch.

(C) The **Climbing Perch** does not build a bubble nest. They need a spacious tank with the water depth adjusted to about 4 inches (10 cm.). The fish embrace in the usual way, quite near the surface. The tiny eggs float to the surface and hatch in a day at a temperature of 78°F (26°C).

## BREEDING THE ATHERINIDAE

### *Telmatherina ladigest*

The breeding tank should be large, well illuminated and contain fine leaved plants and mats of Riccia. The female usually makes the advances when she is ready to spawn. The eggs are released singly with the pair of fish in a side to side position. The eggs hang from the plants by tiny threads. The spawning periods can last for several days or continue over a period of three weeks.

Eggs hatch in 7 to 10 days at a temperature of 82°F (28°C) and fry can be fed with *Cyclops nauplii* initially, followed with Brine Shrimps after about 7 days.

It is advisable to remove plants containing eggs daily, and transfer to an all glass tank for rearing in water about 6 inches (15·2 cm.) deep.

## Breeding the Catfish

The **Catfish** are not easy fish to spawn and not many species have been spawned up to the present time, but *C. paleatus* is one that can be bred, although it may prove inconsistent. To have any success at all, the first consideration must be the condition of the fish. Generally, the catfish are regarded as scavengers, and quite rightly so, but fish intended for breeding should not be considered in this way. Separate them and feed in the usual manner for breeding. Daphnia, tubifex etc., are the best foods for this purpose. In fact, plenty of live foods should be provided.

The breeding tank should be an established one and thickly planted at one end with Sagittaria. The tank should have a capacity of 8–10 gallons and have a fair layer of 'mulm' on the bottom.

Sexing is not easy, but the most reliable sign is that the female is more round and full bodied.

As the female approaches a condition conducive to breeding, her belly takes on a reddish hue and the first ray of the pectoral fins also reddens.

The first indication that spawning is likely to occur is when the male repeatedly swims over the back of the female, just touching her with his barbels.

Later the pair appear to embrace, the male almost on his back, the female in a right-angle position. They remain in this position for possibly 30 seconds, then break away to swim quite independently. The female, upon close inspection, can now be seen to carry about four eggs between her ventral fins. She next looks for a suitable spot to deposit them, carefully examining the plants with her mouth. She then clasps a leaf with her ventral fin and presses the eggs onto it so that they adhere.

This action is repeated probably over a period of two hours, resulting in up to a hundred eggs being deposited. Remove the parents when the spawning is complete.

The eggs hatch in about four days and the young disappear into the sediment for about two weeks. During this period it is unnecessary to provide food.

They will feed on the 'mulm'. If it is impossible to provide the necessary 'mulm', provide a little paste made from boiled oatmeal.

The breeding temperature is approximately 70°F (21°C) and the water should be slightly alkaline (pH 7·2).

## Breeding the Characins

(A) One of the easiest **Characins** to breed is *Hyphessobrycon flammeus*, and for this reason it is a good species for the beginner.

The breeding tank should be cleaned thoroughly and filled with seasoned water to a depth of 8 inches. A tank 12 in. × 6 in. × 6 in. is quite suitable. Cover the bottom with a thin layer of gravel, also washed thoroughly and add some fine leaved plants such as Nitella or Myriophyllum. The plants should be anchored in a horizontal position with short lengths of glass rods or by thin lead strips.

Place the tank in a position where it will receive diffused light, but not in the direct rays of the sun.

Introduce the pair of fish during the evening, they are likely to spawn either during the night or in the early morning.

The male, during the act of mating, will pursue the female vigorously driving her into or over the plants, where she will drop her eggs to be immediately fertilized by the male. Immediately after the spawning is over, both parents should be removed otherwise they will regard their eggs as a suitable meal.

At a temperature between 72°–75°F (22°–24°C) the eggs will hatch in about 48 hours. The tiny splinter-like babies will stick to the sides of the tank or on the plants until the yoke of the egg sac has been absorbed. During this period no food must be given, they will not attempt to eat it anyway. After two or three days when the youngsters become free swimming, they can receive their first food of micro organisms, such as rotifers, or very fine dry food, and hard boiled egg yoke, which can be graduated to Artemia and microworms as the fry develop.

(B) Not all Characins are bred so easily, some species such as *Hyphessobrycon callistus* are very sensitive to strong light, therefore, the breeding tank should be shaded to provide only a dim light. The young of these species should not be fed on dried foods, but micro-organisms and infusoria, until they are large enough to accept newly hatched brine shrimps.

(C) *Hyphessobrycon innesi* requires soft water with a hardness less than 7 German degrees and clinical cleanliness in the tank. No bottom gravel is required, but it is advisable to paint the underside of the bottom to prevent any light entering the tank in an unnatural manner. The water must be crystal clear before the fish are introduced and the tank well shaded from strong light. Once the spawning is completed, the tank should be put into total darkness. Temperatures should be around 70°F (21°C) but never over 73°F (23°C).

(D) The **Poecilobrycons** carefully attach their eggs to the stalks of plants, and require a temperature around 78°F (26°C) otherwise as (C) above.

Because the fry grow rather more slowly than most Characins, they have to be fed microscopic foods over longer periods and this makes the rearing of the fry a little more hazardous.

(E) The genus *Copeina* have a spawning pattern that is quite remarkable. In the wild *C. arnoldi* select a suitable plant *above* the surface of the water, the male then drives the female towards it, and locking or partially locking themselves together, by their fins, they both leap out of the water onto the plant leaves, and deposit the eggs. To prevent the eggs drying out the male squirts water over them more or less periodically.

For aquarium breeding a tank about 24 in. × 12 in. × 12 in. will be required. The depth of water should be adjusted to about 8 inches and have a pH value of 7 or slightly less. Temperature 77°F (25°C) to 80°F (28°C).

As it is difficult to provide suitable aquatic plants above the surface of the water, a sheet of roughened glass or slate can be substituted.

The aquarium should be covered with a sheet of glass.

Position the glass in the aquarium so that about 4 to 5 inches projects above the surface, the rough surface will allow the eggs to adhere.

If the fish are healthy and ready to spawn, they will proceed as described, jumping about 2 inches out of the water.

The procedure is repeated until about 100 eggs are scattered onto the glass or slate.

Once the spawning is over, it is wise to remove the female, leaving the male to tend the eggs by splashing water over them.

When he is not actually splashing the eggs, the male is rather shy and likes to hide himself, therefore, ensure that he has plenty of cover by providing thick clumps of plant at one end of the tank.

When the eggs hatch, usually in 72 hours, the fry drop into the water, it is then prudent to remove the male.

Feed fry with microscopic foods.

(F) *Megalamphodus megalopterus* like most characins requires a clinically clean aquarium, and water slightly acid from Sphagnum peat. Approximately pH 4·5 and a hardness about 7°–10° DH.

Nylon wool and a floor covering made from untangled nylon pot scourers make ideal egg traps that can be boiled and cleaned thoroughly before use to maintain the clinical cleanliness so necessary.

Breeding temperature is 78°F (25°C). After fry become free swimming, early food advised is hard boiled egg yolk squeezed through a piece of muslin into the water containing the fry.


## Breeding the Cichlidae

(A) The **Cichlids** are highly developed fish that care for their young with great diligence. They are however rather pugnacious and this facet of their character usually becomes more accentuated as breeding time approaches. They are somewhat destructive of plants and have a habit of burrowing and rooting among the gravel.

All Cichlids require a diet of live foods and as most of them are quite large, their accommodation must out of necessity by spacious.

The breeding tank should be spacious, not less than 24 in. × 12 in. × 12 in. (60·6 cm. × 30·3cm. × 30·3 mm.). The bottom gravel should be thoroughly cleaned and laid to a depth of about 2 inches (5·1 cm.) a few large flat stones and rockwork caves or a flower pot should be included to provide a retreat. It is pointless adding plants, they will only be uprooted. Next fill the tank with well seasoned water. As most Cichlids breed in water around 77°F (25°C) adjust the temperature to suit.

With some species it will be necessary to separate the tank into two halves by adding a tank separator. i.e. a sheet of glass and some means to fix it in position. Put the male in one half, the female in the other. If the pair are compatible, generally indicated by the heightened colour, wagging bodies and erect fins, the partition can be removed. The reason for the precaution is to prevent unfriendly pairs fighting, which may well result in one being killed.

If a number of the same species is kept in one tank, some will pair naturally. These can then be selected with reasonable confidence and put into the breeding tank without any partition.

If all goes well the courtship will proceed with 'kissing', which is really a mouth to mouth tug of war. If during these preliminary stages one fish should panic, it is liable to be killed by its mate.

In the event of obvious incompatability the pair should be separated, a later try may well prove successful.

If all goes well the pair will proceed to prepare a suitable place for their eggs, they will dig depressions in the gravel and perhaps clean the face of a stone or flat rock. As previously mentioned a flower pot is useful and some aquarist also use a piece of flat marble.

Cichlids are particular about cleanliness, they will clean the finally selected spot with their mouth. A few days before the actual spawning takes place both sexes develop an ovipositor or breeding tube.

The act of spawning consists of the female hovering over the selected breeding spot and touching it with the breeding tube and depositing one or two eggs. The male immediately fertilizes the eggs in the same manner. The activity continues until between 100 or 1000 eggs have been laid.

Both parents now attend the eggs fanning them with the breast fins and tail. Eggs hatch in 4 days at 80°F (27°C) just prior or immediately after the eggs hatch, the parents transfer the fry to a depression in the gravel, and at this stage they resemble a jelly mass rather than young fry. During the period required for absorption of the yolk sac, some 4 to 10 days, the fry are transferrred from one depression to another. Recalcitrant fry are quickly gathered in the mouth of a parent and put back into the nest. The fry, after absorbing the yolk sac, are large enough to accept brine shrimp, micro-worms, sifted daphnia and other small live foods.

Once the youngsters are feeding the parents should be removed.

(B) The **Orange Chromicle** requires large leaved plants, stone archways, and/or a flower pot in their breeding tank. The dark coloured eggs are suspended by individual threads from the leaves or stonework. Otherwise the breeding procedure follows the usual pattern for Cichlids. Breeding temperature about 80°F (27°C). Eggs hatch in five days.

(C) The **Egyptian Mouthbreeder** require a large aquaria, well planted with reasonable space between the plants. Temperature of water should be adjusted to 77°F (25°C). The male fans a depression in the gravel in which the female lays her eggs, the eggs being fertilized as they fall into the nest. Any number of eggs from 20 to 200 may be laid.

Now the departure from the usual Cichlid pattern of breeding behaviour, the eggs are collected by the female and held for safe-keeping in her mouth, they are carried in the mouth until the eggs hatch, and for some time afterwards until the fry absorb their yolk sacs. This can be as long as 14 days, and during this period the female stolidly refuses to eat.

Even after the young become free swimming they are liable to dart back into their mothers mouth at the least sign of danger. The male should be carefully removed after spawning and the female removed as soon as the fry are large enough to look after themselves.

## Breeding the Cyprinidae (Carp-like fish)

(A) Many of the Barbs are easy to breed providing the aquarist gives due consideration to the needs of the fish. In general practice, the following descriptions can be taken as a generality for the family.

The aquarium should be prepared with dense thickets of fine leaved plants with plenty of open space to allow the fish to chase during court-ship. In addition the floor of the aquarium should be covered with large sized pebbles or glass marbles to protect the eggs from being devoured by the parents. Most Barbs will eat the eggs almost immediately they are dropped by the female.

Willow-root is an excellent medium for protecting eggs in the spawning tank, it forms a dense mat into which the eggs can fall. Make certain that the root is well cleaned and boiled. The advantage of willow-root is that it can be stored and used whenever required.

Alternatively fine leaved plants can be laid down horizontally along the bottom of the tank and retained there with glass tubes or rods laid across them.

Having prepared the tank and adjusted the temperature of the water to about 76°F (24°C) it is time to consider the fish.

Healthy strong fish produce the best offspring, so for about a week feed the specimen selected for mating rather more frequently than usual, with live daphnia, shrimp, scrapings of raw beef, and with small quantities of dried flake foods.

Sexes that have been separated are most likely to spawn readily, but if accommodation is limited put the female into the breeding tank a few days in advance of the males. This is a good practice anyway. Most species are egg scatterers. They scatter their eggs in open water or among plants. Rarely are the eggs anchored to plants or any other surface.

When first introduced to the female, the male may appear shy, but courtship will occur as they get to know each other. This takes the form of chasing, and eventually quivering in a side to side position. The eggs are dropped by the female to be immediately fertilized by milt ejected by the male.

Both parents should be removed when the spawning is complete.

The incubation period varies with different species but an average period is 24 to 48 hours. After hatching, the fry usually attach themselves to the glass sides of the tank, or to the plants. They look something like tiny glass splinters. After a few days they become free swimming and from then onwards must be fed on infusoria, and other microscopic foods (see Fry Menu). Dust size dry foods, egg yolk, and white worms mashed to the consistence of a fine paste.

It is advisable to start a culture of infusoria as soon as the fish spawn so that it is available when needed.

(B) Large fish naturally need large aquariums in which to spawn, and sometimes gentle aeration as well. This is particularly true for *Barbus everetti*.

(C) The **Cherry Barbs** are best bred in single pairs. The eggs are usually deposited singly near broad leaved plants to which they are attached by a thin thread. To prevent the parent eating the eggs between spawnings feed enchytrae during·this period.

(D) The **Harlequin** is a difficult fish to breed. First it is necessary to find compatible pairs as not all pairs will mate. The tank should have the base covered with boiled and squeezed peat mulm and a bunch of the broad leafed plants available. The plant Cryptocoryne is ideal and it should be planted in a pot filled with peat moss and positioned in the middle of the tank. Cleanliness is of the utmost importance and so is the water—pH should be adjusted to 5·5 to 6·5 and hardness to 2° DH. Filtering through peat moss will give the required pH. Water temperature 79°F (26°C).

After the usual courting display, the eggs will be found adhering to the underside of the leaves. Parents should be removed after spawning. Fry hatch after 24 hours. Rear fry as for Cyprinids generally.

(E) For breeding the **Scissor Tail** it is recommended to use a water depth of about 5 inches (12·7 cm.) at a pH of 6·6 to 6·8. Temperature 80°F (27°C) and several males used to a single female. Eggs will hatch in 5 to 6 days.

## Breeding the *Cyprinodontidae* (Egg–laying Tooth Carps)

(A) The egg-laying tooth carps are easily distinguished from the live-bearing tooth carps by the absence of the external sex organ, the gonopodium. They are not, however, quite so easily bred, but the satisfaction of a good spawning gives a greater sense of achievement.

The following description of spawning by the egg-layers can be taken as a generality, as in most cases, the spawnings are similar. Where specific departures from this occur, they will be dealt with separately.

For egg-laying tooth carps, your aquarium should be prepared with dense thickets of fine-leaved plants with plenty of open spaces to allow them to chase.

Willow root is an excellent medium for protecting eggs in the spawning tanks as it forms a dense mat into which the eggs can fall, Make certain that the root is boiled before introducing it into the breeding tank. The advantage of willow root is that it can be stored and used whenever required.

Sexes that have been kept separated, are more likely to spawn readily. but if accommodation is so limited that it prevents this, separate them three or four days before introducing them to the breeding tank.

Healthy strong fish produce the best offspring, so feed them rather more frequently than usual for about a week before mating, with scrapings of raw meat, daphnia, shrimp, earthworm, and small quantities of dried prepared food.

Introduce the female a day in advance of the male to let her acclimatize to the new surroundings. When the male is put in he may seem shy at first, but it will not be long before courtship takes place. This takes the form of repeated dashes about the tank accompanied by various actions like fin nibbling and body quivering by the side of the female.

Eggs dropped amongst the plants by the female are fertilized by milt ejected from the male. At the completion of the spawning, the fish, or the plants to which the eggs are attached, should be removed to another tank. If the fish or eggs are transferred the temperature of the water should be consistent.

The incubation period varies with different species. When the eggs hatch the young look like an egg to the top of which a fine body is attached. As the fish develop, the egg-like appendage, which is the yolk-sac, is absorbed. The yolk-sac provides nourishment in the first stages before the fish are able to swim and spend their time keeping out of harm's way hopping about on the sandy bottom, or clinging to the glass sides of the aquarium.

It is this stage, the early feeding period, that is the most critical. The table on page    shows how to feed fry. It is well to start a culture of infusoria as soon as the spawning takes place, so that it is available when needed. It is difficult to state how much infusoria should be given as it varies so much in quality. Experience will provide the best guide.

However, the feeding should be frequent, so that the bellies of the fry visibly bulge.

You will notice that some of the youngsters will develop more quickly than others. Probably some are born with more energy than others, and have the advantage of eating the most and the best food.

### Cynolebias bellottii

(B) Breeding in an aquarium requires a temperature of 68°F (20°C) and slightly brackish water (one teaspoonful of sea-salt per gallon should be added to the aquarium.) After spawning, remove the adults and drain the aquarium gradually over a period of ten days. Leave the sand moist and the tank empty for about three weeks. Then refill over a period of three to four days with clean rain water. The young should hatch in about two days. Feed with brine shrimps or sifted daphnia.

Rearing the fry is not particularly difficult; provided they are well fed with live food they will reach adult size within eight weeks.

(C) For breeding *E. chaperi*, a loose-floating plant like Riccia is needed in addition to normal plants. The aquarium should be placed in a position where it will not get too much sunlight. The best results are obtained if two females are paired to one male. The temperature should be raised to 77°F (25°C) and the females introduced a couple of days in advance of the male.

The female will probably be a little shy at first, but this soon disappears when the male drives her into the masses of Riccia, where they remain side by side and a single egg is dropped and fertilized. The females drop only one egg at a time, 15 to 20 being the average for a day. After about a week the spawning ends.

The eggs are about the size of a pin head and although they are not usually eaten by the parents at this stage, it is advisable to remove the parents or the plants with the eggs attached, before the young hatch. They can be put into a large jar and stood in the aquarium to maintain the water temperature.

It is important for the eggs to be kept in subdued light, as strong light is harmful.

The eggs hatch in about two weeks. Remember that there will be a difference in ages of one week, so the young will be correspondingly different in sizes. They should be transferred to a tank containing only 5 inches (12·7 cm.) of water, until they are strong enough to withstand a greater depth which is usually after a month or so.

Mild aeration helps at this stage. Infusoria need only be fed for a short time and graduation on to brine shrimp ensures rapid growth.

*Rivulus cylindraceus* and *Panchax lineatus* are also species which breed in this manner.

*E. chaperi* prefer slightly alkaline water about pH 7·1.

(D) **Angel Fish** can only be sexed at breeding time by the shape of the genital papillae—the female's being blunt, and the male more pointed.

The aquarium should contain plenty of broad-leafed plants or as alternatives bamboo cane, or glass tubes, the inside of which have been painted green. The eggs, which are adhesive, are laid on the strong plants, or the bamboo. During the period when the young are attached to a leaf, they are continually picked up in the mouth of their parents and sprayed onto another leaf. The conclusions drawn is that this in some way contributes to cleanliness. The decision whether or not to remove the parents after spawning is a difficult one. Sometimes they can be safely left together but there is a fifty-fifty chance that they will be eaten. Eggs hatch in about 48 hours.

The genus *Aphyosemion* comprise fish that naturally inhabit the dark waters of tropical rain forests, where the water conditions change considerably, therefore they should not be subjected to strong illumination or too warm conditions. This is true also when breeding.

The water must be clean and free of infusoria or bacteria. Rinse all food in a strainer before introducing it into their tank, this will inhibit the development of infusoria.

Generally, the water should be soft, slightly acid, and contain humic acid. The addition of ½ oz. of salt to 3 gallons (13·6 litres) of water will inhibit the growth of bacteria.

Some species of *A.* are bottom spawners, others spawn in the plants. The male chases the female vigorously and with the bottom spawners, presses her down near the bottom, there trembling violently, she releases an egg which is caught in the distended anal fin of the male, fertilized and thrown into the mulm.

With plant layers the egg is thrown into a clump of plants.

The eggs, which are sensitive to light, usually take quite a long time to hatch.

For breeding plant spawning species, set up an aquarium with soft, preferably rain water to a depth of 2½ to 3 inches (6·4 to 7·6 cm) and add salt (½ oz. to 3 gallons). Include feather moss, unravelled nylon mops, and thread algae as a spawning medium. Cover glass sides with dark green tissue paper or paint to provide the twilight condition. The adhesive eggs hang from threads. Spawning continues over a period of a few days, 6 to 10 eggs being laid daily. Remove the eggs daily under subdued lighting and place in shallow dishes filled with water from the breeding tank to which $\frac{1}{10}$ grain of Acriflavine to 3 gallons (13·6 litres) has been added. The dish should be kept in the dark until the fry hatch—between 10–20 days. The fry are then transferred to a larger container by means of a glass tube and fed infusoria or dust size dry food.

It is important to maintain the water condition and temperature throughout the cycle.

Bottom spawning species require the same water conditions, but the bottom of the breeding tank should be covered with gravel and a thick covering of feather moss (Feather moss can be anchored to the floor of the tank with glass tubes or rods) and mulm.

The eggs are collected after the spawning by syphoning out with the mulm after being carefully shaken out of the moss, and placed in dishes as for the plant species.

The period of incubation can extend to 3 months, but is is generally between 4 to 6 weeks, at a temperature between 71°–75°F (21°–24°C). These temperatures should not be exceeded—higher temperatures retard or even completely stop the development of the eggs. Infertile eggs, recognized by their whiteness should be removed daily. Fertile eggs should be transferred to clean dishes containing half rain and half tap water. Feed the hatched fry with small quantities of dust sized food. Unhatched eggs should be transferred to other dishes until they hatch and so on.

## Breeding the Poeciliidae (Live-bearers)

(A) The fact that fish can bring forth their young alive is no surprise to aquarist, but it is a source of amazement to the uninformed. Whilst it is true that the young fry enter the world alive, they do not develop in the same manner as mammals.

Mammals perpetuate the species by the medium of the egg, after the egg is fertilized by the male, it adheres to the wall of the uterus drawing sustenance from the females bloodstream for its development, and continues to do so until the offspring are sufficiently developed to enter the world. The period of gestation being constant for every species.

With live-bearing fish the eggs are situated in the egg duct where they are fertilized. Upon hatching the fry are not immediately delivered, but remain in the safety of the mothers body until they reach a stage of development equivalent to the young of egg layers that have absorbed the yolk sac and become free swimming.

Unlike mammals, the period between conception and birth is not of specific duration, it is affected considerably by temperature. As an average the period between conception and birth is between four and five weeks at a temperature of 75°F (24°C). A lower temperature increases the period considerably. For example at a temperature of 68°F (20°C) the period can be extended to eleven weeks. Ideally the breeding temperature should be 80°F (27°C) this induces rapid incubation, and robust fry.

Determination of the sexes is no problem even for novice aquarists. At birth and for a few weeks afterwards, it is impossible to sex, but as the male matures the anal fin becomes more pointed and lengthens into a rigid tube like projection, this is named the gonopodium. The gonopodium is carried normally close to the body and pointing rearwards, but it is a mobile organ that can be angled in almost any direction. The female has a normal anal fin.

Inducing the majority of live-bearers to breed is not difficult, on the contrary, it is more difficult to prevent them breeding when the sexes are mixed. The males court the females with fins erect, and a general alert attitude, they chase the female until the opportunity presents itself for a lightening thrust of the gonopodium.

Females can have up to eight broods from one fertilization, therefore it is unnecessary to remate after the first brood.

Serious breeders keep the males and females separated, and select a pair that they require to breed. Live-bearers normally kept a community aquarium will breed indiscriminately, and will often cross breed between similar species. If the aquarist is interested in perpetrating a particular colour strain or any other feature for that matter, it is imperative that the sexes are housed separately.

Females about to give birth are said to be 'ripe'. This condition can be determined by the appearance of a dark, crescent-shaped area in the females body close to the vent known as the gravid spot.

The appearance of the gravid spot, is accompanied by a general fattening of the belly when viewed from above.

The number of young in a brood is largely dependent upon the size of the female. The larger the female, the larger the number in the brood. Irrespective of the number in a brood, the fry are approximately all the same size at birth.

Live-bearers are notorious cannibals, they will devour their young as soon as they are born. This can be prevented by having an abundance of cover for the youngsters in the form of bunched fine leaved plants, or to use a breeding trap (see Equipment), which restricts the female to a small part of the aquarium, but allows the fry to escape into the wider reaches of the breeding tank. If the breeding trap is large enough more than one female can be accommodated simultaneously.

There are means of making your own breeding trap by inserting two pieces of glass to form a trough with a $\frac{1}{8}$ inch gap in the bottom (see Fig. oo) or alternatively to suspend a series of glass rods to divide the tank top from the bottom, however, breeding traps are so inexpensive it is hardly worth the effort. The preparation for the breeding tank is simple. It need not be too large for most species, and should be filled to a depth of about 8 inches (20 cm.) with matured water, and the temperature raised ·to about 78°F (25°C). The tank should be well stocked with fine leaved plants if a breeding trap is not being used. The use of gravel is optional.

Once the female has given birth to the full brood, both she and the breeding trap should be removed.

Handling live-bearers when they are near the time of delivery can cause premature births. Premature babies have not completely absorbed their yolk sac which can be seen attached to their bellies. Few premature fry survive unless the yolk-sac is very small indeed.

Rearing the young is relatively simple on newly hatched brine shrimps, sifted daphnia, flour size dry foods etc.

Snails can be used to eat surplus food if desired.

(B) The female of the **Mosquito Fish** delivers only one or two young daily, until about twenty are born. The female should not be removed from the breeding tank until after 10 days to ensure a maximum yield of fry.

# FRESHWATER
## TROPICAL FISHES

Now at last the reason for all the care and preparation given to the aquatic home—the fish.

For easy reference the fish descriptions have been arranged under scientific names, irrespective of family, but the family name, in parentheses, has been included following the common name where one exists.

Metric equivalents in the text for inches and degrees Farenheit have been rounded off to the nearest whole figure for convenience, the minor differences due to this approximation are so small that they can be ignored for all practical purposes.

Descriptions of colour have been assessed as accurately as possible, but some fish vary their colour considerably when excited, frightened or when they are in breeding conditions, others may well differ slightly between species in markings or clarity of marking or change with age or maturity.

The scales of the majority of Bony Fishes have a regular arrangement and within certain limits the size of the scale and its disposition are constant to the species. The generally accepted formula for counting scales is to count the scales along the horizontal length (middle) of the fish, and then count the number of rows down from the fore-dorsal fin in traverse series, to the lateral line, and from the lateral line backwards to the ventral fin. Scale counts have not been given for individual fish as it is felt that the majority of aquarists would not require this somewhat scientific information, but the method of doing so is described so that scale counts can be taken if required.

# *Acanthophthalmus semicinctus (Cobitidae),* **Malayan Loach**

Found naturally in the Malay Peninsula and Archipelago the **Malayan Loach**, also known as snake fish, snake worm, half banded coolie and Malayan eel, can at a quick glance be easily mistaken for a tiny eel. Although decidedly eel-like, a second glance soon corrects the first impressions.

The main body colouring is of a salmon pink hue, but this colour will vary with different specimen from pink to beige or orange with a distinct pinkish colouring near the gills. The dark markings are brown and form half bands; these bands are on the upper part of the body and are not regular in shape. They may well have a light spot. Two of the maxillary barbels are on the tip of the snout. Specimen offered for sale in this country rarely exceed 2 inches (5·1 cm.).

*A semicinctus* has sometimes in the past been confused with a similar species—*A. kuhlii. A. kuhlii* can be identified by comparison of the dark markings which extend from the back, right down to the underparts.

Other species in the genus are *A. kuhlii kuhlii,* a sub-species from Java, and *A. kuhlii sumatranus* another sub-species from Sumatra which has less bands and wider interspaces. Borneo's contribution is *A. shelfordi* with dark bands tapering as they near the lower portion of the body. A second row of patchy markings are placed between the main markings.

The Malayan Loach is a scavenger and is quite useful in clearing up any food left uneaten by other fish. It is a nocturnal fish, lying up most of the day behind rocks, or hidden in among the plants. It will, however soon learn to become active during the day, once acclimatized.

This genus likes clean, clear water with a layer of 'mulm' on the floor of the aquarium.

Their food preference is for small live foods, and scraps, for which they forage among the plants, and search the gravel.

Little is known about their breeding habits at present.


# *Aequidens latifrons (Cichlidae),* **Blue Acara**

Also known as the **Blue Spot Cichlid**, this species from Panama and Columbia, is one of the best known Cichlids. Fully grown specimen attain a length of 6 inches (15·3 cm.). But they are mature when only about 3 inches (7·7 cm.) long.

The body colour is mainly of a greenish hue, with darker bands vertically positioned along the sides. Under the eye it has a dark spot and a larger spot about the centre of the body. Irregular lines on the head are blue and have a phosphorescent quality. Scales on the upper body are blue with reddish edges, the lower half is the reverse. Fins are mostly orange to red, sprinkled with blue green markings.

Temperature range between 74°F (23°C) to 78°F (25°C).

Both sexes are similar, but males have the typical long filament to the dorsal. Not a particularly peaceful fish, but neither does it disturb the bottom gravel as much as most Cichlids.

For breeding, see Breeding the Cichlidae.

### *Aequidens maroni (Cichlidae),* Keyhole Cichlid

Originating in British Guiana and Venezuela, this 4 inch (10·2 cm.) species is usually of a mild temperament for a Cichlid. The body colour is yellowish to reddish, with dark blotches, one of which resembles a keyhole. This keyhole is positioned about two thirds down the body and can be vary faint or strongly evident. Each scale has a dark spot.

Males have more pointed anal and dorsal fins. Temperature range between 74°F (23°C) to 76°F (24°C). Given plenty of space, this species will be found to be very peaceful. Like the majority of Cichlids, the **Keyhole** must be fed on live foods.

For breeding, see Breeding the Cichlidae, they are however, not easy fish to spawn and occasionally a pair will not look after their offspring, in such instances it is advisable to remove the parents and rear the fry with microsize-live foods, and supply very gentle aeration.

### *Aequidens portalegrensis (Cichlidae),* Brown Acara

Also known as the **Striped Cichlid**, this species from S.E. Brazil is one of the kinder Cichlids. It grows to about 6 inches (15·2 cm.) and is similar to *A. latifrons* in colouring but it is more subdued. The body is brownish with a bluish sheen, marked with dark bands and blotches. There is a dark spot in the middle of the body and one on the caudal peduncle, the latter being enhanced with surrounding brilliant dots.

Temperature range between 72°F (22°C) and 75°F (24°C). It is not a particularly peaceful species, and will dig around the roots of plants, otherwise it is not very demanding.

For breeding, see Breeding the Cichlidae.

### *Ambassis lala (Ambassidae)*, **Indian Glassfish**

The body colour of *A. lala* is golden in reflected light, with fins yellow to orange, otherwise the body is transparent and very glass-like. The dorsal fin is in two parts, the soft dorsal and anal fin of the male is edged with sky blue. Fine dark dotted lines form vertical bars along the body.

Originating in India, *A. Lala*, rarely exceeds 1½ inches (3·8 cm.) in the aquarium, but it is reputed to grow larger in the wild.

Temperature range between 65°F (18°C) and 75°F (24°C). This species is happiest in established aquariums and they are shown to best advantage in schools with their own kind, but they can be accommodated in communities of fish of similar size.

They require living foods of such a size that they can consume it in one mouthful.

Breeding temperature is about 77°F (25°C). The breeding tank must contain floating plants such as Ceratopteris, so that the pair can mate in the roots. 4 to 8 eggs are released and swirled into the roots where they become entrapped. Fry hatch in 24 hours and remain anchored for a further 4 days, before they become free swimming.

Feeding the very tiny fry is a problem. They need infusoria but in addition they require plenty of Copepod nauplii.

The fry do need plenty of the correct foods otherwise they will soon starve.

The parents do not usually eat the eggs or fry, but they should be removed as a precautionary step.


### *Anabas testudineus (Anabantidae)*, **Climbing Perch**

The **Climbing Perch** has a wide natural range including India, the Malay region, Burma, Siam, South China, Ceylon and the Philippines.

The body colour is rich brown or olive green, the fins are usually tinted similarly to the body, and in some spec...nen the tail is a beautiful dark red. In the wild they can attain a length of 10 inches (25 cm.). Although these are labyrinth fish, they do not conform to the other members of the family. They are able to stay out of water for relatively long periods and can travel overland assisted by the many spines on the edge of the gill cover.

They adapt themselves very well to life in the aquarium, being happy in a temperature between 68°F (20°C) and 85°F (30°C) but they can stand lower temperatures down to 56°F (13°C).

142

Unfortunately they are vicious and have a tendency to try and leave their tank during the hours of darkness.

They can be fed all the normal foods until they grow to about 3 inches (7·6 cm.) thereafter they require quite large live foods.

For breeding, see Breeding Anabantidae (C).

### Anostomus anostomus (Anostomidae), Red Headstander

This species ranges mainly from Guiana. The body shape is long and slender with a slightly flattened head. Its main colour has a reddish tint, marked with three dark brown stripes down the length of the body with a dark yellow-gold in between. The dark areas in the dorsal adipose and other fins near the body are strongly red. These pretty 4 inch (10 cm.) fish, like to swim with their heads down, hence their common name, they are generally quite peaceable, but occasionally a large specimen may indulge in a little chasing of smaller fish.

Temperature range between 75°F (24°C) and 82°F (27°C). Breeding in aquaria has not as yet been accomplished.

*Anostomus anostomus (Anostomidae)*, Red Headstander

143

### *Aphyocharax rubripinnis (Characidae)*, **Bloodfin**

This small fish from Argentina, grows only to $1\frac{3}{4}$ inches (4·5 cm.). It has a silvery body colour strongly reflecting a greenish tint. The fins are all strongly coloured red near their roots. The male, somewhat more slender than the female, has tiny hooks on his anal fin so small that they cannot be seen with the naked eye, but not too small to catch into the threads of a net, so be careful when netting. The adipose fin is present.

The **Bloodfin** is a school species and needs plenty of free swimming space.

These are relatively easy fish to breed. They will often spawn in a school scattering eggs indiscriminately. The adults should be removed immediately after the completion of the spawning, otherwise they will devour the eggs without delay. Breeding temperature 74°F (23°C) normal temperature range 64°F (18°C) to 76°F (24°C). See Breeding Characins (A). Fry will grow rapidly.


### *Aphyosemion australe (Cyprinodontidae)*, **Lyretail**

Found naturally in West Africa, the male **Lyretail** is a particularly handsome fellow. The general body colour is a light brownish-green, darkening on the back to sepia, and lightening to bluish-green on the belly. The body is spotted with irregular carmine marks. Both the dorsal and anal fins are edged with a carmine and blue-green stripe. As may be expected, the tail is most beautiful, the outer rays are pink to orange terminating in white tips and within the outer rays two broad stripes of carmine form a box-like pattern encompassing a blue-green panel and this is spotted with carmine dots. The outer rays of the tail, dorsal and anal fins reduce into filaments.

The female has a similar body colour, and is marked with a few carmine spots on the body and unpaired fins, otherwise she is relatively plain.

This species grow to about $2\frac{1}{2}$ inches (6·4 cm.) and prefer soft, slightly acid water of pH 6·8 and at a temperature between 72°F (22°C) and 75°F (24°C).

The water must be relatively free of bacteria and infusoria, and free of any cloudiness from any source, otherwise the fish will become uneasy, and prone to disease.

*A. australe* is a beautiful and peaceful species, best maintained in aquaria with similar species of *A.*

For breeding, see Breeding the Cyprinodontidae.

*Aphyosemion bivattatum (Cyprinodontidae)*, Banded Fundulus

## *Aphyosemion bivattatum (Cyprinodontidae)*, **Banded Fundulus**

Originating in Tropical West Africa, this species has a body colour of yellow-brown marked with crimson spots. There is a dark stripe extending from the nose, through the eye and along the body to the tail root. A second stripe extends from below the eye, along the lower part of the body and terminates also on the tail root. The dorsal fin is beautifully marked with crimson spots near the base, and streaked with the same colour on the tip. The anal and caudal fins are marked similarly.

The fins are more developed and better marked on the male. This is particularly true of the caudal fin which has extending filaments on the upper and lower lobes.

This species must be kept in old water, pH 7·5. The fish will not take kindly to even slightly new water, and they do require a carnivorous diet, preferably live.

They are a little difficult to keep successfully and not too easy to breed. However, neither is impossible.

Eggs are deposited among clumps of plants and hatch in about 12 days. The ideal breeding temperature is about 72°F (22°C) and the water should be slightly saline.

For breeding, see Breeding the Cyprinodontidae.

### *Aphysoemion coeruleum (Cyprinodontidae)*, **Blue Gularis**

Originating in West Africa this species vary somewhat in colour, but generally the body is a yellow-brown that darkens on the back and lightens to a blue white on the belly. The lips and gill covers are blue but the gill covers are also marked with red streaks. These streaks are also present on the forepart of the body. The rear of the body is marked with red dots, together with a few vertical bars. The dorsal fin is green-blue and tinged with red at the base, the somewhat large anal fin is greenish, dotted red and blue fringed. The caudal fin is reasonably large and has three 'tails'. The upper is blue marked with red dots and streaks; the middle is red and yellow; and the lower is blue-green streaked with red. Females are paler in colour. An overall colour effect of blue is experienced when viewing this species in a good light.

This is not strictly a community fish; it prefers rather special conditions, and although it is not a troublesome species, it will eat fish that are small enough to be taken.

The Blue Gularis is a vicious, predatory species that will attack smaller fish, and occasionally fish of its own size.

It much prefers old water at a temperature not in excess of 74°F (23°C). It does not like to be subjected to very strong light.

Aquariums containing Blue Gularis should be covered to prevent the fish jumping out. Adult fish grow to about 4½ inches (1·5 cm.).

Remember this species is carnivorous and should only be fed with live foods.

Breeding temperature should be about 70°F (21°C). Eggs are laid singly either on, or near the bottom and can take a long time to hatch. Fry are not difficult to raise.

For breeding, see Breeding the Cyprinodontidae.

### *Aphyosemion gardneri (Cyprinodontidae)*

Originating in Tropical West Africa, *A. gardneri* has the typical torpedo shaped body of the genus with dorsal and anal fin positioned well back along the body. The caudal fin has small upper and lower lobes. It is not considered to be a community fish, being of a somewhat vicious nature.

Adult males grow to 2⅜ inches (6 cm.) and females to 1¼ inches (3·2 cm.). Temperature range 68°F (20°C) to 73°F (23°C).

Favoured foods are tubifex, small fishes, enchytrae, mosquito, larvae, and earthworms.

146

Most *Aphyosemion* like soft water with a slightly acid pH value, the addition of humic acid is desirable also. For breeding see Breeding the Cyprinodontidae.

*Aphyosemion gardneri (Cyprinodontidae)*

## *Aphyosemion gulare (Cyprinodontidae)*, Yellow Gularis

This species originating in West Africa, is very similar in many respects to the **Blue Gularis**, in fact the Blue Gularis is believed to be a larger sub-species of *A. gulare*. The latter is only about 2½ inches (6·3 cm.) long when adult.

Body colour is yellow to pale brown marked by dark reddish brown mottling on the forepart of the body, which modifies gradually into vertical bars at the rear of the body. The dorsal fin has a red line and carmine flecks. The anal fin is pale yellow, flecked with carmine. The caudal fin is red, streaked with red-brown on the lower part.

Females are generally less colourful with less mottling and have colourless fins.

It breeds in a similar manner to *A. coeruleum*, but not so readily.

Live foods should be the staple diet of this species, as it is strictly carnivorous. However it might occasionally take a mouthful of dried food. For breeding, see Breeding the Cyprinodontidae.

*Apistogramma ramirezi* (*Cichlidae*) Butterfly Dwarf Cichlid

## *Apistogramma ramirezi (Cichlidae)*, Butterfly Dwarf Cichlid

Here is a dwarf cichlid that is not only very beautiful but also lacks the aggressiveness associated with cichlids. Originating in Western

Venezuela, and attaining a length of only 2 inches (5·1 cm.) the colouring is remarkably beautiful, basically pale violet blue along the dorsal area, they are marked with rows of turquoise blue dots on the sides, and on the fins. When in spawning condition, the female shows a carmine spot on her side.

Temperature range between 72°F (22°) and 75°F (24°C). They prefer soft water but are tolerant to waters of medium hardness. Essentially carnivorous, and relatively easy to breed.

For breeding see Breeding the Cichlidae. Sexes generally difficult to recognize, except during and shortly before spawning when the female develops a short genital papilla.


### *Aplocheilus lineatus (Cyprinidontidae)*, **Panchax**

Growing up to 4 inches (10·2 cm.) this attractively shaped fish from India and Ceylon is a very hardy species, and the largest of the genus.

The body colour of the male is silvery with many rows of bright green and golden spots which extend to the fins, which are red.

The female is pretty, but simpler in colour with several dark vertical bars.

This species should be fed with ample live food especially mosquito larvae.

They breed more or less as other members of the family in densely planted aquaria. The eggs are deposited singly among the plants and hatch in about 12 days at a temperature of 77°F (25°C). The water level of the breeding tank should be lowered to about 6 inches (15·2 cm.).


### *Arnoldichthys spilopterus (Characidea)*, **Striped Panchax**

This attractive little fish from tropical West Africa, grows to about 2¾ inches (7 cm.). It is silvery with a greenish to bluish sheen, marked rather prettily with a chequered pattern. The dorsal fin has a deep black spot and the eye has a vivid red iris. The male is more brilliantly coloured.

This species should be kept in a roomy well covered aquarium. They are lively and swim rather swiftly and occasionally like to jump out of the water. They also like company and it is advisable to keep several of these fish together, but they do not like brightly lit aquariums.

These are peaceful fish, that prefer to take their food floating, or on the water surface.

Breeding in captivity has not been accomplished to the knowledge of the author. Temperature range 75°F –82°F (24°–28°C). *A. spilopterus* likes warmth and it is advisable not to let the temperature drop below 72°F (22°C).

## *Astyanax mexicanus (Characidae)*, Mexican Astyanax

Originating in Mexico and S. United States, this species is not a particularly colourful aquarium fish. Its main charm lies in its hardiness and the fact that it is one of the easily bred Characins.

The body colour is silvery, darkening to olive along the dorsal plane, occasionally specimen are found that reflect a very pale yellow tint. A wide bluish band of colour extends from the upper edge of the gill cover to the base of the tail. It is marked with a dark bar behind the head and a dark spot at the tail root.

In the wild these fish attain a length of 4 inches (10 cm.) but rarely exceed 3 inches (7·6 cm.) in the aquarium.

Breeding *A. mexicanus* is easy. The breeding tank should be spacious and maintained at a temperature of 75°F (24°C). For best results use two males to a female. See Breeding Characins (A).

## *Badis badis (Nandidae)*

The Nandids differ from their related families mainly in skeleton formation. Generally they have large mouths capable of opening to a greater width than other members. The majority of Nandids also have almost transparent caudal fins and clear parts in the rear of their anal and dorsal fins. Nandids are widely distributed.

Strangely, the *Badis badis* is a Nandid that has neither the transparent finnage nor the elastic mouth: it is nevertheless an interesting fish. Fully grown specimen attain a length of 2–3 inches (5·1–7·6 cm.). The male is usually longer, but this is not a reliable indication of sex, neither is the colouring. However, the males do tend to become more intense and darker when in breeding condition, whilst the females remain normal. It is rather difficult to describe the colouring of these fish, as it varies so much with temperament. It can vary between a light red to a dark scarlet, blue and deep mauve. A dark bar runs through the eye. The causes of colour variation are many—the presence of other fish, fright and water conditions for example.

Another characteristic of *Badis badis* is the hollow underparts which give the impression of wasting.

It also adopts unusual positions in the water and when it is immobile it does not seem to mind its body being at any angle.

The *Badis badis* which originates in India, is rather a peaceful fish and is actually shy despite its rather pugnacious appearance. It prefers to hide away among the plants during the day and really becomes active at dusk.

Adult females are fuller bodied than the male, which retains the hollow underparts. These fish prefer live foods which should be generally supplied: dried foods other 'han in small quantities are not advisable.

For breeding, the temperature should be raised to 80°F (27°C) and a clean flower pot laid horizontally on the floor of the aquarium. The eggs are laid on the inside of the upper surface. The female should be removed immediately after spawning. The male will then tend to the eggs by fanning them until the young hatch, which is between 60 and 72 hours. When the young become free swimmers, the male should also be removed.

*Barbus conchonius (Cyprinidae)*, Rosy Barb

### *Barbus conchonius (Cyprinidae)*, Rosy Barb

This species from India, is a hardy barb and has the typical large mirror-like scales which are particularly beautiful during breeding time.

The main body colour is silver with a rich green back. It is marked with a black spot on the caudal peduncle. During spawning the male develops a flush of red bronze, but it is a volatile colour that soon melts away when the spawning is over. Fully grown, **Rosy Barbs** attain a length of 3½ inches (8·9 cm.) The male is slightly smaller and can be sexed easily when desiring to mate by its heightened colour.

Temperature range 65°F (18°C) to 72°F (22°C). Like all barbs they are easily fed on a varied menu of dry and live foods, but should be given vegetable food occasionally. For breeding, see Breeding the Cyprinidae.

### *Barbus cumingi (Cyprinidae)*, **Cuming's Barb**

Found naturally in the forest brooks of Ceylon, this 2 inch (5·1 cm.) species likes warm water between 72°F (22°C) to 75°F (24°C).

The body colour is a silvery yellow and each scale is marked at the base with a dark spot. Fins are yellow to red with a thin flecked design. The body carries a dark shoulder stripe and another stripe on the caudal peduncle.

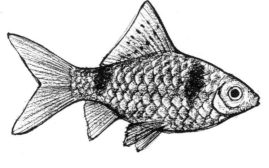

This species prefers a shady aquarium with a dark bottom, and frequent partial changes of water. Although no special water conditions are necessary under normal circumstances, softish water should be used for breeding.

For breeding, see Breeding the Cyprinidae. Breeding is not considered too easy.

### *Barbus everetti (Cyprinidae)*, **Clown Barb**

This is one of the larger aquarium barbs attaining a length of 4–5 inches (10·2–12·7 cm.). It has a yellow-pink body marked with several

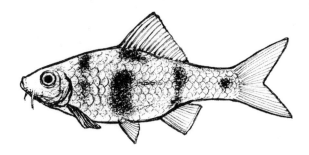

blue grey vertical bars rather blotchily. The fins have a reddish tint.

Originating in Borneo and the Malay Peninsular the **Clown Barbs** are not easy to breed, see Breeding the Cyprinidae (A and B), but they are hardy, easily fed and very attractive.

### *Barbus fasciatus (Cyprinidae)*, **Striped Barb**

Originating in Borneo and Malaysia, the **Striped Barb** is another rather large species growing up to 4 inches (10·2 cm.) in the aquarium and even larger in the wild.

It has a silvery body with an overall tint of yellow marked with four dark horizontal stripes extending the whole length of the body. The colour of the stripes are dark blue or black. The unpaired fins are slightly tinted with red.

This is a reasonably hardy species that requires a temperature range between 72°F (22°C) and 75°F (24°C) otherwise it has no other special requirements.

They are difficult fish to spawn requiring soft and slightly acid water at a temperature of about 78°F (25°C). For further information on breeding, see Breeding the Cyprinidae.

### *Barbus gelius (Cyprinidae)*, **Golden Dwarf Barb**

Ranging from India, this 1¾ inch (4·4 cm.) barb, has a silvery golden to greenish body marked with irregular dark blotches. Males possess a coppery spot on the middle of the body.

Temperature range between 66°F (19°C) and 72°F (22°C). This species is not an easy one to maintain in good health and it is difficult to breed. They are however lively and peaceful and can offer a challenge to the aquarist. For breeding, see Breeding the Cyprinidae (A and C).

### *Barbus hexazona (Cyprinidae)*, **Tiger Barb**

Originating in Malaysia and S.E. Asia, this species grow to about $2\frac{1}{8}$ inches (5·4 cm.) in length. The body is pale yellowish brown marked with six vertical dark bars, these lines commence with a line running through the eye and then more or less evenly spaced along the body. The last bar forms a V and is situated on the tail root.

Adult fish show the best colour, when the anal and dorsal fin of the male become suffused with red, and occasionally a few red specks will be found on the upper half of the body.

This is a peaceful fish, but not too easy to keep in a community mainly because it requires soft and slightly acid water. Little is known about its breeding habits but it can be presumed that it follows closely the procedure described in Breeding the Cyprinidae.

### *Barbus lateristriga (Cyprinidae)*, **Spanner Barb**

Originating in Malay and East Indies, this species is also known as the **T-Barb**. When fully grown they attain a length of $4\frac{3}{4}$ inches (12·1 cm.) in the aquarium, but in the wild they grow much larger, up to 7 inches (17·8 cm.) in fact.

The body colour is silvery grey with a green back and orange belly. The markings consist of two vertical bars between gill cover and dorsal and a horizontal stripe from the tail to just below the dorsal. These markings are blue black and resemble an adjusting spanner. There are also two dark spots on the caudal peduncle and two other spots, one just behind the dorsal and the other on the lower body near the forward edge of the anal fin.

This species does not like low temperatures 70°F (21°C) should be considered a minimum, and whilst they are omnivorous they should be supplied with plenty of live foods.

Breeding is not particularly easy, but they conform more or less to the description given in Breeding the Cyprinidae. A partial change of water in the breeding tank may stimulate a spawning.

## *Barbus nigrofasciatus (Cyprinidae)*, **Nigger Barb**

This species from Ceylon is also known as the **Black Ruby**. It is another barb with large light reflecting scales and whilst it is not particularly brilliant in colouring, it is very interesting for its colour changes during mating periods.

*Barbus nigrofasciatus (Cyprinidae)*, Nigger Barb

Adult fish attain a length of $2\frac{1}{4}$ inches (5.8 cm.). They have a greenish-yellow body with cherry markings around the snout. The sooty black vertical bars numbering three or four, almost disappear when the fish is frightened, but when introduced to a female the male blushes cherry red from mouth to gill cover, whilst the remainder of the body becomes a suffused sooty black.

Temperature range between 68°F (20°C) and 72°F (22°C). The **Nigger Barb** is an exceptionally good tempered species, and relatively easy to breed although they are not considered very productive. For breeding, see Breeding the Cyprinidae.

# *Barbus oligolepis (Cyprinidae)*, Checker Barb

Originating in Sumatra, the **Checker Barb** is a particularly beautiful fish which is known in America as the 'beautiful barb'. The male is basically red brown darkening along the back, lightening to silver along the belly. The scales along the lateral lines are marked with blue black spots, forming a checkered pattern, this checkered pattern is heightened by many light reflecting spots and irregular black dots.

*Barbus oligolepis (Cyprinidae)*, Checker Barb

Fins are yellow, the dorsal of the male is brick red enhanced with a thin black line along the upper margin.

These 2 inch (5·1 cm.) beauties are brilliant and lively fish, requiring a temperature range between 68°F (20°C) and 75°F (24°C). They require a varied menu of live and dry foods and require the addition of soft algae. For breeding, see Breeding the Cyprinidae.

# *Barbus phutunio (Cyprinidae)*, Dwarf Barb

Originating in India, these small 2 inch (5·1 cm.) species are not particularly colourful. They are silvery fish with four or five rather indistinct dark blotches, more or less evenly spaced along the body. Pectoral fins are clear, all other fins have an orange or yellow tint. They do not have any barbels.

Temperature range between 68°F (20°C) and 75°F (24°C). They are peaceful and hardy fish best maintained in schools of their own kind in old water, occasionally livened with additions of fresh water. For breeding, see Breeding the Cyprinidae.

### *Barbus schuberti (Cyprinidae)*

Specimen of *B. schuberti* are often offered in aquarist supply stores. Their scientific name implies that they are a definite species, but in fact they are a golden mutation of *B. semifasciolatus*.

### *Barbus semifasciolatus (Cyprinidae)*, Half Banded Barb

This species from South China, is not one of the most showy of fish, but it has other virtues. It is extremely hardy and can stand temperature down to 64°F (18°C) and it is bred easily.

The body colour is greenish to bronze, marked with six to seven irregular spaced black cross stripes. The fins are tinted pink or yellow. When ready to mate, the body of the male blushes red and the fin colouring becomes more intense.

Adult females grow to about 2½ inches (6·3 cm.) and the males slightly smaller. The temperature range is between 68°F (20°C) and 75°F (24°C).

For breeding, see Breeding the Cyprinidae. **Half Banded Barbs** are a very productive species and the fact that the fry grow quickly make them an ideal fish for beginners.

### *Barbus setivinensis (Cyprinidae)*, Algerian Barb

Here we have a species that is rarely found in home aquaria, it has one big disadvantage—it can grow up to 12 inches (30·4 cm.) long. Originating in North Africa, the body colour is silvery, lightening to white on the underside and darkening to a beautiful coppery brown or olive-green along the back. It has two pairs of barbels, otherwise it is not particularly colourful.

Little is known about its breeding habits, but it can be assumed initially that they breed like most other barbs.

### Barbus terio (Cyprinidae), One Spot Barb

Found naturally in Bengal, Punjab and Orissa, this species is in many respects similar to *B. conchonius*.

The body colour of the male is bronze-yellow, and it is marked with a dark spot above the anal fin and another spot at the tail root. An indefinite line links these two spots together. There is also a reddish spot on the gill cover. Fins tinted orange. The males are more slender than the females. Adults grow to about $2\frac{3}{4}$ inches (7 cm.).

When ready to mate, the body of the male becomes suffused with a beautiful deep orange to red.

For breeding, see Breeding the Cyprindae. They are not, however, too easy to spawn.

*Barbus tetrazona* (*Cyprinidae*), Tiger Barb

### Barbus tetrazona, (Cyprinidae), Tiger Barb

The **Tiger Barb** is a clean well defined species. The general colouring is yellow, striped with four definite black vertical bars, one of which

*Barbus tetrazona (Cyprinidae)*, Albino variety

passes through the eye. Good specimen have a dark base to the dorsal fin varying through red to pale yellow. The ventral fin is red, and the edges of the tail are also streaked with red.

Originating in the Malay Peninsula and Borneo, these barbs grow to about 2 inches (5·1 cm.) and have a temperature range between 68°F (20°C) and 78°F (25°C). They are very active fish and they are best maintained in a school. If put into a community tank they tend to worry the more sedate members, by nipping their fins.

For breeding, see Breeding the Cyprinidae. These are not easy fish to breed they require soft water.


### *Barbus ticto (Cyprinidae)*, the Two Spot Barb

Found naturally in India, the **Two Spot Barb** is not particularly well marked or showy. The body is silvery, marked with a gold edged black spot on the caudal peduncle. Just over the pectoral fins, it has a gold edged stripe almost level with the eye.

Adult fish grow to about $3\frac{1}{2}$ inches (8·9 cm.) the species has no barbels. Temperature range between 72°F (22°C) to 76°F (24°C). For breeding, see Breeding the Cyprinidae. During courtship the body of the male shows a reddish brown sheen.

159

### *Barbus titteya (Cyprinidae)*, **Cherry Barb**

Originating in Ceylon this species grows to about 2 inches (5·1 cm.) in length.

The body colour is a reddish brown, marked with a horizontal blue black stripe with a lighter stripe sandwiched between a darker back. Fins are yellowish, and red to orange in the male. Occasionally, the males give the impression of being overcast with a suffused deep red. They possess a single pair of barbels.

Temperature range between 72°F (22°C) and 78°F (25°C). The **Cherry Barbs** are much happier when kept in the company of their own kind, and are shown to their best advantage in a dark-bottomed tank of their own. The tank should be well planted and contain 'old' or matured water.

For breeding, see Breeding the Cyprinidae (A and C). Although a productive species, they are not considered simple fish to spawn.

### *Barbus vittatus (Cyprinidae)*

This species originates in Ceylon and will grow to about 2¼ inches (5·7 cm.) in length. It is quiet, peaceful and inoffensive. The body is silvery reflecting a yellowish green tint, and marked with a single dark spot on the caudal peduncle. The dorsal fin has a rusty coloured base, all other fins are clear.

Temperature range between 72°F (22°C) and 78°F (25°C). These fish are not too difficult to breed. For breeding, see Breeding the Cyprinidae (A).

### *Belontia signata (Anabantidae)*, **Comb Tail**

Originating in Ceylon, the **Comb Tail** is so named because the rays of the tail extend well past the web. The first rays of the ventral fins are also separated.

This is quite a large species growing to about 4¾ inches (12 cm.). It is basically reddish brown marked with indistinct vertical bars of a darker red.

Unfortunately, it is rather a vicious species otherwise it is not difficult to feed or breed. For Breeding see Breeding the Anabantidae. *B. signata*

160

*Belontia signata (Anabantidae)*, Comb Tail

does not build a nest, the scattered eggs float to the surface, and when the eggs hatch both parents attend the young. Because of their nature, it is advisable to use a large tank for breeding.

## *Betta splendens (Anabantidea)*, Siamese Fighter

There is no other aquarium fish quite like the **Siamese Fighter,** they are real characters that have a dignity of their own. Almost every aquarist will possess at least one male in a community tank even if he has no intentions of breeding them.

The male fighters are the most beautiful, adults develop a most spectacular finnage—a high dorsal, large flowing tail, and a deep anal. Another characteristic feature is the long and pointed ventral fins which are thrust forward when the fish is excited. When in a fighting mood, and this can be stimulated by placing a mirror on the side of the aquarium, in addition to thrusting the ventrals forward, the male will ruffle his gill plates and hold all fins stiffly erected. A truly beautiful sight.

'Cornflower Blue' and 'Fiery Red' are the two main colours, but there are many colour variations including dark blue, green, and red, all

*Betta splendens (Anabantidae)*, Siamese Fighter

with a metallic quality, the colour completely covering the whole of the body and fins.

Some colour varieties have other colours in between the rays of the fins. Females are less colourful and do not possess the large flowing finnage of the males.

These glorious fish are the result of artificial breeding of the somewhat dowdy wild species, the colour of the original being generally darkish brown with rows of bright green spots.

The Siamese Fighter enjoys a temperature range between 78°F (25°C) and about 88°F (31°C) and does not require large aquariums, although it is an advantage not to restrict them. Feeding presents no problems, a varied diet of flake and live foods will keep them in excellent condition.

For breeding, see Anabantidae (A).

### *Botia macracantha (Cobitidae)*, Clown Loach

Originating in Sumatra and Borneo, the **Clown Loach** is golden to orange marked with three clear dark vertical bands. The fins are a beautiful brick red. It has four pairs of barbels. Aquarium species grow to about 6 inches (15·2 cm.).

*Botia macracantha (Cobitidae)*, Clown Loach

The **Clown Loaches** are school fish. Single specimen will often become pugnacious. They do need hiding places such as rocks, and ock caves, and give them clear, oxygenated water.

Breeding habits unknown.

*Brachydanio albolineatus (Cyprinidae)*, Pearl Danio

163

### *Brachydanio albolineatus (Cyprinidae)*, **Pearl Danio**

This species, like most of the Danios, is lively and full of energy, always flashing about the aquarium full of the joys of life. The **Pearl Danio** from Burma is well named, The body colour is similar to mother of pearl, reflecting pastel shades of pink, blue and green. Little hair-like barbels hang down from the upper jaw. Adults grow to about $2\frac{1}{4}$ inches (5·7 cm.). Temperature range between 68°F (20°C) and 75°F (24°C).

For breeding, see Breeding the Cyprinidae (A).


### *Brachydanio devario (Cyprinidae)*

*B. devario* is found naturally in India. It has a greenish body lightening to white on the belly. The forepart of the body is blue and to the rear of this area it is marked with nine or so vertical yellow bars which diminish as they approach the tail. It also has three lateral blue lines with two stripes in between them.

Adults average $3\frac{1}{2}$ inches (8·9 cm.) in length.

For breeding, see Breeding the Cyprinidae (A).


### *Brachydanio nigrofasciatus (Cyprinidae)*, **Spotted Danio**

Originating in Northern Indo-China, the **Spotted Danio** is basically yellowish white with the top half of the body a shade of olive which grows paler in hue as it descends down the body. It has a main horizontal stripe of Prussian Blue extending the whole length of the body and into the tail. Below this stripe it has parallel rows of spots. Smaller spots border the main blue stripe on the upper surface of the body. The males attain a length of $1\frac{1}{2}$ inches (3·8 cm.). The females are a little longer, up to $1\frac{3}{4}$ inches (4·5 cm.). They like warm water between 70°F (21°C) and 75°F (24°C).

For breeding, see Breeding the Cyprinidae. Not too easy to breed.


### *Brachydanio rerio (Cyprinidae)*, **Zebra Danio**

This lively $1\frac{3}{4}$ inch (4·4 cm.) species from Bengal has long been a favourite community fish. It is strikingly marked, vivacious, hardy and not difficult to breed.

The main body colour is silvery white, marked with clearly defined deep blue horizontal lines tha extend into the tail and anal fin.

It is a species that prefers to take its food from near the surface, but it will root around the bottom of the tank.

Temperature range between 65°F (18°C) and 70°F (21°C). For breeding, see Breeding the Cyprinidae (A).

### *Brachygobius xanthozonus (Gobiidae)*, **Bumble Bee**

These tiny 1½ inch (3·8 cm.) fish from India and Indo-China certainly give the appearance of a bumble bee with their yellowish body and dark vertically striped bands of differing widths. Males are brighter in colour, females somewhat plumper.

The ventral fins are united to form a sucking disc which enables them to cling to rocks, glass etc.

It is not a community fish, it should be maintained in water containing one heaped tablespoonful of salt to 4 galls of water (18 litre). Plants are not necessary, but it is advisable to include rockwork.

They are very difficult to breed, requiring very skilled treatment.

This species is almost identical to *B. minus*.

*Bryconalestes longipinnis (Characidae)*, Long Finned Characin

### *Bryconalestes longipinnis (Characidae)*, **Long Finned Characin**

Also known as *Alestestes longipinnis*, this species is basically a shiny silver fish marked with a short black band on the caudal peduncle which extends into the tail. Fins of the male are in part a tint of red, whilst those of the female are yellowish. The eyes are most attractive with their luminous red iris. The dorsal fin is high and flowing, the feature after which the species is named.

Found naturally in West Africa, adult male fish will attain a length of $4\frac{1}{2}$ inches (11·4 cm.) females somewhat smaller.

*B. longipinnis* are lively, and have a tendency to jump out of their tank, therefore, they should be accommodated in spacious aquaria. Breeding habits unknown.

### *Carnegiella strigata (Gasteropelecidae)*, Marble Hatchet

Also known as the **Striped Hatchet Fish**, this species is found naturally in Guiana and the Central and Lower Amazon. It has the typical, thin blade-like deep bellied shape of the **Hatchet Fish**. The body colour is silvery with a yellow-gold tint, it is marked with dark brown to black bars across the forepart. No adipose fin is evident. Adults grow to about $1\frac{3}{4}$ inches (4·5 cm.). Although these are surface fish, they will require space for swimming in the normal areas of the aquarium, and a relatively clear surface without floating leaves. They are peaceful fish, quite at home in a community of similar sized fish.

Under natural conditions these pretty little fish probably eat small flying insect, but in the confines of the aquarium they will take quite readily to dry foods, including small flakes. They like clear water at a temperature of $75°F$ ($24°C$) to $84°F$ ($29°C$).

These are not easy fish to spawn, quite the opposite in fact. Sexing can only be estimated by the broader body of the female when viewed from above.

The breeding procedure is more or less like most Characins. The male courts the female by 'dancing' attendance on her, then a few eggs are spawned with the fish side by side into fine leaved plants. The parents will devour the eggs so remove the pair immediately the spawning is completed.

### *Cheirodon axelrodi (Characidea)*, Cardinal Tetra

This Tetra from the upper Amazon also known as the **Scarlet Characin**, is similar to the **Neon**. It has a luminous green stripe extending from the eye almost the whole length of the body. This stripe is

*Cheirodon axelrodi (Characidae)*, Cardinal Tetra

bordered below by a wide red band from snout to caudal peduncle. The iris is green. Average length of adults 1¾ inches (4·5 cm.).

This is another fish shown best in a tank exclusively dedicated to them, but they can be included with Neons or in any community tank with other fish that are peaceful.

For breeding, see Characins (C).

## *Cichlasoma biocellatum (Cichlidae)*, Jack Dempsey

This is an old aquarium favourite, and it is not surprising when one contemplates its beautiful dark blue body covered with luminous blue green spots on gill covers, fins, and body. Males have the pointed dorsal and anal fin.

Originating in South America and attaining a length of 7 inches (17·8 cm.) it requires a temperature range between 72°F (22°C) and 75°F (24°C).

It is an excellent breeder and parent, but it is also an extremely pugnacious fish, long lived, hardy and an inveterate rooter of plants and gravel. Like most Cichlids it needs a large aquarium and a diet of live food.

For breeding see Breeding the Cichlidae.

### *Cichlasoma coryphaenoides (Cichlidae)*, **Chocolate Cichlid**

The **Chocolate Cichlid** is found naturally in Brazil and Argentina and it is one of the larger aquarium species growing to about 7 inches (17·8 cm.) under normal conditions the general body colour is pale to dark brown with a beautiful metallic purple-brown, the sides are marked by dark vertical bands. It is also marked with three smudges one on the gill cover, a second on the centre of the body, and a third on the caudal peduncle. Fins are generally brownish, the dorsal having a red edge.

This species is rarely found in home aquaria because of its vicious nature. They are agressive fish during mating and this fact makes successful breeding problematical.

### *Cichlasoma facetum (Cyprinidae)*, **Chanchito**

The body colour of this species is very variable but is generally pale brown overlaid with six or seven dark vertical bars. The iris of the eye is red, and fins transparent or brownish red.

Originating in Argentina and growing to about 7 inches (17·8 cm.). Up to 3 inches (7·6 cm.) this cichlid can be included in a community tank, it is hardy and requires a temperature range between 72°F (22°C) and 75°F (24°C). They are not difficult to breed, and show their best colouring during courtship. For breeding, see Breeding the Cichlidae.

### *Cichlasoma festivum (Cichlidae)*, **Festive Cichlid**

Whilst most cichlids are pugnacious and destructive of plants and gravel, the **Festive Cichlid** is the exception. Although it can attain a length of 6 inches (15·2 cm.) it is a peace-loving species very similar to the Angel in habits and character. Although quite variable in colour, it is generally yellowish grey to green, marked with a dark horizontal stripe from the snout to the upper tip of the dorsal fin. The area above the stripe is darker. Vertical bars composed of connecting spots appear on the sides. The caudal peduncle is marked with dark, light edged spots. Males have more pointed fins and a pretty bluish-green throat.

Originating in the calm waters of the Amazon basin, this is one cichlid that can be kept with other fish, especially Angels. They require a temperature range between 72°F (22°C). and 76°F (24°C) and a reasonably large aquarium, well planted and with hiding places among plants and with rocks.

This species requires a vegetable diet in addition to live foods. Boiled and mixed oat flakes is a useful vegetable additive.

Breeding is more or less as described under Breeding the Cichlidae, but it is not always easy to induce them to spawn, they are rather choosy about their mate.

### *Cichlasoma meeki (Cichlidae)*, **Firemouth**

The **Firemouth** is an outstandingly beautiful fish when in breeding colour. The blue green body is patterned irregularly with pale purple and it is marked with a broken blotchy line running from just behind the gill plate to the tail. The most outstanding feature is the fire red or deep orange belly. This colour runs along the belly *right into the mouth*. Another outstanding feature is the bright green edged spot found on the base of the gill plate. Various shades of red are found in the fins.

Originating in Guatemala and Southern Mexico, and growing to

*Cichlasoma meeki (Cichlidae)*, Firemouth

about 4 inches (10·1 cm.) this species enjoys a temperature range between 72°F (22°C) to 76°F (24°C).

Small specimens may be kept in a community tank, but large fish will require a tank of their own.

For breeding, see Breeding the Cichlidae.


## Cichlasoma nigrofasciatum (Cichlidae), Zebra Cichlid

Originating in Central America, this 4 inch (10·1 cm.) cichlid is highly strung and nervous and will dash about the tank if frightened. It is fond of the security provided by archways of piled rocks.

Like most nervous fish the colouring is volatile, but generally the body is yellowish white to silver grey, marked with 8 or 9 dark vertical bars something like a convicts uniform, hence its other popular name 'Convict Cichlid' Sometimes the vertical fins are luminous green.

Requiring a temperature range between 72°F (22°C) and 75°F (24°C) large Zebras are decidedly warlike, their strong jaws are quite capable of crushing the shell of a snail.

For breeding, see Breeding the Cichlids.

*Cichlasoma nigrofasciatum* (*Cichlidae*), Zebra Cichlid

### *Cichlasoma severum (Cichlidae)*, **Striped Cichlid**

Found naturally in Guiana and the Amazon Basin, the colour variation of this species is very wide, the basic body colour can be blue green, dark green, yellow brown, brown or nearly black depending upon mood, temper and the age of the specimen. A dark vertical stripe marks the rear of the body from the dorsal fin into the base of the anal fin. Pale vertical dark bars, eight to nine in number are evident in young fish.

The head and gill covers are lightly marked with irregular dark markings, males are covered with lateral rows of reddish dots. Fins are red brown to orange and in the male both dorsal and anal have long filament-like terminations.

Although they grow to about 7 inches (17·8 cm.) they are not so aggressive as most large Cichlids.

Temperature range between 73°F (23°C) to 77°F (25°C).

For breeding, see Breeding the Cichlidae, (a not too easily bred species).

*Colisa chuna (Anabantidae)*, Honey Dwarf Gourami

### *Colisa chuna (Anabantidae)*, **Honey Dwarf Gourami**

Originating in India, *C. chuna* is similar to *C. lalia*. It is a pretty fish that grows only to 2½ inches (6·3 cm.). Its body colour is tan with a

yellowish overcast, it is marked with a darkish stripe along the sides.
Temperature range between 75°F (24°C) and 82°F (28°C).

Breeding and care is similar to other Gouramis see Breeding the Anabantidae.

### *Colisa fasciata (Anabantidae)*, **Giant Gourami**

The length of this species is about $4\frac{1}{2}$ inches (11·4 cm.). It is found naturally from India to Burma, and because of its large distribution, it is a somewhat variable species.

The body colour is basically a warm brown with blue-green stripes which slant slightly towards the tail. The edge of the gill cover and belly have brilliant blue green markings. Dorsal fin terminates, and anal fin often fringed with red, and tail flushed red to pink.

Because of their large size it is necessary to provide a roomy aquarium, well planted to provide hiding places for the female. The temperature range most suited for this species is between 76°F (24°C) and 82°F (28°C) but for breeding should be stabilized at 80°F (27°C). For breeding, see Breeding Anabantidae (A and B).

Temperature range 75°F (24°C) and 80°F (27°C).

They are not difficult fish to feed, but they do need a varied diet of dried and live foods.

For breeding, see Breeding Anabantidae.

*Colisa labiosa (Anabantidae)*, Thick Lipped Gourami

## *Colisa labiosa (Anabantidae)*, **Thick Lipped Gourami**

Originating in Burma and attaining a length of $3\frac{1}{4}$ inches (8·3 cm.) the **Thick Lipped Gourami** is not so thick lipped as its name suggests, but it does have a rather squat mouth.

The body colour is basically silvery green, with slightly slanting vertical bands of red, more distinct at the rear of the body. Often the middle of the body has a darker shading. When excited the forepart of the belly becomes suffused with dark mauve, overlaid with a pale grey design. The colouring of the fins are most attractive.

Dorsal fin of male is very pointed, whilst that of the female is rounded. Because of the large size of these fish, they require spacious aquariums and plenty of plants in which to hide occasionally as they can be timid, especially the female.

*Colisa lalia (Anabantidae)*, Dwarf Gourami

## *Colisa lalia (Anabantidae)*, **Dwarf Gourami**

Although the Dwarf Gourami is smallest of the Gouramis, about $2\frac{3}{8}$ inches (6 cm.) in adulthood, it is by no means the least attractive. Originating in N. India, it has a beautiful colour pattern of red and blue-green bands running vertically across the body. The fins are blue marked with red dots.

This species is found naturally in India, and likes warmth 76°F

(25°C) to 82°F (28°C). It is a hardy fish that likes a well planted, bright aquarium with plenty of algae.

For breeding, see Anabantids. During the mating play and spawning, males can become a little belligerent.

### *Copeina arnoldi (Characidae)*, **Splashing Tetra**

This is a most interesting fish if only for its unusual breeding habits. It is a peaceful, vivacious and easily fed species from Brazil, that grows to about 3 inches (7·6 cm.) the females a little smaller, about 2½ inches (6·3 cm.). The body colour is red-brown reflecting silver highlights. The fins are yellowish to suffused red, the dorsal of the male has a brilliant white spot at its base with a small black area just to the front of it. The female has a reddish spot. The body is marked with a dark repetitive pattern resulting from the edged scales.

Because these fish like to jump out of the water after small insects, the aquarium must have a cover.

Temperature range 75°F (24°C) to 82°F (27°C). For the unusual breeding procedures, see Breeding Characins (E).

*Corydoras aeneus (Callichthyidae)*, Bronze Catfish

### *Corydoras aeneus (Callichthyidae)*, **Bronze Catfish**

This fish grows to about 2¾ inches (9·5 cm.) and is an excellent scavenger. The head is quite rounded, the body thick set, and the whiskers small. The body colouring is a beautifully shaded bronze-green without any pattern markings. It has two pairs of barbels.

The **Bronze Catfish** is found naturally in Trinidad.

For breeding, see Breeding the Catfish.

### *Corydoras agassizi (Callichthyidae)*

This is one of the slightly larger aquarium catfish, which will attain a length of about $3\frac{1}{2}$ inches (8·9 cm.). It has the typical appearance of a catfish, with a particularly flat underside and spade-like head. The forepart of the dorsal fin is dark grey and the tail rather prettily flecked with orderly rows of spots.

It is found naturally in the Amazon and Western Brazil. This is a difficult species to breed, and no records of successful spawnings are known to the author.

### *Corydoras arcuatus (Callichthylidae)*, **The Streamlined Cory**

Originating in the Upper Amazon, the body colour of this fish is silvery white with a greenish-blue overall sheen. It is marked with a dark curving line from the eye, along the upper part of the body, to the base of the caudal fin. The male fish often has this line starting a little distance behind the eye.

Adult fish attain a length of $2\frac{1}{2}$ inches (6·3 cm.) to the author's knowledge they have not yet been bred in captivity.

This fish is very typical of the Corydoras family, and is obviously much happier when it is a member of a small group.

*Corydoras arcuatus* is usually a lively fellow and an interesting species to observe.

### *Corydoras hastatus (Callichthyidae)*, **Dwarf Catfish**

Originating in the Amazon Basin, this tiny catfish is quite attractive with a grey green body, marked with a dark stripe starting from just behind the pectoral fins and terminating in a large spot on the tail base. The spot is outlined with a horse-shoe of white. Length of adults $1\frac{3}{8}$ inches (3·3 cm.).

### *Corydoras julii (Callichthyidae)*, Leopard Catfish

Originating in East and North-East Brazil the **Leopard Catfish** is quite a popular fish. Its body colouring is a whitish-grey, peppered with black spots. These spots extend over the nose, and also form roughly three lateral lines along the body. The dorsal fin has a black spot on its upper half, and the tail fin also carries a series of almost symmetrical spots. Fully grown specimens are not very large—about $2\frac{1}{2}$ inches long (6·3 cm.). Whilst it is generally accepted that catfish are scavengers and rely mostly on left-overs, the aquarist would be well advised to consider their diet seriously if he would like to attempt to breed them. They are, however, seldom bred.

*Corydoras nattereri (Callichthyidae)*, Blue Catfish

### *Corydoras nattereri (Callichthyidae)*, Blue Catfish

Originating in Central and North Brazil the **Blue Catfish** has a silvery brown body with a translucent overtone of blue. It is marked with a dark stripe from the caudal fin to gill cover. The fins are usually clear and unpatterned, but occasionally the dorsal fin may have a dark tip. The eyes are golden. Aquarium specimen can be expected to attain a length of about $2\frac{1}{2}$ inches (6·3 cm.).

This is not an easy fish to breed, but if you wish to try, use the method described under Breeding the Catfish.

*Corydoras paleatus (Callichthylidae),* **Peppered Cory**

Found naturally in Argentina and S.E. Brazil. This catfish is probably the most common of the catfish. It is not unattractive, the main body colour is a yellowish hue shot with a few green scales. These are more pronounced about the head. The dark overmarking are irregular and coloured blue-black. The pectoral fins are yellow and the anal and ventral fins are opaque ivory, and the tail and dorsal fins are almost clear, but marked with dark flecks. Fully grown aquarium specimens attain a length of 2¾ inches (7 cm.).

*Corynopoma riisei (Characidea),* **Swordtail Characin**

This very attractive fish, about 2 inches in length (5 cm.) exclusive of tail, is found naturally in Trinidad and Northern South America. In colour it is principally silver, marked by a thin horizontal stripe, but it is not the colour, but the long lower lobe of tail and the general well developed remaining fins of the male that makes this Characin so unusual. The male also has a long slender, spoonshaped extension to the gill cover extending back as far as the dorsal.

This is a lively species requiring no special attention, and generally peaceful. Temperature range 75°F (24°C) to 80°F (26°C).

These are not difficult fish to breed, but the exact details of spawning are not as yet fully understood. The mating is very dramatic, the male erecting fins and gill cover extensions in an amorous display.

The female presses the eggs onto spawning spots, usually the underside of broad leaved plants, and continues to care for them.

It is quite safe to leave both parents with the brood, they will not harm them. Rear fry as for Characins.

*Ctenopoma acutirostre (Anabantidae),* **Leopard Bush Fish**

This species is found naturally in Africa. It is basically a reddish to yellow-brown fish marked with irregular dark spots. Adults grow to about 4 inches (10·1 cm.). Its body shape is oval, the dorsal, anal and

177

*Ctenopoma acutirostre* (*Anabantidae*), Leopard Bush Fire

tail forming an almost continual line giving the illusion that the fish is egg shaped, only the upturned snout breakes the contour.

Temperature range between 75°F (24°C) and 85°F (29°C).

Little is known about their care or breeding habits.

### *Cryptopterus bicirrhus (Schilbeidae)*, Glass Catfish

The **Glass Catfish** is an oddity from Malaya. The body is *really* transparent. The skeleton is quite easily seen. If it were not for the silvery sac containing the internal organs, it would be difficult indeed to find the fish in any aquarium.

Another interesting feature is the long anal fin which occupies most of the ventral surface of the body. This fin has a wavy action not unlike a thin reed in quickly flowing water. The two barbels, which are comparatively long, hang from the upper lip. Fully grown specimen in the aquarium rarely exceed 2–3 inches (5·1–7·6 cm.).

It prefers densely planted aquaria, with open spaces, and enjoys small live foods.

Glass Catfish should be fed mainly with live food, but they will

178

eat a small quantity of dried food. They are quite happy in a community tank at a temperature of 72°–82°F (22°–28°C) once they have become acclimatized.

Their breeding habits are unknown.

### *Cynolebias bellotti (Cyprinodontidae)*, **Argentine Pearl Fish**

Originating in La Plata, this attractive species is also known as the **Blue Chromide.** The males have a general body colour of dark slatey-blue which changes to blue-green on the fins. The body and fins are speckled with pearly-white spots.

Females are ochre or yellow-green, marked irregularly with brownish-stripes similar to the graining on marble. The margins of the males' anal, caudal and dorsal fins are dark. Both sexes have a dark stripe through the eye.

Under natural conditions these fish breed in ditches and puddles during the rainy season. The male makes a small depression in the mud, and into the depression the female deposits a single egg which is immediately fertilized and covered by the male. This performance is then repeated. When the pools dry out, the parents perish, but the eggs are protected by the damp mud and remain dormant until the next rains come. The eggs then hatch out and the cycle is continued.

The temperature range for this species is between 64°F (18°C) and 72°F (22°C). They like well illuminated aquariums with soft peaty bottoms, unfortunately they do not live very long even with the best attention, 8 months is considered a maximum life span. They are voracious fish.

For breeding, see Breeding the Cyprinodontidae (B).

### *Danio malabaricus (Cyprinidae)*, **Giant Danio**

This species is found naturally in the clear water of streams or pools of the West Coast of India and Ceylon, where they attain a length up to 6 inches (15·2 cm.) but in the aquarium they only grow to about 4 inches (10·1 cm). The body is basically yellowish to orange, marked with several horizontal wide stripes of blue separated with gold. A few irregular vertical bars appear just behind the gill covers.

They are happy in a temperature range between 68°F (20°C) and

*Danio malabaricus (Cyprinidae)* Giant Danio

78°F (25°C) but because of their large size they should not be included in a community containing very small fish.

This is a fast moving species that rarely rests. For breeding, see Breeding the Cyprinidae. The eggs are adhesive but otherwise they breed like the barbs.

## *Elassoma evergladei (Centrarchidae)*, **Pygmy Sunfish**

This species is brownish with darker spots and rather indefinite vertical bars. The colour is much enhanced during breeding when the males become blue-black with darker bands and luminous spots on both body and fins.

The species is found naturally in the Everglades—Florida, and grows to only 1¼ inches (3·2 cm.). The size and hardiness of the **Pygmy Sunfish** has made it a much favoured species.

They do not like high temperature, 60°F (16°C) to 72°F (22°C) is adequate.

Breeding temperature about 64°F (18°C). The eggs are scattered at random among the plants. Generally the parents do not care for the eggs or fry, and they do not usually harm them. Fry hatch in between 2 and 6 days. Within 2 days they become free swimming when they must be fed small sized live foods.

*Epalzeorhynchus kallopterus (Cyprinidae)*, Trunk Barb

## *Epalzeorhynchus kallopterus (Cyprinidae)*, **Trunk Barb**

This species is found naturally in Borneo, Java and Sumatra, where it grows to about 5½ inches (14 cm.) but in the aquarium it rarely exceeds 4 inches (10·1 cm.).

It is a slender fish with a rather pointed snout and two pairs of barbels. Body colour is silvery marked with a broad black band stretching from the tip of the snout to the caudal peduncle. There is a golden area above the band. The fins are reddish, marked with a pleasing design.

They are omnivorous, but feed mainly from growths and organic detritus on the bottom of their aquariums, therefore, their tank should be abundantly planted.

Temperature range between 73°F (23°C) and 83°F (28°C). Breeding habits unknown.


### *Epiplatys chaperi (Cyprinodontidae)*, Fire-Mouth Panchax

Originating in West Africa it is rather surprising that this species is not more popular in this country, for it is easily fed, extremely pretty and offers quite interesting breeding habits.

The male is the most handsome with diffused vertical bars along the side of the body, and dark edging to the anal fin and base of the caudal fin. The throat and lower lip, best seen from the front, are a fiery red. A peculiarity that makes the sexes easily distinguishable is the pointed extension to the caudal fin of the male.

These fish are quite suitable for community tanks, as they are usually very peaceful, and happy in a temperature range between 70°F (21°C) and 73°F (23°C). Adults grow to about 2¼ inches, females slightly smaller.

For breeding, see Breeding the Cyprinodontidae (C).


### *Etroplus maculatus (Cichlidae)*, Orange Chromide

Found naturally in India and Ceylon the **Orange Chromide** is one of the few Cichlids that can usually be included in a community tank. It grows to about 3 inches (7·6 cm.) and has an orange-gold body which darkens to olive along the back. The lower half of the body is sprinkled with blue black spots. It has a large dark blue spot on the centre of the body, light edged, and evidence of several rather smudgy pale vertical bars broken along the lateral line. The base of each scale carries a red dot. Fins are yellowish and the outer margin of the anal is black edged, ventrals are deep black. Females usually smaller and less brilliantly coloured.

Temperatures range between 72°F (22°C) and 75°F (24°C).

This species is a little sensitive to change in water, and the addition of small quantities of salt increases their well-being, one teaspoonful to about 2 gallons (10 litres). They do not disturb the gravel or plants very much, but may nibble plants if they feel the need for a little vegetable diet. For breeding, see Breeding Cichlidae.

*Etroplus suratensis (Cichlidae),* Striped Chromide

## *Etroplus suratensis (Cichlidae),* **Striped Chromide**

Ranging from the salt and brackish waters along the coasts of India and Ceylon, the **Striped Chromide** will grow up to 16 inches (40·6 cm.) in its natural waters. It is a species that changes colour with maturity and age. Basically it is a green to purple-red, younger specimen have dark vertical bands and more mature specimen have luminous spots.

This species is only really suited for large marine aquaria, it rarely thrives well in freshwater.

Little if anything is known about its breeding habits.

## *Gasteropelecus levis (Gasteropelecidae)*

Originating in Guiana and the Amazon Basin, this species is shiny silver, darkening to olive along the back. It is marked with a narrow stripe extending from the gill cover to the root of the tail, and another edges the body along the base of the anal fin. Fins are clear.

The pectoral fins are well developed into wing-like appendages which enable the fish to skim the water surfaces and virtually take off on short aerial flights.

When viewed from the side, the belly is exceedingly deep, yet when viewed from the front they are knife-like.

Adults attain a length of $2\frac{1}{4}$ inches (5·6 cm.). Hatchet fish are not bottom feeders, but they will accept floating food on or near the surface. They are carnivorous and should not be given dried foods. So far these have not been bred in captivity.

*Gasteropelecus levis* (*Gasteropelecidae*), Silver Hatchet

## *Gymnocorymbus ternetzi (Characidea)*, **Black Tetra**

The **Black Tetras** are found in the Rio Paraguay in Southern Brazil. They are good community fish attaining about 3 inches (7·6 cm.) in length. They are lively, peaceful and prefer to live in a school. Feeding presents no problems, they will accept most live and dry foods.

The body colour is silver marked with several dark vertical bands over the body, one usually through the eye, and another just below the dorsal fin. Younger fish have deep suffused black on the rear of the body, and anal fin, and dorsal fin, but this pales with age. The adipose fin is evident.

Temperature range between 72°F (22°C) and 80°F (26°C), but for breeding this should be increased to 83°F (28°C), see also Breeding Characins (A).

*Haplochromis multicolor (Cichlidae)*, Egyptian Mouthbreeder

## *Haplochromis multicolor (Cichlidae)*, **Egyptian Mouthbreeder**

This species from Egypt is basically metallic green. The gill covers are marked with a blue-black spot, paler around the outer perimeter. The fins have rows of shiny dots, and the anal fin of the male is orange-red tipped. Other colours from blue to orange are found in the fins.

These fish can grow up to 6 inches (15·2 cm) in length but aquarium specimen are usually smaller.

This species will be quite at home in small aquaria, but they are better in spacious accommodation. They need plenty of plants and large stones for hiding themselves.

Diet requirements mainly strong live foods, temperature range between 68°F (20°C) to 75°F (24°C).

For breeding, see Breeding the Cichlidae C. Because of the strain imposed on the female during breeding, it is as well not to breed a female too frequently, two or three times a year is enough.


## *Hasemania melanura (Characidae)*, Copper Characin

The **Copper Characin** from S.E. Brazil, is 2 inches long (5 cm.) when fully grown. As may be expected the colour of the male is coppery. It is marked with a blue-black band on the caudal peduncle, and has white flecking the tips of the fins. The female is less glamorously coloured, her body being silver.

The Copper Characins are peaceful, easily maintained fish that prefer clear water at a temperature range between 68°F (20°C) and 76°F (24°C). They need well planted aquaria, but with plenty of free space for swimming. They will take all kinds of food, but it must be of a relative size.

Not too difficult to breed, see Breeding Characins (A).


## *Helostoma temmincki (Anabantidae)*, Kissing Gourami

Ranging from Central India and Indonesia, the **Kissing Gourami** is an extremely large fish that can grow up to 12 inches (30 cm.) and only the smaller specimens are normally found in home aquaria.

They have a yellowish body which often reflects a greenish tint, with several dark horizontal stripes.

A temperature around 78°F (26°C), a spacious aquarium and plenty of foods will keep them happy, but it is advisable to have only one in a community tank.

If a few specimen are kept together, a pair will often 'kiss' or rather place their lips together, the reason for this peculiar habit is not really understood.

When the fish are about 4 inches (10 cm.) they are ready for breeding. They do not build a nest, the small amber eggs float to the surface and are retained there by oily deposits. The parents may eat the eggs, but rarely the fry.

Feed fry infusoria initially followed by newly hatched brine shrimps, then as for other Anabantidae.

### *Hemichromis bimaculatus (Cichlidae)*, Jewel Cichlid

Originating in Tropical Africa, the body colour of this species is normally an olive green, darker on the back and a pale orange yellow on the belly. The body is marked with a few blurred vertical dark bars, a dark spot just below the dorsal fin about the centre of the body, and a spot on the tail root. Another spot is situated on the gill cover, and a dark line passes through the eye. Luminous metallic blue-green spots are present on the head, body and fins. During mating the lower half of the body becomes a rich red, the upper dark olive with a reddish sheen. The colour of this species may vary a little, dependant upon origin, and the mood of the fish. During courtship the female may well wear the more attractive coat.

The **Jewel Cichlid** will grow to about 5 inches (12·7 cm.) they are very aggressive fish requiring a tank to themselves. Temperature range between 72°F (22°C) and 75°F (24°C).

For breeding, see Breeding the Cichlidae.

They are difficult fish to breed, because they do not pair readily, and it is possible for the female to be attacked and even killed during an attempted or successful spawning.

Sex can only be ascertained during the mating period by the different construction of the genital papillae.

### *Hemigrammus caudovittatus (Characidea)*, Buenos Aires Tetra

As its name suggest, this species is found naturally in the La Plate region around Buenos Aires. It is the largest of the *Hemigrammus* aquarium species, growing to nearly 4 inches (10 cm.). The body is deep, and silvery, marked with a black band on the caudal peduncle crossed by a short bar. All fins except the pectorals are red. The fins of the female are paler.

These fish are hardy, lively and easy to feed, but they tend to nibble the tender shoots of plants. Temperature range between 68°F (20°C) and 74°F (23°C) but should not be allowed to drop below 60°F (15°C) although generally peaceful, they will occasionally become aggressive unless they have plenty of space in which to swim.

Breeding the **Buenos Aires Tetra** is easy, see Breeding Characins (A). Temperature should be 75°F (24°C). The females are slightly larger and fuller. It is an advantage to put two males with a female for mating.

*Hemigrammus erythrozonus (Characidae)*, Glowlight Tetra

### *Hemigrammus erythrozonus (Characidae)*, Glowlight Tetra

This species is found in the jungle waters of N.E. South America. It is a small fish only $1\frac{1}{4}$–$1\frac{5}{8}$ inches (3·2–4·1 cm.) that is shown to best advantage in a school or in company with **Neon** and **Head and Tail Light Tetras** in a not too bright aquarium. The body is greyish brown, vividly contrasted with a glowing red stripe stretching from the eye to the caudal peduncle and sometimes into the caudal fin. The dorsal fin has a red spot on the fore-edge tipped with white.

The males are somewhat slimmer than the females.

The temperature range is 72°F–80°F (22°C–26°C) but it is advisable to maintain a temperature around 75°F (24°C).

For breeding, see Breeding Characins (C). Temperature for breeding 76°F (24°C). Young are not too easy to rear, but will respond to patience.

### *Hemigrammus ocellifer (Characidea)*, Head and Tail Light

The **Head and Tail Light** is found naturally from the Guianas to the Amazon region. It is one of the fish best shown in a not too bright aquarium.

These fish grow to about $1\frac{3}{4}$ inches (4·4 cm.) the females slightly smaller. The body is silvery reflecting a green-grey tint, a pale gold line follows the lateral line, a black wedge shape spot adorns the caudal peduncle. The most striking feature is a brilliant yellow gold spot over the black spot and a luminous yellow and red iris.

The species likes warm water 73°F (23°C) to 80°F (26°C) being an acceptable range, but the temperature should not drop below 70°F (27°C).

Breeding is relatively easy, using two males to a female. See Breeding Characins (A).

### *Hemigramus pulcher (Characidae)*, **Pretty Tetra**

The **Pretty Tetra** is also known as the **Garnet Tetra**. It is a fish that is found naturally in the jungle rivers of the Upper Amazon, hence its glowing colour. This fish grows to about 2 inches (5 cm.) in the aquarium. The colour of the body is reddish to green reflecting light like warm brass, a yellow-green spot marks the shoulder, and it has a short wide black band along the caudal peduncle. This black band is sometimes emphasized with a vivid yellow-gold line along the upper and lower edges. Upper iris red.

The Pretty Tetra is best displayed in a well planted aquarium, lit with subdued light to simulate a jungle river, the effect can be increased by using dark gravel and a dark background. Do not forget however, that the plants do need light.

A collection of **Head and Tail Lights, Glow-Lights,** and similar Tets to the Pretty Tetra make a beautiful and fascinating sight.

The temperature range is between 72°F (22°C) and 78°C (25°C) but for breeding the temperature should be raised to about 80°F (27°C). They are difficult fish to spawn, but the procedure is as described in Breeding Characins (C).

### *Hemigrammus rhodostomus (Characidea)*, **Red Nose**

Also known as the **Rummy–nosed Tetra**, this species originates in the lower Amazon. The body is silvery marked on the caudal peduncle with a black spot tapering away to nothing as it approaches the head and similarly into the tail fin. The tail fin has two white, and two black bars. The most predominant feature is the red snout.

Adult fish grow to about 2 inches (5 cm.) and in general their requirements are the same as other members of the genus. Temperature is around 75°F (24°C).

They are not particularly easy fish to breed, and require a little more attention than most Characins. For breeding, see Breeding Characins (A).

### *Hemigrammus ulreyi (Characidea)*, **German Flag Tetra**

This species from Paraguay is almost identical to *Hyphessobrycon heterorhabdus*, and indeed for some time it was confused with it. The visual differences are a slimmer and less translucent body. To date this fish has not been bred in captivity.

### *Heterandria formosa (Poeciliidae)*, **Mosquito Fish**

This is one of the smallest fish known, the males are only ¾ inch (2 cm.) long, the females slightly larger, about 1⅛ inches (3 cm.) long. Because of their small size they are best kept in an aquarium of their own.

The body colour is basically yellow, marked with a dark horizontal stripe, crossed vertically by a few irregular dark bands. The dorsal fin is marked with a red spot.

Originating in the S.E. of the U.S.A. the **Mosquito Fish** are hardy and can be maintained in quite small containers. They thrive on the normal foods, but they should have access to an abundance of algae. Recommended temperature range between 68°F (20°C) and 75°F (24°C).

For breeding, see Breeding Poeciliidae (B).

### *Heteropneustes fossilis (Clariidae)*

This rather unusual catfish originates in the fresh waters of India and Ceylon, but because of its large size, 26 inches (66 cm.) it will hardly be a suitable specimen for the average aquarist.

It is a dark brown fish, tending towards black, sometimes marked with two paler horizontal stripes. The body is eel-like flattening toward the head, and strongly compressed towards the tail. It has four pairs of barbels. These fish possess a breathing sac which encloses the gills, and permits the fish to breathe atmospheric air. These are a nocturnal species, but will venture abroad during the daylight hours when hungry.

The pectoral fins are capable of giving a nasty sting which can be very painful and often are difficult to heal, so take care when netting.

Temperature range 68°F (20°C) to 73°F (23°C) *H. fossilis* has been bred in very large tanks, but it is unlikely that many aquarist will possess the facilities.

*Heteropneustes fossilis (Chariidae)*

### *Hyphessobrycon callistus (Characidea)*, Jewel Tetra

The **Jewel Tetra** is a Brazilian fish found in the Paraguay River and the state of Matto Grosso. It is probably better known as *H. serpae* to aquarist. It is one of the most beautiful of the small freshwater fishes, having a strong red colouration all over the body and into the fins. The dorsal fin is black, edged with white, the anal fin is edged with black and the ventral fin has a white edge.

The length of these fish is about $1\frac{3}{4}$ inches (4·4 cm.). They are excellent community fish, that enjoy a temperature of between 74°F (23°C) and 78°F (25°C) and plenty of space in a well planted aquarium.

They can be classified as difficult fish to breed, see Breeding Characins (B), breeding temperature around 80°F (26°C).

### *Hyphessobrycon flammeus (Characidea)*, Tet from Rio

Originating in the outskirts of Rio de Janeiro, this species is also known as the **Flame Fish**, and **Red Tet**. Only $1\frac{1}{2}$ inches (4 cm.) in length, it is a real beauty, the forepart of the body is silvery reflecting a green tint, graduating into a beautiful crimson on the rear of the body and into the fins. The anal fin of the males have a black edge. Two or three vertical black bars mark the shoulder. Females are usually slightly larger and fuller in the body.

The **Tet From Rio** likes a temperature between 68°F (20°C) and 72°F (22°C) and a well planted, but not too bright a tank. It is one of the easiest characins to breed, which it will do at a temperature of 75°F (24°C) and preferably with two or three males to a single female, see Breeding Characins (A).

### *Hyphessobrycon griemi (Characidea)*, Red Gold Dot Tetra

The **Red Gold Dot Tetra** is found naturally in Brazil. Its body colour is basically brownish, but it turns a scarlet when excited. Dorsal and anal fins are also scarlet. The anal fin is marked with white, and has an inner black border along the fore and lower margins. Two spots appear on the shoulder. In many respects this species is similar to *H. flammeus* and breeds in much the same way. Use three males to each female. See Breeding Characin (A). Adults usually about 1½ inches (4 cm.) long.

### *Hyphessobrycon heterorhabdus (Characidea)*, Flag Tetra

This is another fish that requires a suitable backdrop to show it to its best advanges. Found naturally in the Amazon, this attractive 1½ inch (4 cm.) species has a greenish brown body brilliantly marked along the lateral line with a narrow red, pale gold, and black band, stretching from the eye to the caudal peduncle. The eye has a gold iris flecked at the top with red. Males have the fin hooks on the anal fin and they are slimmer than the female. The adipose fin is evident.

These are peaceful, moderately hardy fish, that should be shown in a well planted aquarium preferably with dark gravel. They require a temperature around 75°F (24°C) for normal conditions and breeding.

They are not considered easy fish to breed, see Breeding Characins (C).

*Hemigrammus ulreyi* is a similar species.

### *Hyphessobrycon innesi (Characidae)*, Neon Tetra

Found naturally in the regions of the upper Amazon, this tiny fish only 1⅝ inches (4 cm.) long, is a joy to behold in any aquarium. The

*Hyphessobrycon innesi (Characidae)*, Neon Tetra

body has a most luminous quality reflecting colours of blue and green. It has a striking red line stretching from the eye to the caudal peduncle. The sexes are difficult to differentiate the only external differences being that the male is slightly slimmer.

They are not difficult fish to keep and provide a most pleasing picture when shown as a school in a tank exclusively dedicated to them. They are lively and peaceful and they are quite happy in temperatures ranging from 68°F (20°C) to 78°F (25°C).

For breeding, see Characins (C). They are difficult fish to breed, but it can be accomplished.

## *Hyphessobrycon ornatus (Characidea)*, **The Ornate Tetra**

Ranging from Dutch Guiana to the Lower Amazon, these attractive 1½ inch long (4 cm.) fish are best maintained in a small school. The aquarium should be well planted, with shadowy areas, and preferably positioned so that sunlight enters the tank for a proportion of the day. The water should be maintained at a temperature between 74°F (23°C) and 80°F (27°C) and soft.

The body colour is greenish suffused with crimson which on occasion can become quite brilliant. The top of the dorsal fin is black, streaked along the fore-edge with startling white. Ventral and anal fins tinged with crimson.

Temperature for breeding is about 80°F (27°C) but they are not easily bred. It is important to have compatible pairs, see Breeding Characins (A), and water free of infusoria.

*Hyphessobrycon pulchripinnis (Characidae)*, Lemon Tetra

### *Hyphessobrycon pulchripinnis (Characidea)*, **Lemon Tetra**

Originating in the Amazon basin, the **Lemon Tetra's** colour tint is largely due to the vivid yellow and black edging of the anal fin, otherwise the body is very transparent reflecting silver with a faint yellow overtone. The lower half of the iris of the eye is brilliant red.

This species attains a length up to 1½ inches (4 cm.) the males being a little slimmer than the females. The Lemon Tetra has no special demands, it is peaceful, a good community member and easy to feed. It is quite happy in a temperature range between 72°F (22°C) and 78°F (26°C) but it is not an easily bred species, see Breeding Characins (C). It is important that breeding pairs are compatible, not all pairs will accept the favours of the other.

### *Hyphessobrycon scholzei (Characidea)*, Black-Line Tetra

The **Black Line Tetra** from the Lower Amazon is not a spectacular fish, but it is interesting nevertheless because it is one of the easily bred Characins.

Adult fish grow to about 2 inches (5 cm.), the body is silvery sometimes slightly brassy, with a black line running the length of the body from gill cover to tail where it terminates in a diamond shape: usually, the first rays of the females anal fin are more pronounced, but this is not an infallible rule, it is better to use the deeper belly to sex the female.

Temperature range 68°F (20°C) to 80°F (25°C). These are lively and hardy fish that make good community members but individuals are likely to develop the habit of chasing smaller fish.

Easily bred, see Breeding Characins (A). Eggs are adhesive and deposited on feathery leaved plants.

### *Jordanella floridae (Cyprinodontidae)*, Flag Fish

Originating in Florida, *J. floridae* is a hardy species that can live in quite small aquaria.

The name **Flag Fish** was bestowed upon this species because of its resemblance to the American flag. The scale edging is red in colour, corresponding in some degree to the stars on the American flag, in appearance and habit it is rather like a sunfish.

The Flag Fish will eat live foods, but it is more of a vegetarian and to keep it in condition conducive to breeding, algae should always be available. If this is difficult to obtain, boiled spinach is a good substitute. It is the lack of the correct foods that will be responsible for any failure in breeding.

The species is rather aggressive and is really better in a tank by itself, but individuals will settle down in a communal tank, providing the other members are somewhat similar in size.

For breeding, the tank should be planted according to the standard description and the temperature raised to 75°F (24°C). Eggs are deposited either in shallow depressions in the sand, or among the plant roots and hatch in about a week. Remove the female immediately after spawning, but do not disturb the male, who will protect the eggs (he will do this even from the female) and guard the young when they are born.

It is a beautiful and interesting fish with a preference for alkaline water.

Under normal conditions, the preferred temperature is 68°F (20°C).

*Labeo bicolor (Cyprinidae)*, Red Tailed Black Shark

## *Labeo bicolor (Cyprinidae)*, **Red Tailed Black Shark**

This species, which can grow up to 6 inches (15·2 cm.) in length, has a definite shark like body, entirely black, except for a fiery red tail.

The **Red Tailed Shark** is a quarrelsome fellow, very prone to fighting among its own kind, and very territorially minded.

Originating in Thailand, they have horny protrubences around the mouth with which they tear off or rasp the vegetation. Two pairs of barbels are present. The species is not really a community fish as it has a strong tendency to become pugnacious. They are much better maintained in a tank to themselves.

Temperature range between 72°F (22°C) and 80°F (27°C). Their water should be slightly acid and soft. Whilst they will eat prepared dry foods a constant supply of vegetable matter, especially algae, is essential to their well being. Little is known about breeding this species in captivity, except that they lay their eggs in caves or on stones.

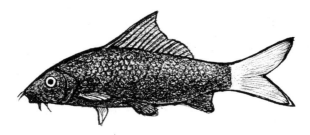

### *Lebistes reticulatus (Poeciliidae),* **Guppy**

How does one describe these fascinating fish from Trinidad, Guiana, and Venezuela when rarely if ever two males are marked the same, it is for this reason that they are known also as **Rainbow Fish.**

These fish are real beauties, so much so that many aquarist breed nothing else. No matter how advanced the aquarist becomes a few Guppies are invariably found among his collection.

The males which grow to about one inch (2·5 cm.) are the possessors of the beautiful colouration, which may be a combination of red, green, yellow or black and blue with dark markings superimposed. The beautiful colours spread also into the fins.

The tail fins also are very variable in shape and by selective breeding many types have becomes more or less 'fixed'. These include the **Cofertail, Speartail, Robson, Roundtail, Doublesword, Top-sword, Bottomsword, Veiltail, Pintail, Lyretail and Triangle.** The final touch is added by a long flowing dorsal fin.

Apart from its obvious attractiveness visually, the Guppy has many other virtues. It is a hardy species that can stand a wide temperature range (but should be maintained in the aquarium at about 74°F (23°C) It has no special demands in respect of food, does not object to a little overcrowding; it is neither pugnacious or timid, and is a prolific breeder. The latter being a particular asset to aquarists wishing to

*Lebistes reticulatus (Poeciliidae),* Guppy

experiment in breeding a particular variety or strain. Determination of the sexes is obvious—the male of course, possess the gonopodium, and the females are usually unadorned by colour and much larger in size—2 inches (5 cm.) being about average.

For breeding, see Breeding Poeciliidae.

*Limia caudofasciata (Poeciliidae)*, Blue Poecilla

## *Limia caudofasciata (Poeciliidae)*, Blue Poecilia

This species from Jamaica is a truly beautiful aquarium fish. They are vividly coloured, and are shown to their best advantage by reflected light and when a number of them are shown together in a single tank.

The colour of the body is generally olive with dark markings along the sides which provides a background for the metallic blue spots flecking the body. The dorsal fin of the male is yellow-orange and has a dark spot at the base. The fins of the female are clear except for a hint of yellow at the base of the dorsal. The belly of the male is slightly golden.

Males grow to $1\frac{1}{2}$ inches (3·8 cm.) females to about $2\frac{1}{4}$ inches (5·7 cm.).

Temperature range 72°F (22°C) to 78°F (25°C). These are hardy fish that respond to the normal foods, but their diet should be in vegetable foods.

For breeding, see Breeding Poeciliidae.

### *Limia melanogaster (Poeciliidae)*, **Black Bellied Limia**

Originating in the small rivers of Jamaica, this species has a body tint of brown or brownish olive green. It is marked with dark vertical bars on the rear half of the body, these usually number six, but can vary between five to eight.

The dorsal of the male is pale yellow marked with a dark band on the margin and another on the base. The female's dorsal is clear and carries only the base marking. The tail of the male is deep orange. Females grow to about $2\frac{1}{2}$ inches (6·5 cm.) males somewhat smaller up to $1\frac{3}{4}$ inches (4·5 cm.). Temperature range 72°F (22°C) to 78°F (25°C). These are hardy fish that respond to the normal foods, but their diet should include vegetable foods.

For breeding, see Breeding Poeciliidae.


### *Limia nigrofasciata (Poeciliidae)*, **Hump-Back Limia**

The **Hump-back Limia** is found naturally in Haiti where it appears in great numbers.

Adult males are blue-green paling to yellow on the belly, the upper part of the body is marked indistinctly with dark vertical bars, and the spines of the dorsal are black also. Irridescent greenish spots are scattered over the bands.

As the male matures the body outline becomes less attractive the forepart of the back develops in a decided hump, and the dorsal fin enlarges. The colouring of the female is similar but somewhat lighter in tint, they grow to about $2\frac{1}{2}$ inches (6·5 cm.) the males are slightly smaller.

They are active and peaceful fish, easily fed on the normal diet of tropical fish, but they do need some vegetable food, especially soft green algae, which should always be present in their tank.

Temperature range 72°F (22°C) to 78°F (25°C). For breeding, see Breeding Poeciliidae. The fry require more attention than most livebearer young, and should, where possible, be given access to natural sunlight.


### *Limia ornata (Poeciliidae)*, **Green Poecilid**

This species is very similar to *L. caudofasciata*. It is a hardy, peaceful, and colourful species. The body colour is basically yellowish-olive

199

mottled with irregular black spots and luminous green dots. The anal and caudal fins are also black spotted.

Originating in Haiti, the males of the species grow to $1\frac{3}{8}$ inches (3·2 cm.) females up to $2\frac{3}{8}$ inches (5·9 cm.). They do not like cool conditions, a temperature about 76°F (24°C) is ideal. Vegetable foods, especially soft algae is a necessary additive to the normal diet for healthy sparkling fish.

For breeding, see Breeding Poeciliidae (A).

### *Limia vittata (Poeciliidae)*, Striped Mud Fish

Originating in Cuba, this is one of the less attractive species of the genus, and because of their relatively large size, that are not considered good aquarium species by some aquarists. The males grow to about $2\frac{1}{2}$ inches (6·3 cm.) and the females to 4 inches (10·1 cm.).

The basic colour of the body is greenish yellow reflecting a bluish tint. The male is marked on the side with irregular dark vertical bars, but these markings may be indistinct, or absent entirely. Fins are orange with dark patterning occurring only on the male. These are fish that like warm water, they are hardy, peaceful, and breed readily. For breeding, see Breeding Poeciliidae.

### *Macropodus chinensis (Anabantidae)*, Round-Tail Paradise Fish

This species is very similar to *M. opercularis*, the most obvious difference being the rounded tail of both sexes.

The body has slightly less red and it is marked less distinctly. The male may be identified by its more vivid colouring and larger fin. At breeding time the male becomes suffused with blue-black, speckled with numerous light coloured dots.

Adult fish attain a length of $2\frac{1}{2}$ inches (6 cm.).

These are peaceful fish that are not worried by low temperatures, 60°F (15°C) to 72°C (22°C) being their recommended range. In fact, the temperature should not be allowed to go above 75°F (24°C).

For breeding, see Breeding Anabantidae (A).

## *Macropodus opercularis (Anabantidae)*, **Paradise Fish**

The main colouring of this species is a deep rusty brown, marked with emerald stripes. The tail of the male only has long pointed filaments trailing from the tips which are usually emerald and terminate in pale blue. Females have a more rounded tail and much shorter fin tips.

Under normal circumstances, the colouring of both sexes is similar, but as mating approaches the colouring of the male becomes vivid, whilst that of the female becomes paler, almost to a drab white.

Found naturally in China, and attaining a length of about 3 inches (7·6 cm.) they can hardly be described as good community fish, they are a pugnacious species that can only be kept with fish of a comparable size.

Although normally requiring a temperature range between 60°F (15°C) and 76°F (24°C) they can live in a temperature as low as 52°F (11°C) which means that they could be cultured in an outside pond during the warm summer months.

**Paradise Fish** are common in the rice fields of China, where they have a plentiful supply of food in the form of algae and mosquito larvae.

For breeding the temperature should be stabilised at 75°F (24°C) otherwise see Breeding Anabantidae (A).

*M. opercularis* concolour. the **Black Paradise Fish,** is a sub-species, being nearly black during courtship.


## *Megalamphodus megalopterus (Characidea)*, **Black Phantom Tetra**

This characin from Brazil is unusual in that the males and females differ widely in colour and finnage. Adult fish grow to about 1¼ inches (3·2 cm.) in length. The female has a soft red body, with pelvic and anal fins also red, the anal fin is bordered with black; dorsal and caudal fins are both black.

The male on the other hand, is dark grey which reflects a pinkish hue, fins are dark grey also. When excited the male is mostly black. Both sexes are marked on the shoulder with a black vertical bar surrounded with an irridescent greenish area.

The most characteristic feature is the large size of the dorsal and anal fin of the male, features after which the species obtain their specific names.

Temperature range between 72°F (22°C) and 80°F (28°C). These

*Megalamphodus megalopterus (Characidae)*, Black Phantom Tetra

are hardy and interesting fish, but they do require a little more care and attention than most characins in respect of water and feeding.

They are not easy fish to spawn, but in general follow the pattern of most characins described under breeding Characins (F).

### *Melanotaenia nigrans (Atherinidae)*, Australian Rainbow

The silversides are common saltwater fish, found in nearly all temperate waters. The **Australian Rainbow** is one of the few that inhabit fresh water permanently. Strangely enough, few of our present-day aquarium fish come from Australia, but this peaceful beauty is one exception.

The body of the Australian Rainbow is mainly silver, faintly overcast with a warmish pink which runs into the centre of the tail. The scales are edged with dark brown and each one is clearly discernible as if it were carefully drawn. The base of the scale has a thicker line, which forms distinct horizontal bars along the sides. In daylight the scales have a spectrum-coloured sheen, which is the reason for the name rainbow.

The eye, with its dark centre, has a phosphorescent outer-circle, which reflects any stray beam of light. The dark spot on the gill cover also has a luminous quality. These fish are ideal aquarium members. They are easily fed and hardy, and can stand a temperature range of between 60°–90°F (16°–32°C).

Sexing is not easy, although the male is smaller and slimmer with more brilliant colouring. They may be bred quite succesfully in the aquarium in the same way as the egg-layers, described under Breeding the Cyprinidae. As may be expected, this species is found naturally in Australia, and will grow to about 4 inches (10·1 cm). in length. *M. maccullochi* is another species that is suitable for aquaria. It grows to about 5 inches (12·6 cm.). It has a reddish to blue-green body which changes according to the light. It is marked with uniform rows of dark red to black dots. Fins are orange brown to red.

### *Mesogonistius chaetodon (Centrarchidae)*, **Black-Banded Sunfish**

Originating in the U.S.A. this 4 inch (10·1 cm.) species has a silvery body marked with not too well defined vertical bars. The male has a shiny spot on the gill cover.

This species does not require too much warmth, a temperature range between 60°F (16°C) and 72°F (22°C) is adequate. It is important to feed live food only. Under no circumstances will they eat dry foods. They do not like strong light and their aquarium should be positioned so that direct sunlight never enters the tank.

Younger fish are the prettiest, and they are happy in the company of other fish, providing they also are calm and sedate specimen.

Breeding temperature is about 64°F (18°C). The pair deposit the eggs during courtship into a depression previously made in the gravel. The eggs adhere to the grains of gravel and hatch in about 5 days. They remain in the depression for a few days and are then driven out by the male using strong motions of the fins to cause violent currents.

The fry then attach themselves to the plants or glass sides of their tank.

The fry require large amounts of infusoria, in addition to microscopic live foods.

### *Moenkhausia oligolepis (Characidae)*, **Glass Tetra**

The **Glass Tetra** ranges from Brazil and Guiana. It is a silvery fish with a yellowish sheen, its only marking is a black spot on the caudal peduncle. The iris of the eye is shiny red.

Like most Characins the males and females are very similar. The males generally are slightly smaller and slimmer. Average length for adult females is 5 inches (12·7 cm.).

It is advisable to only put younger fish in a community tank, fully grown specimen tend to become aggressive and ferocious. A large tank with plenty of space, and a main diet of live foods will keep them healthy. They will however take the occasional pinch of flake food.

Temperature range 70°F (21°C) to 78°F (25°C). Generally they breed as described under Characins (A), but a large tank is a must. They are not an easy species to spawn.

### *Moenkhausia pittieri (Characidea)*, **Diamond Tetra**

The **Diamond Tetra,** found naturally in Venezuela, obtains its common name from the diamond-like reflections from its silvery grey body. These reflections scintillate from hundreds of metallic spots all over the body. These fish are also notable for their tall, striking dorsal fin and red eyes.

The Diamond Tetras are fast swimmers and will often jump in sheer exuberance, therefore, they are best kept with other fast moving fish in a roomy aquarium with a covered top. Although they require ample free swimming space, they also require thickly planted areas as hiding places.

They are peaceful fish, growing to about 2½ inches (6·3 cm.) and best maintained in a community. Temperature range 70°F (21°C) to 76°F (24°C).

For breeding, see Characins (A). They are not particularly difficult to breed, but the males may become a little aggressive.

### *Moenkhausia sanctae filomenae (Characidae)*, **Red Eyed Tetra**

This species ranges from Paraguay and it has much in common with *M. oligolepis.* It grows to about 2½ inches (6 cm.) the males being a little smaller.

The body colour is yellowish with a mother-of-pearl quality. A reticulated pattern on the body is manifest by the dark edging to the scales. The caudal peduncle has a black band with a bright yellow area to the fore. The upper part of the iris of eye is brilliant red.

Temperature range 70°F (21°C) to 78°F (25°C). For breeding, see Characin (A).

### *Molliensia latipinna (Poeciliidae)*, Sailfin Mollie

Originating in North Carolina, Florida and N.E. Mexico, this species obtains its popular name from the large dorsal fin of the male which, on a good specimen, can extend the whole length of the back and be higher than the depth of the body. Unfortunately, the quality and size varies considerably and unless the dorsal fin is outstanding, the real charm will be lost.

These are large fish growing to $3\frac{1}{2}$ inches (9 cm.) in length, the colour of the male is bluish overlaid with a reticulated design and horizontal stripes. Under reflected light the scales have a greenish tint. The dorsal fin is irridescent blue, and tail fin lightish blue with a yellow streak through the centre.

Females are less attractively coloured and do not possess the beautiful 'sailfin'. *M. latipinna* require warm tanks at a temperature between 75°F (24°C) and 82°F (28°C) and being largely vegetarian, they are best kept in large aquaria with plenty of strong illumination to encourage the growth of soft green algae.

If the growth of algae is insufficient and they need plenty, then it can be transferred from another tank. Alternatively they can be given boiled spinach, in addition to vegetable foods they will require all kinds of live and dry foods. Bemax is an excellent additive to the diet.

Because of the large size of these fish, they need spacious accommodation at all time, otherwise they become stunted.

If the fish appear to be unhappy, and show symptoms of closed fins and apparent shimmies, add a little sea salt to their water. Freshly imported specimen will need as much as 5% cooking salt added.

These are excellent aquarium species, being lively and hardy, but if more than one male is contained in a tank, they are likely to tear one another's fins.

For breeding, see Breeding the Poeciliids. Not difficult to breed, but the fry should be well fed and given plenty of room. Specimen showing possible development of a large dorsal should be separated and given special treatment, i.e. vegetable foods and plenty of space.

*Molliensia sphenops (Poeciliidae)*, Marbled Molly

### *Molliensia sphenops (Poeciliidae)*, **Marbled Molly**

The original form of this species is found from Texas to Venezuela, but it is rarely found in aquaria. The form most likely to be found are those with mottled black colouring, or the totally black 'Perma-black Mollies'. The latter are particularly striking with their velvety black livery in which even the eyes are difficult to distinguish.

Care for this species and for its number of sub-species is much the same as for the other members of the genus. They like warmth, and their aquarium should never sink below a temperature of 75°F (24°C). For breeding, see Breeding the Poeciliids. It must be noted, however, that a pair of pure black mollies will not necessarily produce a brood of pure black offspring, it is almost certain that the brood will contain a variation of mottled, but it is possible that some will become completely black as they develop.

### *Molliensia velifera (Poeciliidae)*, **Giant Sail-Fin Molly**

Originating in Yucatan, this species is very similar to *M. latipinna*, except that it is a larger fish, approximately 4 inches (10 cm.). The colour is also similar, but the throat and breast may be tinted orange. The magnificent dorsal of the male is green-blue with a purple sheen,

206

*Molliensia velefera (Poeciliidae)*, Giant Sail-Fin Molly

marked most attractively with blue, red, brown and orange patterning.

The requirements for this species is as for *M. latipinna*. For breeding, see Breeding the Poeciliids, the young are nearly ½ inch (1·3 cm.) when born, and can number up to 100.

## Monodactylus argenteus (Monodactylidae)

The attraction of this fish is derived from its almost circular laterally compressed silvery body. It is *brilliantly* silver with rich yellow in the dorsal and anal fins. A thin line passes through the eye, and a less distinct one curves down the body from the fore of the dorsal fin to the root of the pectoral fins.

Originating in the Indian Ocean, and obtaining a length of some 8 inches (20·3 cm.) in the wild, but more likely to remain about 5 inches (12·7 cm) in the aquarium. This interesting species needs a roomy tank and warm water between 75°F (24°C) and 86°F (30°C). It must be remembered that these are really marine fish and whilst

*Monodactylus argenteus (Monodactylidae)*

they can be acclimatized to fresh water, they will still need salt occasionally. They are sensitive to changes in water

Food consists of live foods only, and these should be small and fed sparingly. They are a little quarrelsome among themselves, but not viciously so. Breeding habits unknown.

## *Nannacara anomala (Cichlidae)*, Golden Eyed Dwarf Cichlid

Originating in British Guiana the males of this $2\frac{3}{4}$ inch (7 cm.) so called dwarf are basically green to brassy in colour, with a dark brown spot on each scale and a blue dorsal fin bordered with red and white. Females are patterned with dark stripes crossing one another to form a chequered pattern. When excited, throat and belly are often deep black.

*Nannacara anomala (Cichlidae)*, Golden Eyed Dwarf Cichlid

Temperature range between 72°F (22°C) and 82°F (28°C).

Breeding is not difficult when compatible pairs are used. For breeding, see Breeding the Cichlidae.

*N. taenia, the* **Lattice Cichlid** is similar to the above.

## *Nannobrycon eques (Hemiodontidae)*, Pencil Fish

The *Hemiodontidae* are Characin-like fish. This fish in common with other species of the genus, swim slowly by vibrating motions of the vertical fins and the body, to all intents and purposes, held rigid. This gives the fish a wooden appearance hence its name **Pencil Fish**.

This particular species originates in the Amazon region, and Guiana. It has a greenish brown body with a dark stripe running the length of the body and into the lower lobe of the tail. Each side of the stripe are two narrower stripes composed of dots joined indistinctly. Between the main stripe and the narrower upper stripe a golden yellow colour is evident.

The Pencil Fish prefers soft, clear water at a temperature between

72°F (22°C) and 77°F (25°C). They are peaceful and best kept with their own species or with closely related species (*Nannostomus*). Foods of all kinds are readily taken, especially Enchytrae and other small live foods. Unfortunately, they ignore foods that sink to the bottom therefore, flakes and free swimming live foods are a 'must'.

The Pencil Fish is a difficult fish to spawn, the temperature of the water should be raised to 82°F (28°C) and be soft. It is not necessary to line the floor with gravel, but a few broad leaved plants in pots, are required for the fish to deposit their eggs on the underside of the leaves. As the parents are avid eaters of their own eggs, a glass or plastic grill should be used to cover the bottom. Otherwise the breeding technique is much the same as for most Characins.

### Nannostomus aripirangensis (Hemiodontidae), Brown Pencil Fish

Originating in the Amazon region of South America, this pretty 1¾ inch (4·4 cm.) **Pencil Fish** is brownish in colour marked by a horizontal stripe from nose to tail which is bordered above by a thin golden line. Above the gold it is coloured red which partly bleeds into the gold. The fins are a reddish hue and sometimes brick red.

Generally, the males are more brilliantly coloured.

Temperature range is between 72°F (22°C) and 78°F (25°C). It is a peaceful fish that prefers to be with its own species. These are difficult fish to breed, conforming more or less to the breeding habits of *N. marginatus*, see also Breeding Characins (A).

### Nannostomus marginatus (Hemiodontidae), Dwarf Pencilfish

The Pencilfish are slender, or very slim fish, this particular little species rarely exceeds 1¼ inches in length (3·1 cm.). It is found naturally in the Amazon and the Guianas, and its principle markings are two very dark brown stripes which run from nose to tail. A broad golden colouration separates these two stripes. The fins are a pretty red-brown at the base and along the edges. Males are usually more brilliantly coloured and somewhat slimmer than the females.

Temperature range is between 72°F (22°C) and 78°F (25°C). It is a peaceful fish that much prefers the company of its own kind and is best maintained in densely planted aquaria with some free swimming space. This is a difficult species to breed, its general requirements are as described for Breeding Characins (A), but it is important that the water should not be too soft or acid, and adjusted to a level of about 4 inches (10 cm). in depth. A good egg trap and spawning media can be made from a mop of nylon yarn, thoroughly clean of course. A plastic grill or glass marbles should cover the floor of the breeding aquarium.

*Nannostomus marginatus (Hemiodontidae)*, Dwarf Pencilfish

## *Nematobrycon palmeri (Characidea)*, Emperor Tetra

The body of the male **Emperor** is silky olive along the back, graduating to beige along the side and ivory white on the belly. A wide velvety black band extends from the snout to the tail where it narrows and forms a centre prong to the trident shaped tail. The rear of the body is flecked above the dark band with metallic tints of red and blue. The long anal fin has a yellow margin bordered by a thin black line. The dorsal fin is sickle shaped marked with a dark leading edge. The eye is most outstanding with its dark pupil and brilliant blue green iris.

This species is native to Colombia and the males will grow to about $2\frac{1}{2}$ inches (6·3 cm.) in the aquarium. Females slightly smaller.

This is a particularly attractive species, hardy and capable of with-

*Nematobrycon palmeri* (*Characidae*), Emperor Tetra

standing a wide temperature range between 68°F (20°C) and 86°F (30°C). It is easy to feed, but requires a varied diet of both dried and live foods.

These are relatively easy fish to spawn. Breeding temperature 78°F (26°C). For breeding see Breeding the Characidae. Note a large tank, about 18 in. × 12 in. × 12 in. is a minimum size, the standard 24 in. × 12 in. × 12 in. is better.

### Nothobranchius guentheri (Cyprinodontidae)

This species is one that should be reserved for the seasoned aquarist, it is not one that is easily kept.

Colour is basically a blue green with a peppering of red dots, and a red edging to the scales. The fins are most beautifully patterned and coloured. The females are quite plain by comparison, being simply a grey to brown. Found naturally in East Africa and Zanzibar the males grow to about $3\frac{1}{2}$ inches (8·9 cm). They require a temperature around 76°F (24°C), and a spacious aquarium well planted with a layer of peat moss on the bottom.

The breeding habits are similar to species of Aphyosemion that spawn on the bottom.

*Nothobranchius guentheri (Cyprinodontidae)*

### *Otocinclus affinis (Loricariidae)*, Dwarf Sucking Catfish

This species originates in Rio de Janeiro. Like all catfish, the **Dwarf Sucking Catfish** is a scavenger, but with a difference—it has a sucking organ. This organ is really an extension of the lips, and a very useful piece of equipment it is, because it enables the fish to climb all over the plants, up one side and down the other, removing algae as it travels.

Although not a highly coloured fish, it has a charm in the streamlined shape of its body. The average length for an adult is $1\frac{3}{4}$ inches (4·4 cm.). The body colouring is a darkish-brown lightening as it approaches the underparts, and it is overlaid with a slightly darker mottling.

Another peculiarity of this fish is that it will sometimes swim upside down immediately below the water surface, clinging to it as it apparently sucks in any floating food.

The sucking catfish is an interesting exhibit in any tank, quite inoffensive and fairly hardy. Unfortunately, it is rarely bred in the aquarium.

### *Pachypanchax playfairi (Cyprinodontidae)*, **Playfairs Panchax**

Found naturally in Zanzibar, Seychelles and E. Africa. The body colour of the male is yellow to yellow-green. The female is similar in colour, but slightly more brown and lighter in tone. The body of the male is well marked with rows of red spots which extend into the dorsal, caudal and anal fins. The caudal and anal fins have a red and black edge. Fins of the male are brownish or yellow, and clear in the female except for a dark spot on her dorsal.

A most distinctive feature of this species is the protruding scales along the front dorsal surface of the body, these scales stand out from the body like the teeth of a saw.

It is not a good community fish as it is somewhat pugnacious and carnivorous. It will also try to leap out of its tank.

This species also seems to like a little salt in the water and one teaspoonful of sea-salt to each gallon of water is approximately the correct proportion.

Adult fish attain a length of $3\frac{1}{2}$–4 inches (8·9–10·2 cm.). They spawn at 75°F (24°C) and will eat their own eggs and young, therefore the plants in the breeding tank must be dense and include floating plants. Adults should be removed immediately after spawning.

### *Phallichthys amates (Poeciliidae)*, **Merry Widow**

Originating in Guatemala, these little fish, males only $1\frac{1}{4}$ inches (3·2 cm.) females up to 2 inches (5 cm.) obtain their popular name from the thin black line edging to the dorsal fin, reminiscent of a mourning card. The body colour is a shade of olive green with dark vertical bars.

A short black line passes through the eye. The gill cover reflects an irridescent blue green.

Females lack the dark margin on the dorsal. The most outstanding feature of the Merry Widow is the long gonopodium of the male, in fact, the scientific name, *phallichthys* means phallus.

Always lively, and easily fed, but should be given a reasonable amount of vegetable foods. Temperature range between 70°F (21°C) and 78°F (25°C).

For breeding, see Breeding the Poeciliids.

### *Phallichthys pittieri (Poeciliidae)*

Originating in Costa Rica and Panama, this species is very similar to *P. amates*. The males grow to about 1½ inches (3·8 cm.). Females over 2⅜ inches (5·8 cm.).

Care and breeding as for *P. amates*.

### *Phenacogrammus interruptus (Characidea)*, Congo Tetra

Found naturally in the Congo, the **Congo Tetras** are quite large, the males up to 3 inches (7·6 cm.) in length and females about 2¼ inches (6·3 cm.). The colour of the body is a silvery reflecting various tints, the fins are slatey violet with lightish margins. The fins of the male are extended, especially the dorsal and the tail, the latter being strongly extended in the middle part. Although these fish can tolerate medium hard water, they are much happier in soft peat filtered water at a temperature range between 72°F (22°C) and 76°F (24°C). They are school fish, and very lively, therefore, they need plenty of swimming space in a well planted aquaria. For breeding the temperature should be 76°F (24°C), a well planted tank which must be spacious. The non-adhesive eggs are laid among the plants. Once the fry become free swimming they will immediately accept Cyclops and Artemia nauplii. These are not easy fish to spawn, but the fry are not difficult to raise once they are free swimming which is some 36 hours after hatching, otherwise see Breeding Characins (A).

### *Pristella riddlei (Characidea)*, Riddle's Pristella

This pretty community fish was introduced in Europe in 1924. It is a fast moving community fish that has been highly regarded ever since.

The females are about $1\frac{3}{4}$ inches (4·4 cm.) when fully grown, males slightly smaller.

Found naturally in N.E. South America, it has an almost transparent body of silver-grey with a soft brown overtone. Characteristic markings are a dark spot just behind the gill cover, black and white patches on the dorsal and anal fins and slightly paler patches on the ventral fins. The base of the dorsal is lemon yellow and terminates in a white point. The forked tail has a reddish hue.

This is a hardy species requiring a temperature range between 68°F (20°C) and 80°F (27°C) and small sized foods. It is one of the more difficult Characins to breed, see Breeding Characins (A), and is best attempted with two males to one female.

### *Pterophyllum scalare (Cichlidae)*, **Angel Fish**

The **Angel Fish** from the waters of the Amazon and Guiana, are so well known that a detailed description is almost superfluous. The long dorsal and anal fins spread gracefully like the wings of a bird, and their slow elegant motions when swimming are so individualistic that the description could fit no other freshwater tropical fish.

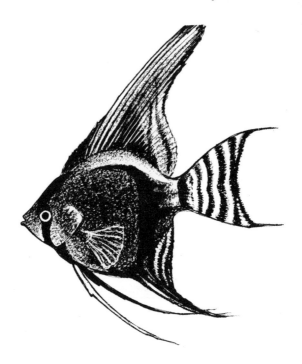

The silvery body, reflecting tints of blue, has many small speckles not unlike freckles. Evenly spaced black vertical bars stripe the body the first one through the eye, the last across the caudal peduncle. One of the body stripes continues into the fins.

Other forms of *P. scalare* are now currently available including the all black Angel, Lace and Veil-tail varieties.

Unlike most Cichlids, they are excellent community members, and do not interfere with the plants. They will however partake of any small fish that offers itself as a meal.

Occasionally Angel Fish will lose their appetite. When this happens try a change of diet, or a partial change of water. Angel fish can grow to about 5 inches (12·7 cm.) long. They require a temperature range between 75°F (24°C) and 82°F (28°C) and water slightly acid. They can be adversely affected by chemicals and over aged water.

For breeding, see Breeding the Cichlidae (D).

*Rasbora daniconius (Cyprinidae)*, Slender Rasbora

## *Rasbora daniconius (Cyprinidae)*, **Slender Rasbora**

This species is not one of the most colourful of the Rasboras but it is a lively, peaceful little fellow with a good shape.

It is mainly a silver fish with a central blue-black body stripe delicately edged on both sides with a thin metallic gold line. The back is olive green and belly white and fins have a hint of yellow.

Originating in India and Ceylon, this species will grow to about 3 inches (7·6 cm.) in the aquarium, but is said to grow larger in the wild.

Temperature range between 72°F (22°C) and 75°F (24°C). For breeding see Breeding the Cyprinidae.

### *Rasbora heteromorpha (Cyprinidae)*, **Harlequin**

The **Harlequin** is a pretty fish with a rather unusual colour pattern. It is silvery fish which strongly reflects a purple tint, but it is the black wedge marking from the centre of the body to the tail that makes this species so distinctive. Males naturally are the most colourful and possess a red eye.

Adult fish attain a length of 1¾ inches (4·4 cm.). Males are slightly smaller and less plump.

*Rasbora heteromorpha (Cyprinidae)*, Harlequin

Originating in the Malay Peninsula, Borneo, Sumatra and Java, it thrives well in the aquarium on prepared dry foods but live foods should be supplied frequently to keep them in the peak of condition.

They are fish that like warmth and a temperature range between 72°F (22°C) and 80°F (27°C) is ideal.

These are not easy fish to spawn. For many years they defied all attempts, but with care and skill they can now be bred.

For breeding, see Breeding the Cyprinidae (D).

*Rasbora maculata (Cyprinidae)*, Dwarf Rasbora

### *Rasbora maculata (Cyprinidae)*, **Dwarf Rasbora**

This species is from Malaya and Indo-China. It grows up to 1 inch (2·5 cm.) in length and has much in common with *R. heteromorpha*, the **Harlequin**.

The body colour is yellowish with a purple red sheen and the belly is greenish to white. It is marked with gold edged black spots. The fins have a tint of red and there is a small ocellated spot on the caudal peduncle. Males can be recognized by their whiter bellies. Temperature range between 74°F (23°C) and 78°F (25°C).

Breeds similarly to *R. heteromorpha*, see Breeding the Cyprinidae (A and D).

This species has been known incorrectly as *R. kalochroma*.

### *Rasbora pauciperforata (Cyprinidae)*, **Red Lined Rasbora**

Ranging from E. Sumatra, the body colour of this species is silvery reflecting a green sheen and marked with a very distinctive red horizontal stripe, bordered on the lower edge by a narrow black line. The females are much plumper than the males.

*Rasbora pauciperforata (Cyprinidae)*, Red Lined Rasbora

Growing to about 1¾ inches (4·4 cm.) in length, they require a temperature range between 70°F (21°C) and 75°F (24°C). To date, there appears to be no record of any successful spawnings.

## *Rasbora trilineata (Cyprinidae)*, Scissor Tail

This species from Sumatra and Borneo rarely exceeds 3 inches (7·6 cm.) in the aquarium, but it does grow longer in the wild.

The body colour is silvery white and somewhat translucent. It has a darkish line running down the middle of the side and another line running from just in front of the anal fin to the base of the lower lobe of the tail. Its most distinctive feature is the tail which is forked, often orange in colour and tipped on each lobe with a black and white bar. The movement of swimming causes the tail to open and close something like the action of a pair of scissors, hence its popular name.

These are definite school fish, hardy, peaceful and sometimes a little shy. They require a temperature between 65°F (18°C) and 76°F (24°C) otherwise they are easy to maintain.

For breeding, see Breeding the Cyprinidae (A and E). These are not a productive species, nor are they easily spawned.

220

*Rasbora trilineata (Cyprinidae)*, Scissor Tail

## *Scatophagus argus (Scatophagidae)*, **Spotted Scat**

Found naturally in the East Indies, *S. argus* has a very slim, laterally compressed body, which is almost disc-like in outline. It is coloured grey to green, or pink to bronze-yellow, and is marked by large circular spots that vary in colour from a dark green to black. The body colour and markings are so variable with this species that they are often erroneously thought to be different species.

There are a number of sub-species, but as these have not yet been accurately classified the aquarist can consider them various sub-species as *S. argus*.

Under natural conditions, these fish are found in brackish water, and for this reason it has not been designated here as a community specimen. It can be kept in a fresh water aquarium, however, if a little salt

221

*Scatophagus argus (Scatophagidae)*, Spotted Scat

is added to the water—one ounce of sea salt to eight gallons of water, or preferably one part of sea water to 20 parts of fresh water. If no salt is added, the water should be maintained in an alkaline condition of pH 7·4 or a little above. Brackish water is, however, preferable.

Although the **Spotted Scats** grow to 12 inches (30·3 cm.) long in their natural environment, aquarium specimen rarely exceed 4 inches (10·1 cm.) They are active, harmless fish and become quite tame when acclimatized.

To date they have not been bred in captivity, and no certain means has yet been determined to differentiate the sexes.

These fish are natural scavengers and are found in estuaries, mouths of rivers, and harbours of tropical ports. They are omnivorous and will eat almost anything.

### Selenotoca papuensis (Scatophagidae)

This fish has a general body colour of silver marked with seven or eight black vertical bands on the upper part of the body. These bands break up into spots on the lower part of the body. The spiny dorsal and lips are black. The body shape is vertically compressed and oval, similar to *Scatophagus argus*. These fish have never been bred in captivity, and there is no known method of determining the sexes. Adult aquarium specimen attain a length of 4 inches (10·1 cm.).

Although it is not considered a community fish, because it normally inhabits brackish water, *S. papuensis* can be acclimatized to fresh water if the transition is gradual. It can then be included in a community of fresh-water tropical fish, providing the other members are about the same size.

Found naturally in New Guinea.

## *Serrasalmus rhombeus (Characidea)*, Spotted Piranha

This ferocious fish from the Amazon is hardly a species for the average aquarist. It must be housed in a large aquarium of its own, or they can be kept in schools if they are well fed, but it is hopeless to put them with any other fish, they will simply tear them to pieces.

The jaws of the **Spotted Piranha** are equipped with very strong razor sharp, wedged shaped teeth that cut into flesh fast and cleanly and they often attack and devour each other. They must be treated with respect by the aquarist, an unwary finger in their tank is likely to receive a very nasty nip. The Piranha originates in Guiana and the Amazon region, fully grown specimens can reach a length of 14 inches (35 cm.) somewhat large for the home aquarium.

The body colour is a somewhat dull grey-green reflecting silver, it is spotted all over the body with many irregular dark spots.

The anal and caudal fins are dark. The belly is edged with saw-like tooth scales.

The temperature range is between 68°F (20°C) and 76°F (24°C). Fish that have been acclimatized can be fed on quite large pieces of raw meat, the fish will snap off appropriate sizes with their sharp teeth. They will also eat live fish, but most aquarist will object to this practice, and I agree with them.

Breeding has not as yet been achieved in the aquarium, in fact, very little is known about their breeding habits. *S. spilopleura* is a similar species with a grey brown body peppered with silver spots and a dark band through the eye to the gill cover.

## *Symphysoden discus (Cichlidae)*, Discus

This beautiful fish from the Central Amazon, is not really a species for the novice, as it requires some skill to maintain them in good health.

The body colour is yellowish brown marked with several vertical dark bars. The beauty of the fish is derived from the overlay of shiny blue green lines that interconnect all over the body from the snout and into the fins, appearing to run horizontally backwards. Females are' similar but a little paler in colour. Sexing can only be determined during the spawning periods by the genital papilla, the males being more pointed.

This species requires large, tall tanks with subdued lighting. Soft, slightly acid water and plenty of tall plants. Temperature range between 77°F (25°C) and 80°F (27°C). Their water should be partially changed weekly (about a $\frac{1}{4}$ of their tank) as they become less resistant to maladies in too old a water.

Feeding can be a problem as they like variety and appear to prefer tubifex worms to most other live foods.

Whilst this species has been bred in captivity, they are particularly difficult and the information available to date does not indicate that recent spawnings have been any easier.

*Synodontis nigriventris* (*Mochokidae*), Upside down Catfish

### Synodontis nigriventris (Mochokidae), Upside Catfish

This very unusual catfish swims for quite long periods on its back, literally upside down. So well adapted is this species to this mode of swimming that its belly colour is darker than its back.

Originating in the Congo and growing to about 2½ inches (6·4 cm.) it is an interesting and peaceful fish that becomes more active during the twilight hours. It prefers densely planted aquariums and not too much light.

Temperature range between 75°F (24°C) and 79°F (26°C). Foods include vegetable foods and small live foods.

This species has been bred, but details are not available.

### Tanichthys albonubes (Cyprinidae), White Cloud Mountain Minnow

Originating in the streams of Canton and in the White Cloud Mountains. This sparkling little fish only 1¾ inches (4·4 cm.) in length was known as the 'poor man's Neon Tetra' when the Neon was expensive and in short supply.

Body colouring is between a silvery olive and violet blue, with a fluorescent line of electric blue-green running from just behind the eye, along the side of the body to the tail. The dorsal fin has a red base and a streak through the tail.

These are excellent community fish requiring a not too warm environment, 64°F (18°C) to 68°F (20°C) is an ideal temperature range for them.

Hardy, easy to feed and vivacious, this minnow should be given plenty of space in which to swim. Long aquariums filled with about 40 of these attractive fish are a pretty sight indeed.

Sex can be determined by the longer dorsal of the male. For breeding, see Breeding the Cyprinidae.

### Telmatherina ladigesi (Atherinidae), The Celebes Rainbow Fish

The **Celebes Rainbow Fish** as may be expected, is found naturally in the Celebes Islands. It is a school fish that is shown to best advantage with a number of their own kind in large, rather long aquaria. They are transparent but reflect a yellowish, or blue-green tint under

*Telmatherina ladigesi (Atherinidae)*, The Celebes Rainbow Fish

fabourable lighting. The belly, back, and parts of the fins are a pale lemon yellow.

The soft dorsal is small and completely separate from the spiny dorsal which is comparatively large and has the first few rays extended well past the web, the anal fin is almost a duplicate, but inverted of course. The extended rays are dark in colour.

They grow up to about 2 inches (5·1 cm.) females a little smaller.

It is a fish that requires reasonable warm conditions—a temperature range between 75°F (24°C) and about 80°F (27°C) is ideal for them.

They are peaceful, hardy and very lively and will eat most live and prepared food, which they prefer to take from the surface or in mid depth, they prefer not to feed from the bottom.

For breeding see Breeding the Atherinidae. Rearing fry requires patience and some skill on the part of the aquarist.


### *Tetraodon fluviatilis (Tetraodontidae)*, Green Puffer

Found naturally in India, Burma and the Malay Peninsula in fresh and brackish water, the **Green Puffer** is an unusual addition to the aquarists collection. Generally the body colour is greenish on the dorsal surface and side, paling to whitish, yellow or grey on the underside. It

*Tetraodon fluviatilis* (*Tetraodontidae*), Green Puffer

is marked with more or less round dark spots. The colour is strongly variable.

Growing to about 7 inches (17·5 cm.) this species is rather vicious when fully developed, but small specimen are relatively peaceful.

Their most interesting feature is of course, their ability to puff themselves into a ball. This they do by taking in air by the mouth until the belly is inflated fully. Fright will cause them to do this when taken out of the water. When fully inflated tiny spines stand out all over the belly. When returned to water deflation is rapid.

Temperature range between 70°F (21°C) to 80°F (27°C). In nature, this species feeds by scavenging, therefore, it will eat almost anything. Not difficult to keep, preferably in an aquarium with their own kind. They spawn in brackish water, eggs laid on rocks and guarded by the male. They are most difficult to induce to spawn and rearing the fry requires skill and patience. First food infusoria, followed by egg yolk and later daphnia.

### *Thayeria obliqua (Characidae)*, Penguin

The **Penguin** comes from the Amazon river in tropical South America. It has a silvery body, with a deep black line running from

*Thayeria obliqua (Characidae)*, Penguin

behind the gill cover along the length of the body down into the lowe₁
half of the tail fin. When swimming slowly the body lies at an angle
with the tail lower than the head, this attitude accentuated by the black
line is responsible for its penguin-like appearance. It grows to about
2¾ inches (7 cm.).

This is a peaceful fish fond of company, but it does require some free
space for swimming, and some well planted areas for a refuge.

Temperature range 72°F–80°F (22°C–26°C).

For breeding the temperature should be raised to 85°F (29°C).
See Breeding Characins (C).

### *Trichogaster leeri (Anabantidae)*, Pearl Gourami

Also known as the **Lace Gourami,** this species is one of the larger
aquarium fish growing to 4 inches (10 cm.). Originating in Siam,
Malay Peninsular and Sumatra. It is a most attractive fish with a body
colour of turquoise suffused with a mosaic of pearly dots which extends
into the fins, and gives the impression of fine lace. An irregular dark
brown line runs from the mouth through the eye and becomes indistinct as it approaches the tail. Ventral fins are long and slender and
usually carried forward to the body.

When in breeding condition the belly of the male becomes brick red.

*Trichogaster leeri (Anabantidae)*, Pearl Gourami

**Pearl Gouramis** are timid fish that tend to hide behind the plants and rocks.

Temperature range between 76°F (24°C) and 86°F (30°C). They prefer live foods, but these should be graded to suit the small mouth of the species.

They make good parents, neither males or females being inclined to eat eggs or young, and rarely does the male attack the female during courtship.

For breeding, see Breeding Anabantidae (A). Temperature for breeding 80°F (27°C).

## *Trichogaster pectoralis (Anabantidae)*, Snakeskin Gourami

Found naturally from Indo-China to Malaysia, this rather rare species grows to about 12 inches (30 cm.) in the wild and also provides a popular fish dish in Ceylon. Aquarium specimen rarely exceed 6 inches (15 cm).

The **Snakeskin** has a greenish brown body overlaid with pale yellow to gold wavy bars. It is marked with a dark brown to black

*Trichogaster pectoralis* (*Anabantidae*), Snakeskin Gourami

broken line along the sides. Fins are varying tints of yellow. The eye is outstandingly yellow.

Sexes can be distinguished by the much higher dorsal fin of the male.

These fish are hardy and very good natured and have the same requirements as *T. leeri.*

They are among the easier of the bubble nesters to breed, see Breeding Anabantidae (A), neither parents eating eggs or fry. Breeding temperatures 80°F (27°C).

### *Trichogaster trichopterus (Anabantidae)*, Three Spot Gourami

Originating in India, the Malay Peninsular and Indo-China this species is an unbelievable powder blue in colour, overlaid with a pale wavy pattern. It is marked with two black dots on the body, one about the centre, the other on the caudal peduncle. The eye forms the third spot from which this fish gets its popular name.

It is quite a large fish attaining a length of 5 inches (12·7 cm.). The ventral fins are long and threadlike which are usually stretched forward as if used like the whiskers of a cat.

It is a species that needs a reasonably warm aquarium between 75°F (24°C) and 80°F (27°C) and is very easy to breed.

For breeding, see Breeding Anabantidae (A).

*Trichogaster trichopterus (Anabantidae)*, Three Spot Gourami

*Trichopsis vittatus (Anabantidae)*, Croaking Gourami

## *Trichopsis vittatus (Anabantidea)*, **Croaking Gourami**

This species grow to about $2\frac{1}{2}$ inches (6·3 cm.) and are found naturally
in the Malay region. They obtain their name from the sound they make

at breeding time—a kind of croaking produced by vibrating the air in the labyrinth.

This species is also known as *Ctenops vittatus*.

The body is basically yellow reflecting a green tint, marked with dark bands the length of the body. Fins have a hint of red—the eye is the most attractive feature which is deep red, and brilliant blue. Males are more highly coloured and have the vertical fins terminating in threads.

They are a peaceful, somewhat shy species requiring a temperature range between 72°F (22°C) and 75°F (24°C) which should be increased to 85°F (30°C) for breeding. They are not particularly easy to breed, but conform to the normal breeding habits of the Anabantids, see Breeding Anabantidae (A).

*Xiphophorus hellerii (Poeciliidae)*, Swordtail

### *Xiphophorus hellerii (Poeciliidae)*, Swordtail

Originating in E. Mexico, the **Swordtail** is a good showy aquarium fish that prefers slightly alkaline water.

The Swordtail is a shiny green marked with red horizontal stripes, the red line along the centre of the body is particularly distinct. The extension of the tail forming the sword is green to orange red.

The red variety, obtained by hybridizing with a red Platy, has a deep orange body and a long tail spike varying from orange to yellow, bordered by a thin black line. Albino Swordtails are usually of a lightish colour and the sword-like tail fin is also paler than the other varieties, and like all true albinos, the eyes are pink. There are other varieties including the **Wagtail** and **Tuxedo**.

Sexing is of course, very simple, only the male possess the 'sword'. Males grow to about 3¼ inches (8·2 cm.) excluding the sword and females to about 4¾ inches (12 cm.).

Temperature range between 68°F (20°C) and 75°F (24°C).

Care and breeding is similar to that for most of the live-bearers.

*Xiphophorus maculatus (Poeciliidae)*, Platy

### *Xiphophorus maculatus (Poeciliidae)*, Platy

Originating in E. Mexico and Guatemala, this species was previously known as *Platypoecilus maculatus*, but the close relationship between *Xiphophorus* and *Platypoecilus*, born out by their readiness to cross breed and other factors, was the reason for combining both genera in the genus *Xiphophorus*.

The males grow to about 1½ inch (3·8 cm.) and the females to about 2 inches (5·1 cm.), the original form is yellow grey, but by selective breeding of a number of colour sports, the aquarist of today can avail himself of a vivid variety of colour that is almost unbelievable.

**Blue Platy, Red Platy, Black Platy, Wagtail Platy, Golden**

233

**Platy, Variegated Platy, Spotted Platy,** and the **Tuxedo Platy** are a few of the most popular varieties.

Temperature range between 68°F (20°C) and 80°F (27°C) but they can stand a little lower temperature for short durations.

These lively, pretty fish, will eat all kinds of foods both prepared and live. Unfortunately they are not always hardy, and whilst they may thrive in one aquarium, they may well degenerate when transferred to another.

For breeding, see Breeding the Poeciliidae. When desirous of maintaining a particular colour strain the sexes must be kept separated and only those mated with the necessary characteristics.

*Xiphophorus variatus (Poeciliidae)*, Variegated Platy

## *Xiphophorus variatus (Poeciliidae)*, **Variegated Platy**

Originating in Mexico, this species was previously known as *Platy-poecilus variatus*. It should not be confused with *X. maculatus*. The male and female are both the same size, approximately 3 inches (7·6 cm.) in length. It is in the colour that the main difference occurs. Females usually have a dull brownish green body with a dark zigzag line along the sides, and only the male has the wonderful variegated colours which can combine yellow, blue, red, and green in one fish.

Temperature range between 68°F (20°C) and 80°F (27°C). This

234

species is hardy, and will eat both live and prepared foods, they are particularly fond of algae and will occasionally nibble the plants.

For breeding, see Breeding the Poeciliidae. When selecting pairs for breeding, never choose a small male—the bigger and brighter the colour the better. Females should be selected by their body colour and should not be used until some time after they reach their full maturity. Fry take rather a long time to develop to their full maturity.

# The Microscope

It is not necessary to own a microscope to keep fish. It is, however a useful piece of ancillary equipment for the hobbyist who wishes to concern himself with aspects of fishkeeping that are not obvious by casual observation. A good reliable instrument, quite suitable for most tasks can be obtained for only a few pounds, but if you wish to be really scientific, then by all means obtain a high quality instrument.

A microscope is basically a magnifying glass, either with a single, double, or compound lens system. The type required for the aquarist need not be of a very high power, a magnification of 10 times is quite sufficient.

A compound microscope consists of a frame on which is mounted the stage, i.e. a platform to hold the specimen, and a tube containing the lens system mounted at right angles to the stage, the tube is raised and lowered by a screw to enable the microscope to be focussed. A small hole in the centre of the stage enables light to be reflected by a mirror through transparent specimens on the stage. Solid objects, of course, will require illuminating from the top side of the stage. The tube carries a lens at its bottom extremity, near the object under scrutiny, this lens is called the objective, the opposite end of the tube carries another lens called the eyepiece or ocular. Sometimes one or two lenses are incorporated within the tube. The ocular is usually marked with its magnification thus 5× or 10×, meaning 5 times, or 10 times as the case may be. The objective lens is similarly marked. To obtain the magnifying power of a microscope it is only necessary to multiply the power of the objective by the power of the ocular. For example a 10× ocular and 25× objective will give a magnifying power of 250 times. A few glass slides on which to place the specimen are usually supplied with the microscope, but additional slides will prove inexpensive to buy. A few cover glasses will be required if you intend to mount specimens.

236

When using the microscope it is advisable to get into the habit of focussing the instrument upwards and away from the slide, otherwise it is possible to push the objective lens through the slide, and this may well damage the glass of the objective lens.

The application of the microscope to disease diagnosis is generally beyond the average aquarist, especially diseases caused by bacteria and viruses. Bacteria are extremely small single-celled organisms, and viruses are even smaller requiring an electron microscope to make them visible. Also it is necessary to have some knowledge of staining methods, culture growth, and general laboratory techniques, however, we can use the microscope to advantage for determining a few things such as the richness of an infusoria culture.

The organisms in an infusoria culture usually congregate near the surface of the water drawn there by the presence of light.

To examine these organisms, remove a drop of water, taken from the surface with a fountain pen filler or by dipping a glass rod just below the surface, and transfer it, to a glass slide. Place the slide under the microscope with the drop just below the objective lens, and above the hole in the centre of the stage. Looking through the eyepiece adjust the mirror for maximum brilliance, then focus—remember to focus upwards. The minute infusorias will be seen in lively clusters. Rich cultures will be swarming with life, experience will soon indicate the various concentrations, and so indicate to the aquarist the richness of the culture.

Your infusoria culture will reveal a small protozoan, known as paramecium, or the slipper animalcule because of its general slipper shape. These creatures are about 1/100 of an inch in diameter, and are useful as a food for newly hatched fry. Rotifers, which can be found in ponds containing daphnia are also good subjects for examination. Sometimes they will be discovered attached to the bodies of daphnia.

Both infusoria examination and rotifers only require a magnification of 10 ×.

Micro organisms found in most aquarium waters

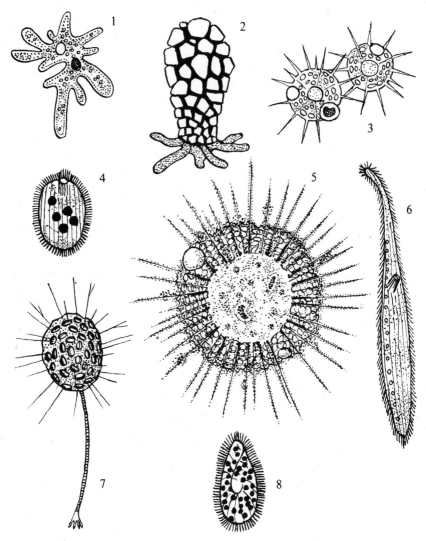

Amoeba proteus; 2.Difflugia pyriformis; 3.Actinophrys sol; 4.Prorodon teres;
5.Actinosphaerium eichhorni; 6.Dileptus anser; 7.Cladrulina elegans: 8.Paramecium
bursaria

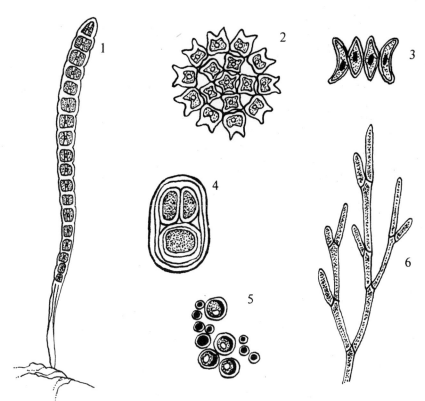

1. Ulothrix zonata; 2 Pediastrum sp., 3. Scenedesmus acutus;4.Chroococcus giganteus; 5. Protococcus olivaceus; 6.Cladophora sp.

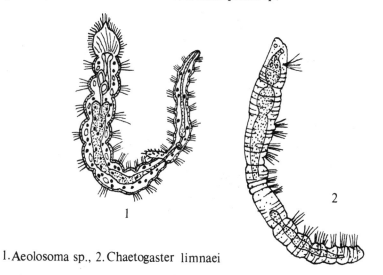

1.Aeolosoma sp., 2.Chaetogaster limnaei

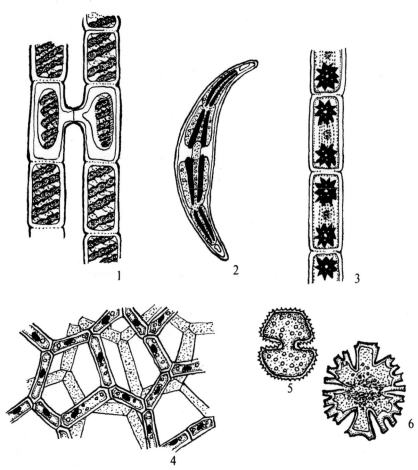

1. Spirogyra sp., 2.Closterium Ehrenbergi; 3. Zygnema sp., 4.Hydrodictyon utriculatum; 5.Cosmarium botrytis; 6. Micrasterias apiculata

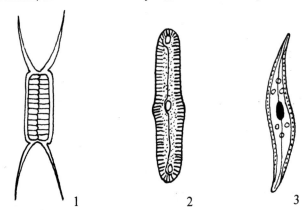

1. Attheya zachariasi; 2. Pinnularia viridis; 3. Pleurosigma acutum;

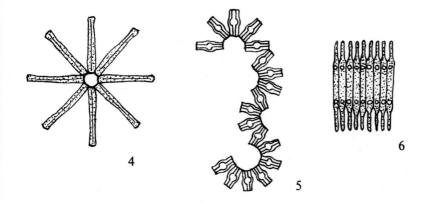

4. Asterionella gracillima; 5. Tabellaria fenestrata; 6. Fragilaria crotonensis

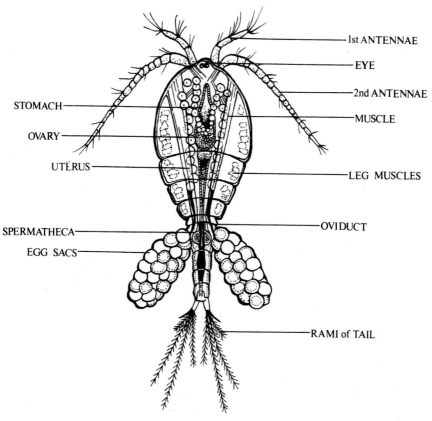

Anatomy of the Copepod *Cyclops albidos*

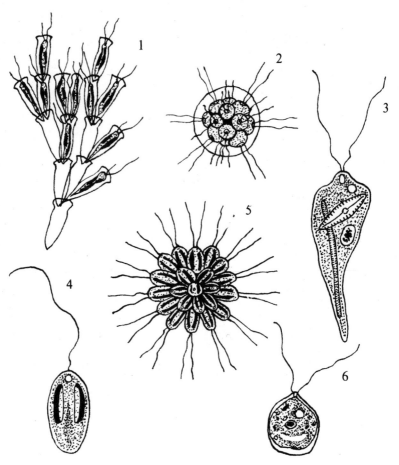

1.Dinobryon sertularia; 2. Pandorina morum; 3.Heteronema nebulosum;
4.Chromulina; 5. Synura uvella; 6. Chlamydomonas

# APPENDIX

| Specific name | Common name | Family | °F aver. temp. | Breed- ing temp. | Aver. l'gth in ins. | |
|---|---|---|---|---|---|---|
| Acanthophalmus semicinctus | Malayan Loach | Cobitidae | 78° | — | 4 | Malay Pen. & Archipelago |
| Acanthophalmus kuhlii kuhlii | | Cobitidae | 78° | — | 4 | Java |
| Acanthophalmus kuhlii sumatranus | | Cobitidae | 78° | — | 4 | Sumatra |
| Aequidens latifrons | Blue Acara | Cichlidae | 76° | 78° | 6 | Panama and Colombia |
| Aequidens maronii | Keyhole Cichlid | Cichlidae | 75° | 80° | 4 | Brit. Guiana & Venezuela |
| Aequidens portalegrensis | Brown Acara | Cichlidae | 74° | 78° | 6 | S.E. Brazil |
| Ambassis lala | Indian Glassfish | Centropomidae | 70° | 76° | 2½ | India |
| Anabas testudineus | Climbing Perch | Anabantidae | 75° | 78° | 10 | India, Burma, Siam, Ceylon, Phillipines |
| Anostomus anostomus | Red Headstander | Characidae | 73° | — | 4 | Guiana |
| Aphyocharax rubripinnis | Bloodfin | Characidae | 72° | 78° | 1¾ | Argentina |
| Aphyosemion australe | Lyretail | Cyprinodontidae | 70° | 72° | 2¼ | West Africa |
| Aphyosemion bivattatum | Banded Fundulus | Cyprinodontidae | 75° | 72° | 2½ | Tropical W. Africa |
| Aphyosemion coeruleum | Blue Gularis | Cyprinodontidae | 75° | 70° | 4½ | West Africa |
| Aphyosemion gardneri | | Cyprinodontidae | 70° | 73° | 2⅜ | Tropical West Africa |
| Aphyosemion gulare | Yellow Gularis | Cyprinodontidae | 70° | 73° | 2½ | West Africa |
| Apistogramme ramirezi | Butterfly Dwarf Cichlid | Cichlidae | 73° | 83° | 2 | Western Venezuela |
| Aplocheilus lineatus | Panchax | Cyprinodontidae | 76° | 78° | 4 | India and Ceylon |
| Arnoldichthys spilopterus | Striped Panchax | Characidae | 78° | — | 2¾ | West Africa |

| Specific name | Common name | Family | °F aver. temp. | Breed-ing temp. | Aver. l'gth in ins. | |
|---|---|---|---|---|---|---|
| Astyanax mexicanus | Mexican Astyanax | Characidae | 73° | 75° | 3 | Mexico |
| Badis badis | | Nandidae | 73° | 80° | 2 to 3 | India |
| Barbus conchonius | Rosy Barb | Cyprinidae | 70° | 72° | 3½ | India |
| Barbus cumingii | Cumings Barb | Cyprinidae | 74° | 78° | 2 | Ceylon |
| Barbus everetti | Clown Barb | Cyprinidae | 75° | 84° | 4 to 5 | Borneo and Malay Pen. |
| Barbus fasciatus | Striped Barb | Cyprinidae | 74° | 78° | 4 | Borneo, Malaysia |
| Barbus gelius | Golden Dwarf Barb | Cyprinidae | 70° | 72° | 1¾ | India |
| Barbus hexazona | Tiger Barb | Cyprinidae | 74° | 78° | 2⅛ | Malaysia and S.E. Asia |
| Barbus lateristrigo | Spanner Barb | Cyprinidae | 75° | 80° | 4¾ | Malay and E. Indies |
| Barbus nigrofasciatus | Nigger Barb | Cyprinidae | 70° | 80° | 2 | Ceylon |
| Barbus oligolepis | Checker Barb | Cyprinidae | 71° | 78° | 2 | Sumatra |
| Barbus phutunio | Dwarf Barb | Cyprinidae | 71° | 78° | 2 | India |
| Barbus schuberti | | Cyprinidae | 71° | 75° | 2½ | South China |
| Barbus semifasciolatus | Half Banded Barb | Cyprinidae | 71° | 75° | 2½ | South China |
| Barbus setivinensis | Algerian Barb | Cyprinidae | 71° | 75° | 12 | North Africa |
| Barbus terio | One spot Barb | Cyprinidae | 71° | 75° | 2¾ | Bengal, Punjab and Orissa |
| Barbus tetrazona | Tiger Barb | Cyprinidae | 73° | 80° | 2 | Malay Pen. and Borneo |
| Barbus ticto | Two Spot Barb | Cyprinidae | 74° | 76° | 3½ | India |
| Barbus titteya | Cherry Barb | Cyprinidae | 75° | 80° | 2 | Ceylon |
| Barbus vittatus | | Cyprinidae | 75° | 80° | 2¼ | Ceylon |
| Belontia signata | Comb Tail | Anabantidae | 75° | 78° | 4¾ | Ceylon |
| Betta splendens | Siamese Fighter | Anabantidae | 75° | 82° | 2⅜ | Singapore, Malaya, and Indo-China |
| Botia macracantho | Clown Loach | Cobitidae | 75° | — | 6 | Sumatra and Borneo |
| Brachydanio devario | | Cyprinidae | 73° | 75° | 3½ | India |
| Brachydanio nigrofasciatus | Spotted Danio | Cyprinidae | 73° | 75° | 1¾ | N. Indo-China |
| Brachydanio ábolineatus | Pearl Danio | Cyprinidae | 71° | 75° | 2¼ | Burma |
| Brachydanio rerio | Zebra Danio | Cyprinidae | 68° | 75° | 1¾ | Bengal |
| Brachygobius xanthozonus | Bumble Bee | Gobiidae | 78° | 86° | 1½ | India and Indo-China |

| Scientific Name | Common Name | Family | Temp | Temp | Size | Distribution |
|---|---|---|---|---|---|---|
| Bryconalestes longipinnis | Long Finned Characin | Characidae | 75° | 78° | 4½ | West Africa |
| Carnegiella strigata | Marble Hatchet | Characidae | 77° | 85° | 1¾ | Guiana, Central and Lower Amazon |
| Cheirodon axelrodi | Cardinal Tetra | Characidae | 76° | — | 1¾ | Upper Amazon |
| Cichlasoma biocellatum | Jack Dempsey | Cichlidae | 74° | 77° | 7 | South America |
| Cichlasoma coryphaenoides | Chocolate Cichlid | Cichlidae | 74° | 77° | 7 | Brazil and Argentina |
| Cichlasoma facetum | Chanchito | Cichlidae | 74° | 77° | 7 | Argentina |
| Cichlasoma festivum | Festive Cichlid | Cichlidae | 74° | 77° | 6 | Amazon Basin |
| Cichlasoma meeki | Firemouth | Cichlidae | 74° | 77° | 4 | Guatemala and S. Mexico |
| Cichlasoma nigrofasciatum | Zebra Cichlid | Cichlidae | 74° | 77° | 4 | Central America |
| Cichlasoma serverum | Striped Cichlid | Cichlidae | 75° | 80° | 7 | Guiana, Amazon Basin |
| Colisa chuna | Honey Dwarf Gourami | Anabantidae | 73° | 84° | 2½ | India |
| Colisa fasciata | Giant Gourami | Anabantidae | 73° | 84° | 4½ | India to Burma |
| Colisa labiosa | Thick Lipped Gourami | Anabantidae | 77° | 84° | 3¼ | Burma |
| Colisa lalia | Dwarf Gourami | Anabantidae | 73° | 86° | 2⅜ | N. India |
| Copeina arnoldi | Splashing Tetra | Characidae | 73° | 78° | 3 | Brazil |
| Corydoras aeneus | Bronze Catfish | Callichthyidae | 75° | 78° | 2¾ | Trinidad |
| Corydoras agassizi | | Callichthyidae | 75° | — | 3½ | Amazon and W. Brazil |
| Corydoras arcuatus | Streamlined Cory | Callichthyidae | 75° | — | 2½ | Upper Amazon |
| Corydoras hastatus | Dwarf Catfish | Callichthyidae | 75° | 80° | 1⅜ | Amazon Basin |
| Corydoras julii | Leopard Catfish | Callichthyidae | 76° | — | 2½ | E. and N.E. Brazil |
| Corydoras nattereri | Blue Catfish | Callichthydae | 76° | — | 2½ | Cent. and N. Brazil |
| Corydoras paleatus | Peppered Catfish | Callichthyidae | 76° | 70° | 2¾ | S.E. Brazil, Argentina |
| Corynopoma riisei | Swordtail Characin | Characidae | 77° | 80° | 2 | Trinidad, Northern S. America |
| Cryptopterus bicirrhus | Glass Catfish | Schilbeidae | 77° | — | 2 to 3 | Malaya |
| Ctenopoma acutirostre | Leopard Bush Fish | Anabantidae | 80° | — | 4 | Africa |
| Cynolebias bellottii | Argentine Pearl Fish | Cyprinodontidae | 68° | 68° | 2¾ | La Plata |
| Danio malabaricus | Giant Danio | Cyprinidae | 73° | 80° | 4 | India and Ceylon |
| Elassoma everglades | Pygmy Sunfish | Centrarchidae | 66° | 64° | 1¼ | Florida |
| Epalzeorhynchus kallopterus | Trunk Barb | Cyprinidae | 78° | — | 4 | Borneo, Java and Sumatra |
| Epiplatys chaperi | Fire Mouth Panchax | Cyprinodontidae | 71° | 77° | 2¼ | West Africa |

245

| Specific name | Common name | Family | °F aver. temp. | Breed-ing temp. | Aver. l'gth in ins. | |
|---|---|---|---|---|---|---|
| Etroplus maculatus | Orange Chromide | Cichlidae | 74° | 84° | 3 | India and Ceylon |
| Etroplus suratensis | Striped Chromide | Cichlidae | 72° | — | 16 | India, Ceylon |
| Gasteropelecus levis | | Gasteropelecidae | 75° | — | 2¼ | Amazon Basin and Guiana |
| Gynanocorymbus ternetzi | Black Tetra | Characidae | 76° | 83° | 3 | Rio Paraguay |
| Haplochromis multicolor | Egyptian Mouthbreeder | Cichlidae | 71° | 77° | 6 | Egypt |
| Hasemania melanura | Copper Characin | Characidae | 72° | 78° | 2 | S.E. Brazil |
| Helostoma temmineki | Kissing Gourami | Anabantidae | 78° | 78° | 6 plus | C. India and Indonesia |
| Hemichromis bimaculatus | Jewel Cichlid | Cichlidae | 73° | 77° | 5 | Tropical Africa |
| Hemigrammus caudovittatus | Buenos Aires Tetra | Characidae | 71° | 75° | 4 | Buenos Aires |
| Hemigrammus erythrozonus | Glowlight Tetra | Characidae | 76° | 77° | 1¼ | N.E. South America |
| Hemigrammus ocellifer | Head and Tail Light | Characidae | 76° | 78° | 1⅜ | Guiana and Amazon |
| Hemigrammus pulcher | Pretty Tetra | Characidae | 75° | 80° | 2 | Upper Amazon |
| Hemigrammus rhodostomus | Red Nose | Characidae | 75° | — | 2 | Lower Amazon |
| Hemigrammus ulreyi | German Flag Tetra | Characidae | 75° | — | 1½ | Paraguay River |
| Heterandria formosa | Mosquito Fish | Poeciliidae | 71° | 78° | 1 | S.E. of U.S.A. |
| Heteropneustes fossilis | | Clariidae | 71° | — | 26 | India, Ceylon |
| Hyphessobrycon callistus | Jewel Tetra | Characidae | 76° | 80° | 1¾ | Brazil |
| Hyphessobrycon flammus | Tet from Rio | Characidae | 70° | 73° | 1½ | Rio de Janeiro |
| Hyphessobrycon griemi | Red Gold Dot Tetra | Characidae | 72° | 73° | 1½ | Brazil |
| Hyphessobrycon heterorhabdus | Flag Tetra | Characidae | 75° | 75° | 1½ | Amazon |
| Hyphessobrycon innesi | Neon Tetra | Characidae | 73° | 70° | 1⅝ | Upper Amazon |
| Hyphessobrycon ornatus | Ornate Tetra | Characidae | 77° | 80° | 1½ | Dutch Guiana, Lower Amazon |
| Hyphessobrycon pulchripinnis | Lemon Tetra | Characidae | 75° | 77° | 1½ | Amazon Basin |
| Hyphessobrycon scholzei | Black-Line Tetra | Characidae | 74° | 75° | 2 | Lower Amazon |
| Jordanella floridae | Flag Fish | Cyprinodontidae | 68° | 75° | 2¼ | Florida |
| Labeo bicolor | Red Tailed Black Shark | Cyprinidae | 76° | — | 6 | Thailand |

| | | | | | | |
|---|---|---|---|---|---|---|
| Lebistes reticulatus | Guppy | Poeciliidae | 74° | 78° | 1 | Trinidad, Guiana, Venezuela |
| Limia caudofasciata | Blue Poecilia | Poeciliidae | 75° | 78° | 2 | Jamaica |
| Limia melanogaster | Black Bellied Limia | Poeciliidae | 75° | 78° | 2½ | Jamaica |
| Limia nigrofasciata | Hump-back Limia | Poeciliidae | 75° | 78° | 2½ | Haiti |
| Limia ornate | Green Poecilid | Poeciliidae | 76° | 78° | 1⅜ | Haiti |
| Limia vittata | Striped Mud Fish | Poeciliidae | 76° | 78° | 2½ | Cuba |
| Macropodus chinensis | Round-tail Paradise Fish | Anabantidae | 66° | 73° | 2½ | Eastern China and Korea |
| Macropodus opercularis | Paradise Fish | Anabantidae | 68° | 75° | 3 | China |
| Macropodus opercularis concolor | Black Paradise Fish | Anabantidae | 68° | — | 3 | China |
| Megalamphodus megalopterus | Black Phantom Tetra | Characidae | 76° | 78° | 1¼ | Brazil |
| Melanotaenia nigrans | Aust. Rainbow | Atherinidae | 75° | 78° | 5 | Australia |
| Mesogonistius chaetodon | Black Banded Sunfish | Centrarchidae | 66° | 64° | 4 | U.S.A. |
| Moenkhausia oligolepis | Glass Tetra | Characidae | 74° | 78° | 5 | Brazil and Guiana |
| Moenkhausia pittieri | Diamond Tetra | Characidae | 73° | 78° | 2½ | Venezuela |
| Moenkhausia sanctae filomenae | Red Eyed Tetra | Characidae | 74° | 78° | 2½ | Paraguay |
| Molliensia latipinna | Sailfin Molly | Poeciliidae | 78° | 80° | 3½ | N. Carolina, Florida, N.E. Mexico |
| Molliensia sphenops | Marbled Molly | Poeciliidae | 78° | 80° | | Texas to Venezuela |
| Molliensia velifera | Giant Sail-fin Molly | Poeciliidae | 78° | 80° | 4 | Yucatan |
| Monodactylus argenteus | | Monodactylidae | 80° | — | 5 | Indian Ocean |
| Nannacara anomala | Golden Eyed Dwarf Cichlid | Cichlidae | 77° | 80° | 2¾ | British Guiana |
| Nannobrycon eques | Pencil Fish | Hemiodontidae | 74° | 82° | 1¾ | Amazon |
| Nannostomus aripirangensis | Brown Pencil Fish | Hemiodontidae | 75° | 86° | 1¾ | Amazon |
| Nannostomus marginatus | Dwarf Pencil Fish | Hemiodontidae | 75° | 80° | 1¼ | Amazon and The Guianas |
| Nematobrycon palmeri | Emperor Tetra | Characidae | 78° | 80° | 2½ | Colombia |
| Nothobranchius guentheri | | Cyprinodontidae | 76° | 76° | 3½ | East Africa and Zanzibar |
| Ococinclus offinis | Dwarf Sucking Catfish | Loricariidae | 72° | — | 1¾ | Rio de Janeiro |
| Pachypanchax playfairi | Playfairs Panchax | Cyprinodontidae | 75° | 75° | 3½ to 4 | Zanzibar, Seychelles, E. Africa |

| Specific name | Common name | Family | °F aver. temp. | Breed-ing temp. | Aver. l'gth in ins. | |
|---|---|---|---|---|---|---|
| Phallichthys amates | Merry Widow | Poeciliidae | 74° | 78° | 1¼ | Guatemala |
| Phallichthys pittieri | | Poeciliidae | 74° | 78° | 1½ | Costa Rica, Panama |
| Phenacogrammus interruptus | Congo Tetra | Characidae | 74° | 76° | 3 | Congo |
| Pristella riddlei | Riddles Pristella | Characidae | 74° | 78° | 1¾ | N.E. South America |
| Pterophyllum scalare | Angel Fish | Cichlidae | 78° | 80° | 5 | Amazon and Guiana |
| Rasbora daniconius | Slender Rasbora | Cyprinidae | 74° | 78° | 3 | India and Ceylon |
| Rasbora heteromorpha | Harlequin | Cyprinidae | 76° | 79° | 1¾ | Malay Pen., Borneo, Sumatra, Java |
| Rasbora maculata | Dwarf Rasbora | Cyprinidae | 76° | 80° | 1 | Malaya and Indo-China |
| Rasbora pauciperforata | Red Lined Rasbora | Cyprinidae | 73° | — | 1¾ | E. Sumatra |
| Rasbora trilineata | Scissor Tail | Cyprinidae | 70° | 80° | 3 | Sumatra and Borneo |
| Scatophagus argus | Spotted Scat | Scatophagidae | 74° | — | 4 | East Indies |
| Selenotoca papuensis | | Scatophagidae | 75° | — | 4 | New Guinea |
| Serrasalmus rhombeus | Spotted Piranah | Characidae | 72° | — | 14 | Amazon |
| Synodontis nigriventris | Upside Down Catfish | Mochokidae | 77° | — | 2½ | Congo |
| Symphysoden discus | Discus | Cichlidae | 78° | 84° | 5½ | Central Amazon |
| Tanichthys albonubes | White Cloud Mountain Minnow | Cyprinidae | 66° | 72° | 1¾ | Canton |
| Telmatherina ladigesi | Celebes Rainbow Fish | Atherinidae | 77° | 80° | 2 | Celebes Islands |
| Tetraodon fluviatilis | Green Puffer | Tetraodontidae | 75° | — | 7 | India, Burma, Malay Pen. |
| Thayeria obliqua | Penguin | Characidae | 76° | 82° | 2¾ | Amazon |
| Trichogaster leeri | Pearl Gourami | Anabantidae | 80° | 82° | 4 | Siam, Malay Pen., Sumatra |
| Trichogaster pectoralis | Snakeskin Gourami | Anabantidae | 77° | 80° | 6 | Indo-China to Malaysia |
| Trichogaster trichopterus | Three Spot Gourami | Anabantidae | 77° | 80° | 5 | Malay, India, Indo-China |
| Trichopsis vittatus | Croaking Gourami | Anabantidae | 74° | 86° | 2½ | Malay Region |
| Xiphophorus hellerii | Swordtail | Poeciliidae | 72° | 78° | 3¾ | E. Mexico |
| Xiphophorus maculatus | Platy | Poeciliidae | 74° | 78° | 1½ | E. Mexico, and Guatemala |
| Xiphophorus variatus | Variegated Platy | Poeciliidae | 74° | 78° | 3 | Mexico |

# INDEX

251